READING IS NOT A SPECTATOR SPORT

MARY HELEN PELTON

Illustrated by
JOAN GARNER

1993
TEACHER IDEAS PRESS
A Division of
Libraries Unlimited, Inc.
Englewood, Colorado

To the children in my life—Sammy, Molly, baby Nicole, Joanne, Casey, and Jason—and to their parents—Jill and Duane Glover, Dawn and Don Malene, Jackie and Jim DiGennaro—who are making sure that their kids are participants in the reading game.

TEACHER IDEAS PRESS
A Division of Libraries Unlimited, Inc.
P.O. Box 6633
Englewood, CO 80155-6633
1-800-237-6124

Library of Congress Cataloging-in-Publication Data

Pelton, Mary Helen White.
Reading is not a spectator sport / by Mary Helen Pelton ; illustrated by Joan Garner.
xix, 264 p. 17x25 cm.
Includes bibliographical references and index.
ISBN 1-56308-118-0
1. Reading (Elementary) 2. Education, Elementary--Activity programs. 3. Children--Books and reading. I. Title.
LB1573.P45 1993
372.41--dc20
93-26165
CIP

Contents

Preface

There's no better way to reform and expand your mind on a regular basis than to get into the habit of reading good literature.... You can get into the best minds that are now or that have ever been in the world.... The person who doesn't read is no better off than the person who can't read.

—Stephen Covey, *The Seven Habits of Highly Effective People* (1989, 296)

With Pepsi and popcorn in hand, I curl up on the sofa to watch, maybe to cheer. Mostly I watch, I sleep, and then I dream.

In the dream that comes, I'm there—Number 303 at the shortstop position. I run onto the field. The cheer of the home crowd feels tangible and alive. The turf squeaks, the shoes grip, and the ball in my glove feels solid like victory.

I hit the ball and the vibrations of the bat course through my forearms into my shoulders and across my back, making every muscle alive and ready for the dash, for the race to first. Who will claim the base—the gladiator of the field or Pegasus racing the hurled sphere? I live inside each of my teammates as if their movements were my own.

When the game is over, I may weep, laugh, embrace, hide in shame, or sit quietly to reflect on what was or is to be—in another game, in another world, or in a time not our time. And I am whole, for it is not the victory that is important. It is the playing, the feeling, the being. It is the game.

Thus is it with reading. We do so much more than watch and wait. We are not mere spectators in the reading game. In the gap where the mind meets the text is the response, the action. The gap is filled not with a simple transfer of meaning; rather, in the interaction between the reader and the text is the being, the life. Nancie Atwell (1987, 154) says, "When we invite readers' minds to meet books ... we invite the messiness of human response ... personal tastes, personal habits, personal experiences. But we also invite personal meaning." And the chance that our kids will grow up to be different people.

We must create a learning environment that invites the response, one that surrounds kids with books and invites them to interact with print in hundreds of creative, probing, and enlightening ways. At its core is the readers' response.

This book is about the response—finding it, stimulating it, nurturing it, living it, surrounding students with opportunities to experience it. This book is about

- Meeting people who were NOT spectators, people who discovered a new vision of life itself in that mysterious place where the mind meets the text
- Inviting teachers to coach, to care, to cultivate the response; helping teachers live the joy and the pleasure of reading
- Getting the playing field just right, creating a literacy environment that invites kids to participate as members of, as Frank Smith says, the "literacy club"
- Inviting kids to respond to literature through writing, drama, storytelling, and art
- Building the team through cooperative learning activities
- Using thematic units and reading centers to place reading and books in a larger context
- Making TV-reading-writing connections
- Promoting reading through special events and incentive programs
- Preparing parents and administrators for their roles as talent scouts, cheerleaders, promoters, and role models
- Opening up the world of reading to include print materials such as comics, magazines, newspapers, pamphlets, and reading games
- Learning what local communities and national organizations can do, and are doing, to support and promote reading

Reading is like sports: Unless you are willing to participate, you can't play the game. This book is about inviting children to participate in the joy, the adventure, the laughter, the tears, the knowing, the sharing, the new ways of seeing—in the place where the mind meets the text. It is about the people, the events, and the hundreds of ways that we as teachers, parents, and administrators can support our players.

As we look out at the playing field and see our children take their positions with books in hand, we know that they are true participants in the great game of reading, not just spectators. There are no losers in the reading game. The only way to lose is not to play, for Reading Is Not a Spectator Sport.

References

Atwell, Nancie. 1987. *In the Middle: Writing, Reading, and Learning with Adolescents*. Portsmouth, NH: Heinemann.

Covey, Stephen R. 1989. *The Seven Habits of Highly Effective People*. New York: Simon & Schuster.

Smith, Frank. 1991. Speech delivered to a teacher workshop in Grand Forks, North Dakota.

Acknowledgments

Although I put the words of this book on paper, I didn't write it alone. I express my deep appreciation to the many people who shared their wisdom, knowledge, and experience with me—the people who helped make this book live:

- Kyle Archbold for his story "Why Houses Have Chimneys."

- Sandy Fischer, a third-grade teacher in Enderlin, North Dakota, now living in Fargo. Ms. Fischer gave me a copy of her third grade's "How and Why Tales." From this wonderful collection, I selected Kyle Archbold's story.

- Jon White Owl for his stories "Why the Pheasant Is So Handsome" and "Legend of the Spider Girl."

- Prairie Rose Greyeagle for her story "The Beat of the Drum."

- Linda Vizenor, teacher at the Wahpeton Indian School in Wahpeton, North Dakota, who supervised and inspired the creation of the class book *Indian Legends*, from which I selected stories by two of her students.

- Jeanne Swartz, librarian at the Wahpeton Indian School, who gave me a copy of *Indian Legends* and who provided me with the list of books on picture writing.

- Nan Campbell, Jeanne Erickson, Terry Hager, Cheryl Hoekstra, teachers at Winship School in Grand Forks, North Dakota, for sharing their experiences with me in their multigrade, integrated, theme-based curriculum.

- Sharon Gates, Beth Randklev, Ginny Bollman, and Mike Johnson, all elementary principals in Grand Forks, who shared their perspective on the principal's role in creating readers and for sharing the many innovative ideas that abound in their schools.

- Judy Hager and Peggy Koppelman, school librarians in Grand Forks, for their help in describing the ELBA Program and the Young Authors' Project, for their ideas about book fairs, and for being such wonderful models of what school librarians can be.

- Jackie DiGennaro, a teacher in Sitka, Alaska, for sharing several of her creative ideas with me. Although she is my sister and my friend, I feel I can still say with conviction that her classroom is one where kids can't help but participate.

- Madonna Schaner, formerly the librarian at Christ the King Elementary School in Mandan, North Dakota, for sharing her ideas on the interactive book fair.

- Joann Kitchens for sharing her recipe for monster cookies and for her invaluable help in typing and editing the manuscript.

- Kim Bristow, who also helped type the manuscript.

- Pat Johnston, the reading consultant for Grand Forks Public Schools, for her many suggestions, ideas, and leads, as well as for her careful explanation of the Back Pack Reading Program.

- Becky Thompson, teacher at Century Elementary School, for her inspiring explanation of Century's Young Authors' Project.

- Mary Ellen Peters, librarian in the Bisbee-Egeland (North Dakota) School District, for her creative idea about the Garfield Dinner Club.

- Walter Besler, high school principal in Cando, North Dakota, for his suggestions about ways high school principals can promote reading.

- David Darby from the Carson Group, managers of Pizza Hut's BOOK IT! program, for information and insights on that program.

- James Wendorf, director of programs for Reading Is Fundamental (RIF), and Ruth Graves, president of RIF, for giving generously of their time to talk with me about the organization. Not only did they share with me their time and RIF's marvelous publications, they also inspired me to move forward on this book. RIF, under their leadership, is truly making a difference in the lives of millions of children.

- Patricia Sylvester Spencer, high school teacher in Cedar Rapids, Iowa, for granting me permission to use part of her article in this publication.

- June Gray, former educator in Saginaw, Michigan, for her suggestions about the Battle of the Books.

- John Y. Cole, executive director of the Center for the Book, for the invaluable information not only about the Center for the Book but also information about their partners and programs.

- Gwen Kirk, from the NAA Foundation, for the information about the many programs and activities of the NAA Foundation, including the Newspaper in Education programs.

- Valerie A. Becker, from Chrysler, for her enthusiastic review of the activities associated with the Chrysler Learning Connection.

- Robert Brands, marketing manager of Osram Sylvania, Inc., for the information he provided about the company's America's Official Reading Time™ program.

- Joy Webster Peterson for the insight into the reading and literacy programs being promoted by Cargill.

- My colleagues and friends in the Division of Continuing Education at the University of North Dakota for their encouragement and support.

- Suzanne Barchers and David Loertscher, my editors, for their advice, knowledge, and expertise.

- Neil Price, chair of Science and Audiovisual Instruction at the University of North Dakota, for the resources that helped greatly in the development of chapter 16, on the role of the library media specialist.

- The hundreds of teachers who have participated in my university class, Turning Kids on to Reading, for the inspiration and reality tests for the information contained in this book.

- The hundreds of children and young adults who have shared a classroom with me and participated with me in the great sport of reading.

- Finally, and most important, my husband, friend, and first editor, Ray Pelton, for his unfailing encouragement, insight, patience, and diligence. Not only did he read and reread every word of this document, he also taught me everything I know about sports (which, by the way, is just about enough to get me through the metaphors in this book—but not much farther).

1

People Who Have Played and Won

Readers! Take your positions and Play Ball! No spectators allowed in this sport, this great reading game. In much of this book, we'll explore how to make sure our kids are participants and not spectators.

Before we get into the hundreds of things teachers and parents can do to help their players, let's give reading a very human face through the stories of players who have played and won. Reading changes lives as sports change lives. The stories cause us to reflect on the resilience of the human race and admire the courage of those who challenge the barriers that could have made them spectators.

Because this book is built around sports metaphors, we'll start with some athletes who refused to accept spectator status, then take a brief look at some outstanding players in the game of reading representing many different fields of endeavor.

In Sports

Jim Abbott

Jim Abbott takes the pitcher's mound. He winds up and throws. Only when he moves his catcher's glove back to his left hand do you notice that he is missing his right hand. In an interview in *Time* magazine Abbott says, "Growing up, I always pictured myself as a baseball player.... I never thought to myself, 'Wow, I only have one hand'" (Callahan 1989, 78). As a pitcher on the U.S. Olympic baseball team, he helped the United States bring home the gold medal in 1988. He is now one of the starting pitchers for the California Angels. Initially his opponents tested him, thinking they could slip bunts past him before he switched his glove. That's all changed. Fans, opponents, and teammates no longer think of him as an excellent one-handed baseball player. They think of him as an excellent baseball player.

Gail Devers

No one could believe it. Eighteen months before the 1992 Olympics, Gail Devers couldn't walk, and her physicians were going to cut off her feet. *Newsweek* magazine reported that she would have lost them within 48 hours if a doctor hadn't finally halted the radiation treatments she had been receiving for Graves's disease, a debilitating thyroid condition. But a miracle occurred. Eighteen months later, Gail Devers not only won the gold medal in the 100-yard dash, but she also set a world record doing it. *Newsweek* reports, "It was the first time anybody in sports ever used the word 'miracle' as an understatement" (Deford 1992, 29).

Kenny Walker

Kenny Walker, an all-American football player, chosen as Big Eight Defensive Player of the Year, runs out onto the Nebraska Cornhuskers' field. The crowd rises and applauds him as they've never done before. They raise their hands, spread wide their fingers and quickly rotate their wrists back and forth. It's called the "deaf clap." When his signer, Mimi Mann, first worked with Kenny, she knew nothing about football, but she learned the sport while he adjusted to college life. It was a remarkable four-year journey and a remarkable friendship. At Walker's last game, a huge banner was unfurled in the stands: "Thank you Kenny and Mimi."

In Reading

The parallels between reading and sports are striking. Both reading and sports have changed, and in some cases saved, the lives of people who learned to participate. Like sports, reading is not static. It is not passive. It requires discipline and good coaching. The following stories introduce people who have played and won in the game of life. Reading made the difference.

Ben Carson

Ben Carson wrote a book, *Gifted Hands* (1990), that tells his remarkable story. Carson was raised in inner-city Detroit by a mother with a third-grade education. His future didn't look bright. He lacked motivation. He had terrible grades and a pathological temper that threatened to put him in jail. Sonya Carson wouldn't accept that for her son. When she saw his horrible fifth-grade report card, she laid down the law. Ben and his brother Curtis couldn't play outside until they learned their multiplication tables, and the boys could watch only three TV programs a week. She required the boys to go to the library and read at least two books every week. At the end of each week, she insisted that they give her a report on each book.

That's impossible, thought Carson. He had never read a whole book in his life. How could he possibly finish an entire book in one week?

The boys grumbled and dragged their feet. The seven-block journey to the library seemed endless. But Sonya Carson had spoken and neither boy even thought about disobeying.

"'Bennie,' she said again and again, 'if you can read, honey, you can learn just about anything you want to know. The doors of the world are open to people who can read. And my boys are going to be successful in life because they're going to be the best readers in the school'" (37).

Then Ben Carson began to go through a metamorphosis. First he read books about nature, animals, and science. His science teacher, noticing his interest, gave him special projects, such as helping the other students identify rocks, animals, and fish. Before too long he became the fifth-grade expert in anything of a scientific nature.

He began improving in all his school subjects and looking forward to his trips to the library. Soon the library staff recognized Ben and his brother and offered suggestions on books that might interest them. Carson said, "I thrived on this new way of life, and soon my interests widened to include books on adventure and scientific discoveries. By reading so much, my vocabulary automatically improved along with my comprehension. Soon I became the best student in math when we did story problems" (38).

One day Ben was thinking about how much the smartest kid in the class, Bobby Farmer, knew about flax. "Bobby sure knows a lot about flax. He's really smart. Suddenly, sitting there in the classroom with spring sunshine slanting through the windows, a new thought flashed through my mind. I can learn about flax or any subject through reading. It is just like Mother says—if you can read, you can learn anything" (39).

Ben moved not only to the top of the class but eventually to the top of his field. Carson received a full scholarship to Yale and graduated from the University of Michigan Medical School. At age 33, he became the director of pediatric neurosurgery at Johns Hopkins Hospital. He pioneered extremely complex and delicate surgeries. Maranda was typical of the children he saved.

Maranda had her first grand mal seizure at 18 months, a convulsion characteristic of epilepsy sometimes described as an electrical storm in the brain. Nothing seemed to help. By the time Carson heard of Maranda, the 100 or so seizures a day she was experiencing were making the right side of her body useless. She couldn't eat or sleep. It appeared that Maranda could next expect paralysis on one side of the body, mental retardation, and eventually death. Her only hope was a hemispherectomy, which would remove half of her brain. Carson and his team saved not only Maranda but also 30 other children who had no hope of surviving. Fortunately, when this surgery is performed on young children, the other half of the brain tends to readapt, taking on some of the function of the missing part. Carson (with a team of 75 other professionals) performed his most dramatic and best-known pioneering surgery when he successfully separated Siamese twins who were joined at the back of the cranium and shared converging veins.

Carson isn't content to have "made it" himself. He puts aside time from his demanding schedule to talk to young people. He wants talented Black teenagers to see that it can be done if they THINK BIG. When he talks to students, he explains the meaning of each letter in THINK BIG. Not surprisingly, the **B** stands for **B**ooks.

Will Durant

Will Durant and his wife, Ariel, won the Pulitzer Prize for their 11-volume *Story of Civilization*, which popularized history. In his memoirs, *Transition: A Sentimental Story of One Mind and One Era*, published in 1927, he remembers a young girl named Irene and his introduction to literature.

Irene's lovely hand held the immense volume of *Pickwick Papers*. Was he more attracted to the soft hand that touched the book or the book itself? He remembers, "I begged it from her, and that night, against the protest of my parents, I burned the midnight oil.... I read every word and marvelled that I had lived twelve years without discovering the book" (1927, 42). He asked her for additional books, but she had no more by Dickens. Her father was giving her *David Copperfield* for Christmas. Perhaps he'd like to borrow it then.

Will couldn't possibly wait until Christmas. Within a week he had accumulated 14 pennies and walked three miles to a bookstore. He asked the grouchy proprietor for the cheapest edition of *David Copperfield*. The owner went into a rear room, worked his way among stacks of broken-down books, and emerged with a weathered copy.

"That will be twenty five cents," he said.

Durant looked heartbrokenly into the coins in his hand. "But mister, I've only got fourteen cents."

Unmoved, the proprietor turned away to help another customer. A tall handsome gentleman had watched the interchange. He put his arm around Will's shoulder and asked him how much he needed. Durant describes the final scene:

> "Eleven cents," I replied.
>
> "Is that all? Here you are; when you get rich you can pay me back."
>
> ... I was so grateful that I could not speak. I accepted the eleven cents as a gift from God, and walked out of the store in a daze. I trudged home in ecstasy over the kindness of Providence, the goodness of human nature, and the pleasures in store for me in the 860 pages I carried under my arm. From that day I became a tremendous reader (43).

Mary Helen Pelton

In first grade, there were the Swans, the Bluebirds, and the Buzzards; I was a Buzzard. In second grade, there were the Gazelles, the Zebras, and the Turtles; I was a Turtle. In third grade, the teacher grew more subtle. There was Group One, Group Two, and Group Three. Only people who had had their heads in the schoolyard sandbox for the first two years of school could have missed that Group Three was a synonym for Turtles or Buzzards; I was a Group Three.

Now don't get me wrong. It wasn't that I couldn't read. I just couldn't read orally. It seemed oral reading was all that mattered. Teachers didn't seem to care whether or not you understood what you read. Evidently the rule of life was, If you could say the words, you "got" it and if you couldn't, you didn't.

My mother and father had read to me daily since I was a baby, and I knew good oral reading when I heard it. It had pizzazz—inflections, voices, pauses, pacing—and it made sense. The only way I could do the same when I read aloud was to read down about three lines so I'd have the sense of the story and could interpret the meaning. I did not necessarily (and most probably did not) read the words, which was all rather unfortunate as far as my reading group placement went. I'd proceed glibly along, merrily making meaning but hardly ever reading what was on the page. "Oh dear," said the teacher, shaking her head, "she is obviously a Buzzard."

I never read at school after the unfortunate time in fourth grade when I had to do a book report. For two weeks I stayed after school laboring over The Report with one of those big pencils that were great if you had hands the size of baseball gloves. Why do they do this to little kids?, I thought. The best way to avoid

The Report, I decided, was to never read a book, at least not one the teachers knew about. But how I read at home! My allowance was carefully saved for trips to Minneapolis and Dayton's bookstore. I couldn't wait to buy the next book in the Dana Girls series. I might have continued in the Nancy Drew/Dana Girl genre had not two events occurred.

My mom took me to the library, where from a dusty shelf I took a worn, uninteresting-looking book with a burgundy cover with the interesting title *The Angry Planet*. All afternoon I read curled up on the sofa. I came to the place where the dear little space creature died, and I wept. That week our fourth-grade teacher, Mrs. Zimmerman, read *Henry Huggins* and I laughed right out loud.

Then I had an "aha" experience. Books could make you laugh and they could make you cry. They were more than the formula fiction of Nancy Drew. They held a part of you—your emotions, your imagination, your fears, your dreams—and I knew their power. I was hooked on books for life.

I still had a long way to go, however. My self-esteem as a reader (and therefore as a student) was very low. I remember a conversation with my father to the effect that had I the misfortune to have been born in Germany, where 10-year-old students were tested then tracked for life based on their scores, I most certainly would now be in training to sweep out dismal, rat-infested prewar factories in Hamburg.

Because I couldn't read aloud, I must not be able to read. Teachers for years had told me so. It seems odd to me now that I accepted the label of "poor reader" and, with that, assumed I was dumb. It never occurred to me that the reading I had done outside of school had helped me become a pretty good silent reader.

Thank heaven for Loreen Adsit, my sixth-grade teacher. She changed my life because she believed in me. "Mary Helen," she said, "you are not nearly as stupid as you think you are. [She probably didn't say it quite that way, but that's the way I remember it.] Tomorrow we're going to take a standardized test and you're going to get a perfect score on the reading section." When the test scores came back, my score in the reading section was perfect and I was a Buzzard no more.

Mrs. Adsit did two other things. At Christmastime she read the class *The Birds' Christmas Carol*. At the end, she cried and we cried and I understood how literature through the story experience can bind us together into a family of literary sojourners in a moment of shared emotions.

The other thing she did came later. Fifteen years after I left her class, I sent her a wedding invitation. She gave us a delicate ornament for the Christmas tree. It was a Christmas Spider with the story of the Legend of the Christmas Spider included. Each time I put the spider in the limbs of the tree, it inspires me as an educator: I must always believe in children, especially those who stop believing in themselves. Mrs. Adsit helped me win, and I have spent my life as an educator trying to help others do the same.

Richard Wright

Richard Wright's literary reputation became secure with the publication of *Native Son* and *Black Boy*. In his 1937 autobiography, *Black Boy* (reprinted in 1966), he recounts begging the schoolteacher who lived with the Wright family to tell him about what she was reading. "She whispered to me the story of 'Bluebeard and His Seven Wives,' and I ceased to see the porch, the sunshine, her face, everything. As her words fell upon my new ears, I endowed them with a reality that welled up from somewhere inside of me.... The tale made the world around me throb, live. As she spoke, reality changed, the look of things altered, and the world became peopled with magical presences.... My imagination blazed" (1966, 47).

But Wright never got to hear the end of this gripping tale. His grandmother stepped out onto the porch and shouted, "You stop that, you evil gal! I want none of that Devil stuff in my house!" (47).

Even though he argued and begged, his grandmother wouldn't let her finish the tale. "Not knowing the end of the tale filled me with a sense of emptiness, loss.... I vowed that as soon as I was old enough I would buy all the novels there were to read and read them" (48). He reports slipping into the teacher's room when no one was looking and taking the book to the back of the barn and trying to read. He could not decipher enough words to make the story have meaning. But he would learn. He asked his mother the meaning of every strange word he saw and his journey toward literacy began.

Wright left home when he was 17, and with the small amount of money he earned as an errand boy, he bought secondhand magazines and books, read them, and then resold them. One morning he saw a newspaper article furiously denouncing H. L. Mencken. "I wondered what on earth this Mencken could have done to call down upon him the scorn of the South" (267). Wanting to find out more about Mencken, he knew of the huge library near the riverfront, but he also knew that Blacks were not allowed to use it. Finally he screwed up enough courage to ask a white man on the job whether he could use his library card. Wright then wrote a note to the library over that man's signature to the effect that he was sending the "boy" to pick up books for him: "Dear Madam: Will you please let this nigger boy have some books by H. L. Mencken?" (270).

When he got home, he began to read. As he read the clear clean sentences, he realized, "This man was fighting, fighting with words. He was using words as a weapon, using them as one would use a club. Could words be weapons?... Then, maybe, perhaps I could use them as weapons?" (272). Wright had tried writing but was beaten by the experience. The feeling surged again, and he hungered for books, "new ways of looking and seeing ... something that made the look of the world different" (272).

He forged more notes, and trips to the library became frequent. "Reading grew into a passion. I knew of no Negroes who read the books I liked and I wondered if any Negroes ever thought of them. I knew that there were Negro doctors, lawyers, newspapermen, but I never saw any of them" (275). Sometimes he would stop reading, but he would hunger for books, "books that opened up new avenues of feeling and seeing, and again I would forge another note to the white librarian. Again I would read and wonder as only the naive and unlettered can read and wonder, feeling that I carried a secret, criminal burden about with me each day" (275-276).

Cushla

The story of Cushla comes from *Cushla and Her Books* by Dorothy Butler (1975). Cushla's parents began reading to her when she was four months old. By the time she was nine months old, she responded to the sight of certain books and conveyed to her parents which were favorites. By the age of five she had taught herself to read.

But Cushla was far from a typical bright child. Born with a chromosome defect, she had multiple handicaps, including deformities of the heart, spleen, kidney, and oral cavity. She suffered violent muscle spasms that prevented her from sleeping more than two hours a night. Due to her lack of upper-body muscle tone, she couldn't hold anything in her hands until she was three years old. It soon became obvious that her vision was hazy beyond her fingertips and that she suffered from hearing loss.

Cushla was tested many times, but until she was three, the doctors diagnosed her as "mentally and physically retarded" and recommended that she be institutionalized. Her parents refused and continued to try to find ways to stimulate her.

What could they do during those long hours of sleeplessness? When she was four months old, her parents introduced books. They would hold them very close to her and she would focus intensely, trying to "take in" each picture, as much as her limited vision would allow.

Even after she began to sleep for longer periods, her parents decided to continue the practice. Cushla couldn't occupy herself in normal ways—crawling, pulling herself up, exploring objects, tasting, or watching everyday activities. Without one-on-one help, she would exist in a state of almost total noninvolvement. She had to have constant attention if she was to experience her environment at all. And Cushla loved books.

Butler's book provides a fascinating chronicle of the books and Cushla's reaction to them. It is a story of the tenacity, love, and patience of Cushla's parents and extended family and of a very sick little girl who was loving, courageous, and determined. On August 1, 1975, at the age of three years, eight months, Cushla was retested. On the Stanford-Binet Intelligence Scale, Cushla performed in the above-average IQ range.

Butler, Cushla's grandmother, says in the postscript to her book,

> Seven years ago, before Cushla was born, I would have laid claim to a deep faith in the power of books to enrich children's lives. By comparison with my present conviction, this faith was a shallow thing. I know what print and picture have to offer a child who is cut off from the world, for whatever reason.... It is in the hope of recruiting more human links between books and the handicapped children of the world that Cushla's parents have agreed to the publication of her story. We are all confident that a much older Cushla will want to help with this recruitment. We think that Cushla's belief in books as bridges may be even stronger than ours (1975, 107).

Cushla and the others whose stories I've shared can read. But what about the estimated 25 million Americans who cannot read well enough to negotiate the daily business of life? What about the functional illiterates of this country? Walter Anderson, in his book *Read with Me: The Power of Reading and How It Transforms Lives* (1990), interviewed volunteers—three women and four men—at the second national Adult Literacy Congress in Washington, D.C. In their own voices they recount the pain they faced as functional illiterates and the amazing grace of learning to read as adults. Robert Mendez and Linwood Earl Johnson are two of those interviewed.

Robert Mendez

Robert Mendez had pretended to read all his life. He manipulated his teachers and became active in organizations like the pep club, drama club, and art club. Then one day he realized that he was living a lie. He was trapped in a low-level job. He kept making excuses to avoid promotion. In reality he was terrified of the written test he'd have to take; then people would know that he couldn't read. He had to do something. He heard on the radio about an adult literacy program where there were no classrooms, just a friend and tutor. Robert and his tutor succeeded. Robert learned to read.

When asked what he had gained, Robert said, "Self-respect—the understanding that I have control over my life, for the first time.... When you can read, you're free. You're free to make mistakes, free to make the world change. Reading has changed my world forever" (Anderson 1990, 108). Later he talks about a special moment. He was reading a Mickey Mouse number book to his three-year-old and he started to cry. The little boy asked, "Daddy this isn't a sad book. Why are you crying?" (109).

Linwood Earl Johnson

Linwood had spent a lifetime denying that he was illiterate, having become adept at fooling others. One day he made a decision. He joined the Volunteer Literacy Program in Nashville. His tutor, Sharon Hollaway, said he made incredible progress. When asked how he felt about himself once he had learned to read, he said, "Like a six-year-old waking up on Christmas morning. My life is like a rose blossoming. It opens more and more every day, I read books, newspapers, everything I can." And when the interviewer asked what his dreams were now, he replied,

> Before I entered the literacy program, I had a single goal. I wanted to learn to read. Now I have several. First, I'm going to return to high school to earn my diploma—and I know I'll be able to read it when I receive it. I'm going to kneel down like I did before I joined the literacy program and I'm going to ask God to help me in the right direction, because after high school I'm going to enroll in college.... And, well, I have another dream, something I really want to do. I want to teach someone else how to read (Anderson 1990, 100).

John Corcoran

The story of John Corcoran, written by Gary Smith, appeared in the August 1990 issue of *Esquire* magazine.

Who would ever have known? John Corcoran was a millionaire, a college graduate, a former high school teacher, and, yet, before their wedding he confessed to his fiancée, Kathy, that he couldn't read. He faked, cheated, and conned his way through school. As a teacher he was noted for his innovative methods—oral tests, films, videos, lots of guest speakers. When his real estate business took off, he quit teaching and felt safe. He could hire people to do his reading and writing. Then one day his real estate market turned sour and he walked into Carlsbad City Library and confessed to the woman in charge of the tutoring program, "I can't read." Then he cried.

Within 14 months, his land development company began to revive and John was learning to read. He read every book or magazine he could get his hands on, every road sign he passed. Then one day he remembered one more thing he could finally do. In his office, he carefully removed a ribbon-bound sheaf of papers that had been tucked away in a dusty box. A quarter of a century later, John Corcoran sat down to read his wife's love letters.

These are poignant, inspiring stories of individuals, of readers, but we can't leave this chapter without reflecting on other important actors in these mini-dramas. The stories would have been different had it not been for the supporting cast—the parents, the teachers, the tutors, the friends, a co-worker, and an unknown stranger. Like baseball, it's not just the field and the players, it's much more. The following chapters explore the "much more," the many ways teachers, parents, librarians, administrators, organizations, and communities can support their players so they will win as they participate in the game.

References

Anderson, Walter. 1990. *Read with Me: The Power of Reading and How It Transforms Lives*. Boston: Houghton Mifflin.

Butler, Dorothy. 1975. *Cushla and Her Books*. Boston: Horn Book.

Callahan, Tom. 1989. "Dreaming the Big Dreams: One-Handed Jim Abbott Shines at Spring Training." *Time* 133 (March 20): 78.

Carson, Ben, with Cecil Murphrey. 1990. *Gifted Hands*. Grand Rapids, MI: Zondervan.

Deford, Frank. 1992. "A Track Full of Miracles." *Newsweek* 120 (August 10): 29.

Durant, Will. 1927. *Transition: A Sentimental Story of One Mind and One Era*. New York: Simon & Schuster.

Wright, Richard. 1966. *Black Boy*. New York: Harper & Row.

Literature Resources

Wright, Richard. 1940. *Native Son*. New York: Harper.

2

The Teacher as Coach

No teacher begins the school year saying, "Hey, terrific, another school year. I can't wait to get my hands on my students so they can LOSE in a big way." Even the most curmudgeonly sort want the kids to win, to learn, if for no other reason than it would be most unpleasant to have the same crowd in third grade year after year. A class of third-graders whose voices are changing and are shaving would most certainly reflect poorly on the teacher. Joe Potley had a losing team year after year and he got traded to another school. Eva Kilton's team had such a losing streak that she was retired early. That's what can happen to poor coaches.

We have to assume that 99.9 percent of teachers want very much for their students to win; yet, when we examine current practice in many classrooms across the nation, we see a program for failure.

During my first year of teaching, the school began with a dynamic inservice speaker. He said something I have never forgotten. Thundering into the microphone, he charged, "Ladies and gentlemen, we've raised a generation of kids who can read but don't." We even have a word for it now, "aliteracy." In the foreword to *Aliteracy: People Who Can Read but Won't*, editor Nick Thimmesch (1984, ix) says,

> As difficult as the problems of the functional illiterate may be, aliteracy may be the more dangerous problem because of its potential effects on the future of our nation. Aliteracy reflects a change in the cultural values and a loss of skills, both of which threaten the processes of a free and democratic society. Literacy has two critical functions in a pluralistic society. First it knits a people together, giving them a common culture. Of equal importance, literacy provides students with the intellectual tools used to question, challenge, understand, disagree and arrive at a consensus.

It is through reading that we come together. It is through reading that we stay free. Indeed, reading is not a spectator sport.

How did aliteracy become a problem? As educators, as parents, let's look. In many classrooms across the country, I see programs that produce kids who have the technical skill to read but choose not to play the game—the superb baseball players who can hit, run, and field but choose to watch instead. Decades of research tell us what NOT to do. If only we would listen.

Things You Don't Want to Be Caught Dead Doing If You Want Kids to Win

Insist on Round Robin Reading

The nemesis to reading enjoyment most often mentioned by both researchers and students is the pernicious practice of round robin reading (Berglund, Telfer, and Heimlich 1991; Callaway 1981; Bruckerhoff 1977; Carlsen and Sherrill 1988; Lynch 1988; Durkin 1983; Robertson 1974; Gilliland 1978; Karlin 1971). In his article about reading comprehension, Douglas Lynch (1988, 98) explores the research of several reading theorists. "Round robin reading is vehemently discouraged as 'pedagogically outdated as the dodo,' placing the teacher in the role of a 'vulture' with 'hawk-like' qualities."

For the fortunate few who may never have experienced this surefire cure for insomnia, let me describe the ritual. "It's time for the blue birds," calls the teacher. "Bring book three. Take your places in the semicircle. Now, boys and girls, open to page 35."

She peers over her half glasses. "That's page 35, Gregory. Now is everyone on that page? Today we are going to read an exciting story about how Sally takes Puff for a ride in the red wagon." Gregory rolls his eyes, puts his Ninja Turtle on the picture of the wagon in the book and races it into Brad's left elbow. "Gregory," the teacher says, "since you seem to be having trouble paying attention today, you may start by reading the first sentence. Then we'll continue around the circle with each student reading a sentence. Brad, you'll be second. When we run out of boys and girls, we'll start over again with Gregory. Gregory, you may begin. Gregory! Kathy, help him find his place in the book. Gregory, I'll keep the turtle until the end of the day. Please show him where to begin, Kathy." Round we go in the circle, reading one sentence at a time, with no one paying attention except the reader.

Even worse, notice how the little boy with the lisp cringes when the teacher and the children laugh at his pronunciation of *chicken*. See the Japanese child, a new immigrant to the United States, tremble in humiliation as she tries to get her tongue around these strange new sounds. John, a poor reader, begins to act up before it's his turn to read. He is hoping he will be sent to the principal's office before he has to risk the horror of public shame as he struggles to read words his peers find unbelievably simple.

In their article "Twelve Easy Ways to Make Readers Hate Reading (and One Difficult Way to Make Them Love It)," Thomas Estes and Julie Johnson (1983) observe a creative "solution" to the problem that some children cannot or will not keep their place during round robin reading time. They observed a teacher orchestrating her new twist on round robin reading "word by word—first child, first word; second child, second word; ... eighth child, eighth word; first child, ninth word. With expression please. Ludicrous you say? But why more ludicrous than sentence by sentence or even paragraph by paragraph" (8 9).

The criticism of round robin reading by both researchers and students falls into three basic categories:

1. Round robin reading encourages subvocalization.
2. Round robin reading inhibits reading comprehension.
3. Round robin reading has a devastating effect on the self-esteem of some students, making them hate reading in particular and school in general.

The research on this topic includes a study that collected thousands of reading autobiographies written by students in a young adult literature class over three decades. Robert Carlsen and Anne Sherrill share this research in their book *Voices of Readers: How We Come to Love Books* (1988).* As we examine the preceding criticisms, the reader will hear the voices of Carlsen and Sherrill's students.

1. *Round robin reading encourages subvocalization* (Durkin 1983). One of Carlsen and Sherrill's students said, "This oral reading resulted in a persistence in vocalizing when I tried to silent read. This persisted even into college and was a difficult and slow thing for me to overcome" (32).

2. *Round robin reading inhibits reading comprehension* (Durkin 1983; Lynch 1988). Another of Carlsen and Sherrill's students said, "I recall how frightened I would be to be called on to read orally. Usually I would read ahead and try to anticipate the passage I would be required to read.... If anyone were to ask me what I had read orally, I'm sure I wouldn't have remembered a thing" (1988, 33). Round robin reading may confuse students by leading them to believe that the purpose of reading is to read "word by word" rather than to comprehend the meaning of the text (Durkin 1983). Ken Goodman (1973) distinguished "recoding" (moving from the graphic code to the oral code) from "decoding" (moving from the graphic code to meaning with no intervening pronunciations). Sometimes students are so busy matching the letters to the sounds that they have no understanding of what they are reading. But how can that be? Surely if they can say the word they know what it means. Let me tell you about Heidi's German mother.

Even though Heidi's mother spoke no English and her American grandchildren spoke no German, she was determined to do "grandmotherly things" when she visited Heidi's family in Southwest Harbor, Maine. I stopped by the house one day and was astonished to hear Grandmother reading Little Red Riding Hood in lively English that rolled and lilted with her soft, round German accent. "Heidi," I said. "I thought your mother couldn't speak English. How did she learn in two days?"

"She can't speak English," replied Heidi, "but she can pronounce the words. She understands the sound-symbol relationship in English but she doesn't have the slightest idea what she's reading." I'm happy to report it didn't seem to bother the children. They had their grandmother and their story and they wanted nothing more at that moment.

*Material from Robert G. Carlsen and Anne Sherrill, *Voices of Readers: How We Come to Love Books* (Champaign-Urbana, IL: National Council of Teachers of English, 1988), copyright © 1988 NCTE, is reprinted with permission.

3. *Round robin reading has a devastating effect on the self-esteem of some students, making them hate reading in particular and school in general.* As Hilary Holbrook (1983, 29) says, "For some students learning to read is risky business." Certainly a few students bask in the spotlight of the semicircle, anxious to show their less able peers their skill; however, the literature abounds with heartbreaking stories of how much even good students were hurt by round robin reading (Carlsen and Sherrill 1988; Berglund, Telfer, and Heimlich 1991).

Does oral reading have a place in the school curriculum? Of course it does, but it should be taught just like any other skill—like bouncing a ball or public speaking. Let me emphasize once more: Fluent oral reading IS NOT synonymous with reading for meaning. Oral reading has its place, but not in mind-dulling, ego-destroying round robin reading. We'll talk more about appropriate places for oral reading in chapter 5.

Emphasize Isolated Skills During Reading Instruction

Suppose we were to emphasize isolated skills in sports. We would drill the team on shooting baskets, have them practice passing and dribbling, draw diagrams of plays, talk to them about offense and defense, but never have them actually play the game. The idea behind the so-called whole language movement is that you simply cannot learn to read by staying out of the game. You have to get kids into print wholistically and not in isolated bits. Proponents emphasize that language should be whole, meaningful, and relevant to the learners. We can't possibly achieve this if we focus our reading instruction on isolated skills. In "12 Easy Ways to Make Reading Hard," Frank Smith (1974) points out that well-meaning educators have tried to make the task of reading easy by breaking it into small bits. In other words, by isolating print from its functional use, by teaching skills out of context, and by focusing on written language as an end in itself, we make the task harder, if not impossible, for some children. Goodman (1986, 9) agrees: "Many so-called 'skills' were arbitrarily chosen. Whatever research they're based on was done with rats and pigeons—or with children who were treated in research like rats and pigeons. Rats are not kids; rats don't develop language or think human thoughts. Artificial skill sequences turn schools into mazes for children to stumble through."

Students in Byron Callaway's study (1981, 216) also report isolated drill as a major turn-off to reading. Children don't need skill drills to learn to read. In his meta-research study *The Power of Reading*, Stephen Krashen (1993, 2)* found that "in 38 of 41 studies, students using free voluntary reading did as well or better in reading comprehension tests than students given traditional skill-based reading instruction."

---

*Material from Stephen Krashen, *The Power of Reading: Insights from the Research* (Englewood, CO: Libraries Unlimited, 1993), copyright © 1993 by Stephen Krashen, is reprinted with permission.

Emphasize Phonetics to the Exclusion of Meaning

Although simple, well-designed phonics instruction may be advisable in the first and second grades, some researchers (Anderson et al. 1985) believe too many teachers allow this to become their total reading program. Suzanne Barchers (1990, 54) offers this advice: "Phonics is not taught for the sake of being known.... It is carefully integrated into the program when the instruction is logical and meaningful. The teaching of generalizations about words, beginning sounds, unusual blends ... occurs with examples from books using words." Let me repeat, phonics instruction must take place in the context of authentic, joyful, meaningful reading. Krashen (1993, 85) agrees: "Reading for meaning, reading about things that matter to us, is the cause of literate language development."

Teachers must remember that phonics is itself a bit of guesswork. English is a language that doesn't lend itself to phonetic rules. Our language is put together from so many other languages that few absolutes exist. Think of the beginning **g** sound in **g**oat, **g**et, and **g**o versus **g**entle or **g**erm; or the sound of **c** in **c**ity and **c**yclone versus **c**andy or **c**arrier. Consider also the sound of "ough" in the following words: dough, cough, rough, through, and sough. Why in the world do we pronounce the suffix *-tion* as *shun*? Or where is the **r** in colonel? Nancie Atwell, in *In the Middle: Writing, Reading, and Learning with Adolescents* (1987, 216), observes that competent readers don't depend on phonetics. Children and adults alike usually use one of several strategies when they encounter a word they don't know. They skip over the unfamiliar word. They guess at the meaning of the word. And finally, they use the least preferred strategy—they sound the word out. Phonics is the least efficient choice, yet it is the method we most often teach. Guessing is actually the most efficient way to read and learn to read. Both Atwell (1987) and Smith (1974) call it "informed guessing," making reasonable guesses from a relatively small set of possibilities. What readers already know about written language helps them make predictions about new information.

Make Sure You Find Material That Is Irrelevant or Boring

This one just boggles my mind. Why in the world would teachers persist in making kids read irrelevant, boring material? Participants in a sporting event would head for the locker room if the sport were boring or irrelevant to them. Adults wouldn't read irrelevant, boring material (unless, of course, they were taking a college class from someone who had not read this book). Why should we expect more from our students? A major complaint among students in Carlsen and Sherrill's *Voices of Readers* (1988, 136) was teachers who do not consider students' age or interests. Students in Callaway's study (1981, 216) were discouraged by irrelevant or biased material. Children's and young adult literature is available in such breadth and depth that there is no excuse for teachers to give students boring, irrelevant reading material. Thousands of new books are produced every year. Certainly a teacher can accommodate a wide range of interests and abilities.

I'm an optimist who believes that with the right stimulation anything can be made interesting to students. While student teaching in Atlanta, Georgia, I carefully reviewed the basal reader for the next week. Three days of lessons were built around a mindless, vapid story of a duck who was likewise mindless and vapid. "You've got to liven this up, Mary Helen. If your supervisor comes in to see 30 children asleep at 9:45 in the morning, the university might suggest that you explore another line of work." I bought a kiddie swimming pool, and after three days of telephone calls, I located a place to purchase live ducks.

On Monday I built the tension by telling my students that some special friends were going to visit the classroom to help them get started on their story. On Tuesday the children were greeted by three baby ducks happily paddling around in the kiddie pool. After enjoying the ducks (and asking seemingly hundreds of questions about them), the children couldn't wait to get to their story.

After they silently read the story, you could see it in their faces—first puzzlement, then the "you've got to be kidding" look. The unvoiced message was, You brought in real live baby ducks for THAT unbelievably stupid story? They were disappointed, and so was I.

On impulse, I grabbed a copy of *Make Way for Ducklings* by Robert McCloskey (1941) and read it aloud. Then two students, with my permission, headed for the library to find more duck stories, and one scurried to the library for more books by McCloskey. We wrote down questions about ducks, then brainstormed how we could find the answers. More kids headed for the library. Two children called the hatchery where I got the ducks to find out how much to feed them, where to purchase the best duck food, what quantity was needed, and how much it cost. They were off on a math lesson figuring our budget for baby duck management. One forward-thinking child (actually, an adult in a child's body) began making lists of possible "homes" for our ducks after they got too big for the kiddie pool. Later the children explored all the possibilities, except the one that said, "Provide Easter dinner at the homeless shelter."

As two children pored over a dictionary of names, looking for appropriate ones for our new class additions, I began to wonder whether a person could flunk student teaching for failing to complete the basal. As you may have guessed, there is a moral to this story. Certainly, material can be made more interesting with a little creativity, but don't advertise a nonexistent product, and if you do, be prepared. Your customers may move to plan B with or without you. If you advertise a big game, it's a good idea to have the event on the appointed day.

Make Sure You Require Book Reports

"As a reward for finishing this book you get to do a book report. Make sure all the words are spelled correctly and check your punctuation and capitalization. Aren't you excited?" says the teacher. Or, "You've played a great game, team. Now I want each of you to write a play-by-play account of the game. Check your spelling, I'll be counting off one point for each split infinitive. Doesn't that sound like fun?"

Carlsen and Sherrill (1988, 154) report, "Book reports were almost universally disliked by the respondents. Book reports did more to kill the young person's interest in reading than to promote it. Some writers were traumatized by oral presentations even when the presentations were about books they actually enjoyed reading." The survey of research by Berglund, Telfer, and Heimlich (1991) agreed. Book reports were a universal turn-off.

Students in the Carlsen and Sherrill study (1988) resorted to all kinds of subterfuges when faced with doing the mandatory book report. One student had such good luck with an oral book report on Hemingway's *Old Man and the Sea* (1952) that he gave the same report for the next two years. Other students reported such devious practices as building the report on the TV version of the story; copying the ready-made, vivid, complete summaries from *Classic Comics*; or using Cliffs Notes. I'm sure Mr. Cliff has written more book reports than we'd like to admit. A student said, "Book reports ... destroyed the enjoyment I derived from reading. I loved to read just for the sake of reading and learning something new. But reading came to mean remembering insignificant details in order to make a book report" (102).

My story was similar. As I mentioned in the previous chapter, I once made the mistake of reading a book in school. Then we had to do a book report. Two things worked against me. First, I had an excellent memory, and second, the teacher didn't tell us what a book report was. (She'd probably done so many when she was in school that book reports fell into the category of "doesn't everyone know?") The concept of summarizing or picking out the main idea was foreign to me, so I remained after school night after night painstakingly rewriting the whole story. It was a rather dull story about a goldfish, as I recall, and it wasn't one bit better in the retelling than it was in the initial encounter. I vowed never to read a book in school again.

The book you are reading contains myriad alternatives to book reports. I can think of only one reason why you should ask students to write traditional book reports. Here is the one reason. As a middle school teacher, I never assigned book reports; however, Mrs. Kinney, the mother of a former student, didn't agree with me, and I had to admit she had a point. "Do you realize," said she, shaking her finger at me, "your students are at a terrible disadvantage when they get to high school? My daughter Martha just received a *D* on her first high school book report. Students from every other eighth-grade class in the entire county know how to do them but YOURS!"

Had I been courageous, I would have marched to the high school to convince my upper-division colleagues of the folly of book reports and handed over my personal copy of "167 Alternatives to Book Reports." I was, however, already considered a bit of a radical, so I took the low road. After my first-period class was settled, I said, "Folks, today we're going to learn how to do book reports." A hand went up. "Anna, before you ask, this will be a 'one time only' traditional book report. This is what will be expected of you next year in high school, and I want you to have one practice run before you leave. We'll do one together, then you'll do one on your own."

Make Sure You Analyze the Books Ad Nauseum and Accept Only the Correct Interpretation (the Teacher's Version)

Okay team, I think we'd better analyze the video of the game one more time. I have to make sure you understand everything about the play. What did the opponents really do when they dropped the wing back to the safety's position? We'll look at it one frame at a time.

Yes, team, we'll review those play-by-plays until the video becomes a tool in aversion therapy. "Please, please coach, if you promise not to show that play one more time, I promise I'll never play ball again."

And, of course, the only analysis of the plays that is acceptable is that of the coach. After all, what do players know, they just play the game.

Students in Carlsen and Sherrill's book (1988, 101) said that they enjoyed books until they were "analyzed to death." And, of course, the only intrepretation of the literature that was considered to be correct was the teacher's.

Carlsen and Sherrill (135) also report teaching techniques that instilled in students a long-lasting dislike of the classics: dissecting the work paragraph by paragraph, symbol hunting, and reading line by line slowly. Students were happier when they were permitted to read at their own pace, simply enjoying a book and figuring out meanings or discovering symbols for themselves. A little analysis goes a long way.

Don't Let the Kids Read—Build Your Program Around Worksheets and Dittos

This is very important. You have to have something for the kids to stuff in their backpacks at the end of the day, something to adorn refrigerators. If you just sent a book home, the parents might not think you are doing anything but READING.

Think about it this way. You have a team, but you never let them get on the playing field. Every "practice" period, the players draw diagrams of plays, they do a word find of baseball words, they fill in the blank: "A bat is to ____________." Sarah, who is such a nice little girl, obediently fills in "hit." Mary, who is thoroughly disgusted by the whole game, fills in "catch, then turns into a teacher-eating Dracula, with hideous dripping fangs." She's hoping to get some kind of a reaction from you, and she's also curious to see whether you read any of the 7,005 worksheets produced each day.

Then you wonder why your team hasn't a clue how to play the game once they get on the field. By this time, half of them don't care either. Mary is running around doing a vampire impression. Beth is trying to remember "A catcher is to...." Joe is trying to see how many new words he can make out of the Coca Cola sign on the baseball field fence. Kelley's father, a professional baseball player, is going to put Kelley in a private school where they know how to teach the game. And Scott, whose Mom plays baseball with him at home, can't figure out why all these other kids are so DUMB.

In *Becoming a Nation of Readers* (Anderson et al. 1985), researchers reported that children spent 70 percent of their total reading time filling in the blanks in workbooks or on ditto sheets. The commission raised questions about the quality of worksheets and clearly noted that time spent completing worksheets is not related to year-to-year gains in reading proficiency. The board of directors for the International Reading Association passed a resolution in 1988 stating that there is little value in workbooks and ditto sheets and recommended that children read or write during the time usually devoted to these activities.

Make Sure You Have Permanent Ability Grouping

Again, let's think about sports. You have all the talented kids on team one, the average athletes on team two, and the kids who have trouble even finding their tennis shoes on team three. It may be good for the talented kids to a point. But when it comes down to playing the game with others, it would be better if the talent were dispersed. If the teams had a mixture of talent, players would be learning from each other and cooperating. What fun is it for the talented team to always wash over the less talented teams? What are they learning?

And the less talented teams? They can benefit greatly from playing with the talented kids, learning from them and modeling them. When all the team members have trouble finding the playing field, there is less motivation to "sharpen up," to get into the game. But what about the average kids? Wouldn't they be OK by themselves? "What a terrible thing not to be special in any way—not especially good, but especially bad, not possessing special talent, not having special needs. All children bring gifts and talents and all children have special needs" (Cochrane et al. 1984, 135).

Does that mean the coach always works with heterogeneous groups? Certainly not! Some kids need extra help on batting, some on fielding, others on strategy. The important thing is that the players not be "locked in," always working with the same kids.

As they reflect on ability grouping in reading, Orin Cochrane and colleagues (1984, 134) say this: "There is simply nothing good that can be said about placing children in permanent groups.... In fact, permanent ability grouping is undoubtedly the most harmful educational practice in use today." Children get the message that they are in the top group or bottom group. Research shows that the groups seldom change. If you are a Buzzard in first grade, you'll probably be a Buzzard in sixth grade as well. "These self-fulfilling prophesies of doom deny children their chance to be uniquely human.... Usually the bottom group gets far less actual reading and writing time than the top group.... The teacher expects little from the bottom group, so she gives them little to challenge them.... There is nothing at all that is good about permanent ability groups in schools" (134). And kids expect less of themselves. I can remember thinking many times, I can't do that, after all I'm just a Buzzard. What did you expect?

If you want your kids to win, please listen to the decades of research telling us what to avoid. Measure these suggestions against your own experience. Challenge any practice in your classroom or in your school that hurts children, that turns them away from real reading. And remember, if your team loses year after year, you may get traded or retired; and it could be that the team dying to get you is the Buzzards.

Winning Coaches and Winning Teachers Do These Things

It's time to turn away from what not to do and unleash the power that's in every good coach and teacher to create winning players.

Know Kids and Know Books and Know How to Bring the Two Together

One day a student I had taught four years earlier stopped by to see me. After we finished talking about after-high-school plans and the usual "how's it going" kinds of things, he turned to go. He paused at the door, stood reflectively for a moment, then with a studied intensity said, "You know why you are so good?" Because it was obviously a rhetorical question, I remained silent. "You knew kids and you knew books and you knew how to put them together."

"What do you mean?" I asked.

"Well, first of all," he began, "every day when the kids came in, you asked them what was up, how they were, what things they were doing outside of school. If we looked sad or angry, you asked us what was bothering us, what we were afraid of—stuff like that. You observed us, listened to us, and put all the data into this incredible computer brain of yours. And the kids observed you, too. [I lived directly across the street from the school, so this was not difficult.] Every time we'd go by your house, we'd look through the window and we'd see you surrounded by books, reading—we didn't think you ever did anything else—reading on the floor, reading on the sofa, reading on the porch, reading in the backyard, reading at the table."

He continued, "Then presto, it all began to make sense. First you'd come in each day and say, 'I read this terrific book last night about ... does anybody want to borrow it?' But that wasn't the best part. Maybe you'd catch a kid in the hall, or whisper to them in library, or sit down beside their desk and say, 'I know you've been worried about ... here's a book about a boy who felt the same way. You may get some ideas from it' or 'I know you really liked the science fiction movie last night. This book is about a space alien who....' And on you'd go all day long. You probably gave me 50 or 60 books to read and I liked every one. That's why you're good, you knew kids and you knew books and you knew how to put them together."

It seemed like such an easy, natural way. And how do you "know kids"? During my early years of teaching I had the kids fill out an interest inventory answering questions such as:

What do you usually do after school or on weekends?

Do you collect anything?

What's your favorite TV program?

What do you like best about school?

What do you like least?

What makes you happy?

What makes you sad?

What kinds of books do you like to read?

What is your favorite book?

Do you have any hobbies?

Do you have any pets?

But later, I found a much better way. I talked to the kids—at noon, after school, in the halls, before school, while they were in the lunch line, while they were waiting for the bus. I talked and I listened to them. Why not have a "lunch date" or a "breakfast date" with a different student each day, either at school, at a fast food restaurant, or in your room? Why not have a student talking-and-listening buddy when you are on playground duty? While the kids are helping you after school with your bulletin boards, talk to them and listen to them. You may feel more comfortable with interest inventories at first, but you don't really need them. You just have to want to know your kids.

And how do you know books? Quite simply, you read them. I started at ground zero with no knowledge of children's books, but I read fast! Until you have read every book that could possibly be of interest to your students, go to your school or public librarian, who can not only advise you on what the kids are reading, but also show you indexes containing excellent book reviews that will guide you after you have exhausted your own reading list. In case you don't have a library close by, I have included in appendix A a publications list, indexes, and selected booklists. Again, if you listen to kids, you'll find out what they are reading, what they like, and why they like it. Soon you'll find yourself pulling your chair up next to students and saying, "I haven't read this yet, but Greg was telling me that it's about...."

Like a good coach, you have to know the abilities and interests of your players; you have to know the playing field; you have to know a little bit about the game. Then your job as a coach is to make connections and to do everything you can to make the kids love it so they'll keep playing long after they've moved on to other playing fields and other coaches.

Read Aloud to Your Students No Matter What Their Ages

Among the primary findings in *Becoming a Nation of Readers* (Anderson et al. 1985, 23), one declaration rang clear: "The single most important activity for building the knowledge required for eventual success in reading is reading aloud to children." Jim Trelease (1989), one of the best-known advocates of reading aloud to children, calls reading aloud "advertising," a commercial for the joy of reading. Study after study demonstrates the powerful positive effect of reading aloud to students (Berglund, Telfer, and Heimlich 1991; Artley 1975; Bruckerhoff 1977; Jett-Simpson 1980; Livaudes 1985; Beers 1990; Lesesne 1991, 61).

When we read aloud to students, we share a very special moment in time. We slip away to distant lands and places. We meet characters we mutually love and hate. We laugh together, we cry together. We delight our audience and, most important, we give them reasons to want to read. As Carlsen and Sherrill (1988, 45) said, "The association of literature and the human voice has a powerful influence on a young person's interest in reading."

Some teachers think their students are too old to be read to. Where in the Book of Life is it written, "Thou Shalt Read to Your Students Only 'Til They Can Read by Themselves"?

I owe my enduring love of Shakespeare to Mr. Bennett, one of my high school English teachers. Shakespeare was written to be performed, to be heard. The words would flow in magical rhythms from his lips, "The quality of mercy is strained...." Or he would cackle as the witches chant, "Double, double toil and trouble, fire burn and cauldron bubble." Or he would screw up his face in agony, "To be or not to be, that is the question. Whether it is ..." In my own silent reading of Shakespeare, I would have missed the power, the flow, the emotion, had it not been for Mr. Bennett. The oral presentation also helped me understand the language and meaning in ways not possible had I simply read it on my own. Afterward, when we had our silent reading assignment, I could still hear the poetry of the language as if Mr. Bennett were still reading right next to me in my room.

I owe my enjoyment of poetry to Cynthia Pope Haarhues, my roommate during my early years of teaching. I hated poetry. The mere thought of it conjured up memories of memorizing dull poems by dull poets and performing them badly during those endless hours when 30 bored eighth-graders recited the same three poems in singsongy cadences. When I read poetry silently, I couldn't hear the lovely rhythms. Then C-C, as we called her, introduced me to a new world. Preparing for her English class, she read "Jabberwocky," "Eletelephony," and "The Cremation of Sam McGee." I loved it. I was a poetry convert, all because I had heard it "sung" in C-C's deep, lovely voice. Now I have a collection of delightfully funny poetry pleasing to children of all ages. Try starting out the day with some of Silverstein's, Prelutsky's, Moss's, or Nash's poetry. You, too, may win some converts.

So you're convinced. You're ready to put aside a little bit of each day to read aloud to students. Oral reading is a skill that takes practice. Here are a few suggestions for doing it well.

Tips for Reading Aloud

1. Read only selections you enjoy yourself. If you don't like the book, poem, or story, chances are you won't convince your students to enjoy it either.

2. Read the story through at least once beforehand. Look up unfamiliar words and practice pronouncing difficult names. It's also a good idea to preview the story so you're not surprised by the content. Parts that may be objectionable are easier to rephrase if you know ahead of time that they're coming.

3. Visualize the characters in the story and try to develop different voices for each. When I receive thank-you notes from students following my storytelling performances, the thing they mention most often is, "I like the way you changed your voice and became all the different characters."

4. Make sure you have the children's attention before you begin. Ninja turtles and laughing boxes may have to be put in an out-of-the-way place until the end of the reading aloud time.

5. Take your audience in and keep them with you by looking up from your reading to establish eye contact. With a little practice you won't have to worry about losing your place.

6. Change the modulation of your voice to fit the mood of the story. I love students' rapt attention when I whisper or the tension in their bodies as the story gets louder as it moves toward a climax.

7. Change the speed of your reading and your voice quality to match the action of the story.

8. Use pauses to build suspense or to cause your audience to reflect on what has just been said.

9. Use your body and facial expressions to show emotion: fear, sorrow, anger, puzzlement, surprise, love.

10. If the story has long descriptive passages, cut or summarize them. Action and dialogue hold your audience best.

11. You may wish to share with students pictures that are important to the story. Many primary teachers have developed the "hold up the book so it faces the children and read over your shoulder" technique. I do that only if the words alone can't carry the story. Otherwise, I prefer to let the children provide their own pictures through their imaginations.

12. After you have finished reading or telling the story, leave the book out so students can visit it on their own. I recently told Paul Goble's *Buffalo Woman* (1984) to a group of students at the Wahpeton Indian School. I looked up after the session to see a junior high boy gently caressing the book. He was the boy who hadn't wanted to come to the session.

Reading aloud gives children reason to read on their own, just as seeing the pros in action inspires budding athletes to take to the field. When children hear, feel, and experience the world of literature through the oral reading of an inspired adult, or when they see a sport played by the very best, they have reason to join in—spectators no more.

Allow Time for Children to Read in School

Research suggests that the amount of independent, silent reading children do in school is significantly related to gains in reading achievement (Anderson et al. 1985, 76). Krashen (1993, x) builds a powerful case for the critical importance of free voluntary reading. After reviewing more than 225 research studies, he concludes that children who don't develop the habit of reading for pleasure "simply don't have a chance—they will have a very difficult time reading and writing at a level high enough to deal with the demands of today's world." Reading is like any other sport. It requires practice. The more you practice, the more proficient you get. It sounds so sensible, doesn't it? Apparently not, because something quite different is happening in schools. John Goodland (1984, 107) conducted one of the most comprehensive studies of the American classroom. In his seven-year study, *A Place Called School*, Goodland found that only 6 percent of the time in the elementary classroom is devoted to reading, 3 percent in the middle school, and 2 percent in the high school. In *Becoming a Nation of Readers* (Anderson et al. 1985, 76), researchers report that in typical primary classrooms only seven or eight minutes a day are devoted to silent reading. Can you imagine a sports team that practices only seven minutes a day, five days a week? How competent would they be? I think the team might be named the Buzzards.

More bad news—students aren't reading at home either. In a study of fifth-graders (Anderson, Fielding, and Wilson 1988, 285-303), 50 percent of the children read books an average of four minutes a day or less, 30 percent read two minutes a day or less, and fully 10 percent reported never reading at all. In contrast, the children averaged 130 minutes a day watching TV, or about one-third of the time between the end of school and going to bed. Yet, the same researchers found that the average number of minutes per day reading books was the best predictor of reading comprehension, vocabulary size, and gains in reading achievement between the second and the fifth grades.

Fortunately, this is a very easy problem to solve (unless you have an administrator who thinks reading is goofing off, in which case giving him or her this book might help). We simply have to allow time for children to read independently in school. When we provide time for kids to read in school, we make a strong statement about the value of literacy. When reading is the central activity taking precedence over homework, family, social interaction, and recreation, and when students can enter the world of literature uninterrupted to visit places unimagined, we say reading is our highest priority. In its recommendations, the commission in *Becoming a Nation of Readers* states, "Priority should be given to independent reading. Two hours a week of independent reading should be expected by the time children are in the third and fourth grade" (Anderson et al. 1985, 82).

Independent reading time, most commonly called Silent Sustained Reading (SSR), has many other names: DEAR (Drop Everything and Read), SQUIRT (Sustained Quiet Un-Interrupted Reading Time), DIRT (Daily Individual Reading Time). No matter what the time is called, the principle is the same. During SSR time everyone reads, both the teacher and the kids. If the program is implemented schoolwide, the "everyone reads" extends to the secretary, the custodian, the principal, the physical education teacher, the art teacher, the aides—and if the classroom gerbil and goldfish could be taught to read, they'd be included, too. Any teacher who dares to correct workbooks or anything else during SSR gets traded to the Buzzards that very afternoon. Students likewise must read; no other activities are allowed.

The whole idea is that even 15 minutes of reading a day can put the child well into a book, increasing the likelihood that reading might continue at home. This opens new possibilities for reading, including enjoyment, pleasure, and a new form of recreation. Based on his review of over 225 research projects, Krashen (1993, 84) reaches this powerful conclusion:

> When children read for pleasure, when they get "hooked on books," they acquire, involuntarily and without conscious effort, nearly all of the so-called "language skills." They will become adequate readers, acquire a large vocabulary, develop the ability to understand and use complex grammatical constructions, develop a good writing style, and become good (but not necessarily perfect) spellers. Although free voluntary reading alone will not ensure attainment of the highest levels of literacy, it will at least ensure an acceptable level. Without it, I suspect that children simply do not have a chance.

Be a Role Model for Students

The students must see you reading and enjoying it. Ask the kids what they are reading and tell them about your books, like the one you finished last night that was so scary you couldn't go to sleep, or about the one that made you cry so hard you had to redo your makeup before you could go to your church meeting.

I used to stand by my door with book in hand while on hall duty, both reading and watching. Kids from all the classes, not just mine, got into the habit of asking me to tell them about the book. Tell them about an interesting article you read in a newspaper or magazine. Better yet, read it to them. Tell them why you like to read cookbooks or maps. Share your literary life with them.

Never was the power of role modeling made more clear to me than by two experiences I had during SSR. I was totally lost in my book, *A Whale for the Killing*, by Farley Mowat (1972). A pregnant whale goes into a cove near a village during an unusually high tide. The tide drops, imprisoning the whale in the cove. While her mate and her calf call to her outside the cove, the people of the village decide to use her for target practice. She endures gunshots and having boats run across her back. Mowat knows she is growing weaker by the day and tries to focus the attention of the world on these acts of barbarism. Antibiotics are finally flown into the village to save her. But it is too late. The whale dies.

That noble, beautiful creature is gone, I thought, and I began to sob—not soft, gentle, ladylike sniffles, but gut-wrenching, gasping sobs. Then I remembered where I was and looked up. Thirty seventh-graders gazed at me with their heads cocked quizzically to the side, like your dog does when he's deeply concerned about you but isn't quite sure what's wrong. Every child in the room signed up for the book.

Another time, I laughed so hard I had to stop reading to wipe the tears out of my eyes. The book was *Dinky Hocker Shoots Smack* by M. E. Kerr (1972). The book is not about drugs, as the title might imply, but rather about the hilarious foibles of being a teenager. Naturally the kids lined up for the book. The next day two indignant adolescents charged into my room and said, "Boy are you sick. This isn't funny at all." Well, I guess teenage foibles aren't funny if you're living them. They must be funny only in retrospect. Naturally this spurred more kids on to see just how sick their teacher was.

Talk to the students about your reading strategies. Tell them you sometimes skip over the boring parts or words you don't know. Tell them that it's OK to give up on a book after you've given it a fair try. Let them know what you wonder about—for example, "I finished *Killing Mr. Griffin* last night. It didn't seem realistic. I had a hard time believing that kids would give in to peer pressure the way they did in the book. Has anyone else read it? I'd be interested in your reactions."

Atwell (1987, 48) says, "I show them what I'm reading, and I talk about and lend my books. I tell them reading is an old habit, one that shaped my life and gives so much meaning I don't know if I could go on living if I suddenly couldn't read." If the coach doesn't like the game, why should the players? Let them see you love it. Lead by your example. Play hard at the reading game and invite the children to join you, not as spectators but as participants in your literary life.

Surround Students with Literature

This is easier said than done in some schools. The researchers in *Becoming a Nation of Readers* (Anderson et al. 1985, 78) report:

> Analyses of schools that have been successful in promoting independent reading suggest that one of the keys is ready access to books. However, fully 15 percent of the nation's schools do not have libraries. In most of the remaining schools, the collections are small, averaging just over 13 volumes per student. In 1978 schools that did have libraries were adding less than a book a year per student, which does not even keep up with loss and wear.

I despaired when I arrived to take a position as a middle school reading teacher in Northeast Harbor, Maine. There were no books, no library, no magazines, no posters, not even any workbooks or dittos. Thank heaven for the wonderful public librarian, for the Maine state librarian, for the community who supported our book drive, and for the kids and parents who pooled their scarce resources to buy books from book clubs. I hired kids to work after school for me so that they could buy books. I pooled the dividends to buy four or five classroom copies of especially popular books. I asked the newspaper to let us have day-old newspapers for the classroom. I asked parents, doctors, and dentists to give us old magazines. I found discarded basals in the basement of the school, and we cut out stories that were "real" literature and bound them for the classroom or for the kids to take home. Kids wrote books that other kids could read. "Literature" doesn't have to be books. I collected anything that had print on it—manuals, pamphlets, cookbooks, sheet music, maps, posters, and the like.

One day the principal said, "You are going to get me in more trouble than any teacher I've ever had."

"How so?" I asked.

"Your kids are buying and reading so many books the parents are going to be upset," he replied.

"If you would give me a budget to buy paperback books, it would help solve the problem," I answered. And he did.

Ask your administrator to allow you to use your workbook and ditto budget for paperback books. Let the kids help you pick out the books to order.

You can't play baseball without a field or basketball without a hoop. Why would you expect kids to read without access to books? If the books aren't accessible, find them.

Treasure Your School Library and Fight for a Good One

The library media specialist and the media center are critically important to children and teachers as they participate in the great sport of reading. Although the classroom library, which affords immediate access to books, has been proven to increase the numbers of books students read, another interesting statistic has emerged. It seems that reading begets reading. The more books the children check out of the classroom library, the more they also check out of the school library. A good library is essential if teachers and students are to move beyond the textbook in science, social studies, literature, art, music, and other subjects. Not only should teachers schedule times to visit the library, they also need to involve the library media specialist in planning for thematic units and student-directed research projects. Chapter 16 offers additional information on school and public libraries.

Give Students Freedom of Choice in Reading Materials

"Oh dear," we say as we wring our hands and fret. "What about controlled vocabulary? What if it's too easy or too hard? What if all they read are series books?" I say, "So what if?" I can't understand why we expect children to be so different from adults. It's just plain common sense that people who have a choice in their activities are more motivated to engage in them. Wouldn't you be more motivated to read a book that interested you than one I think would be "good for you"? Again, researcher after researcher supports freedom of choice as an important motivation for independent reading (Lesesne 1991, 61; Callaway 1981; Berglund, Telfer, and Heimlich 1991; Carlsen and Sherrill 1988; Sullivan 1991, 40).

Sullivan, in her article "The Natural Reading Life: A High-School Anomaly," reports asking her students to write reading histories. She couldn't wait to get home to read them, and then she cried. In account after account, she found a recurring thread: "I loved reading when I was young; school made me hate it" (40). The general theme continued. About the time students lost control over the choice of reading material and the pacing, they began to hate reading. Sullivan describes her view of a natural reading life, a life we should wish for our students: "A natural reading life is an organic one in which personal choices lead to personal connections and meaningful discoveries ... within which we have permission NOT to complete a reading that bores or frustrates us. In a natural reading life, one reading experience leads to another.... It is a life in which the reader is in control" (45). Atwell (1987, 61) concurs, saying that her students told her time and again that the freedom to choose had turned them into readers. The students in Carlsen and Sherrill's study (1988, 149-150) said much the same thing. Those students who were given freedom of choice "were enthusiastic about reading because they were encouraged to read what they liked and because blocks of time were set aside for them to do so."

Daniel Fader and Elton McNeil, authors of *Hooked on Books* (1968)* tell a poignant story of a student at the W. J. Maxey Boys Training School. It seemed that any book that had sex in the title guaranteed its popularity. Therefore, the librarian reported doing a brisk business in books such as *Ann Landers Talks to Teenagers About Sex*; *Sex and the Adolescent*; *The Art of Dating*; *Facts of Life and Love for Teenagers*; *Love, Sex and the Teenager*, and similar titles. One day an English teacher watched one of his poorest readers choose Hawthorne's *Scarlet Letter* from the rack. Knowing how difficult it would be for the boy to read and not wanting him to be discouraged, he asked him if perhaps he had chosen the wrong book. Fader and McNeil (65) relate the conversation: "'Ain't this the one about the whore?' asked the boy. 'And don't that big "A" stand for whore?' When the teacher had to admit that this description was more or less correct, the boy had heard enough. If it was a book about a whore, it was a book for him."

Several days later the same boy returned with *The Scarlet Letter* in hand and two sheets of notebook paper:

> On those two sheets, front and back, were all the words—and their definitions—the boy hadn't known in the first eleven pages of the book. He had clearly spent the weekend with Hawthorne and the dictionary.... The two sheets of notebook paper represented at least six hours of work.... This was a boy who may not have spent six hours reading since he was nine years old, and had no apparent idea of how to use a dictionary when he came to the Maxey School. Motivated by Hawthorne's whore, he fought his way through the entire book [it took him months].... His conversations with his English teacher were full of his view of what was happening to Hester Prynne. Proceeding as slowly as he did through the story of her life, she took on dimensions of reality for him which authors dream of imparting.... His valediction of Hawthorne's heroine may not have been couched in the author's own phrases, but it conveyed an understanding of the book that no one could improve upon; "That woman," he announced as he returned the book, "she weren't no whore" (65-66).

*Material from Fader and McNeil is reprinted by permission of The Putnam Publishing Group from *Hooked on Books: Program and Proof* by Daniel N. Fader and Elton B. McNeil. Copyright © 1968 by Daniel N. Fader and Elton B. McNeil.

This boy read that book because he wanted to, because he chose to read it. Fader and McNeil (66-67) remark,

> Semiliterate readers do not need semiliterate books.... Reading is a peculiarly personal interaction between a reader and a book, an interaction differing in each case as widely as readers may differ from each other in breadth of experience and quality of mind. But in no case does this interaction demand an understanding of every word by the reader. In fact, the threshold of understanding—of meaningful interaction—is surprisingly low, and even many complex books can be pleasurably crossed by many simple readers.

I had the same experience when my students read *A Whale for the Killing* (Mowat, 1972). Although the book might have been classified as too difficult for many of my readers, student after student worked through the book, if only to find out how a mere book could have such a powerful emotional impact on their teacher.

"But all my students will choose are the series books," you protest. I started my reading habit with the Dana Girls series, but one day (probably after about book 15 of the Dana Girls) I read a "real" book. I tried to go back to finish the rest of the series, but suddenly the formulaic nature of the fiction seemed shallow and vapid. I yearned for power, emotion, surprise—and I read Dana Girls no more. The important piece of this story is that I got into the reading habit with formula fiction but I grew out of it. Your students will, too. But like any good coach, you have to promote the sport, give students choices, and encourage them to grow. The following poem by Carol Combs Hole summarizes this point:

Sam at the Library*

My librarian
Said to me,
"This is the best book for grade three."
That was the year I was in third,
So I took the book
On her good word.
I hurried home, crawled into bed,
Pulled up the covers over my head,
And turned my flashlight on
And read.

But the book was awful
And icky and bad.
It wasn't funny;
It wasn't sad.
It wasn't scary or terribly tragic,
And it didn't have even an ounce of magic!
No prince,
No dragon,
No talking cat;
Not even a witch in a pointy hat.
Well!
What can you do with a book like that?

My librarian
Tried once more:
"This is the best book for grade four."
That was the year I was in fourth,
So I took her word
For what it was worth;
And I took the book back home to bed,
Draped the covers over my head
Turned my flashlight on,
And read.

But the book was dull as a Brussels sprout.
I couldn't care how the story came out.
It didn't have baseball
Or football or tennis,
It didn't have danger and lurking menace,
Or wicked kings like the ones in history,
And it didn't have even an ounce of mystery!
No midnight moan,
No deserted shack,
No great detective hot on the track,
Nobody tortured on the rack.
So naturally
I took it back.

My librarian
Used her head.
When I was in grade five, she said,
"Sam, it's silly to try to pretend
You like the books I recommend,
When it's perfectly,
Patently,
Plain to see—
Your taste and mine will never agree.
You like sports books—
I can't stand them.
I don't like mysteries—
You demand them.
You think fairy tales are for babies.
You hate dog stories worse than rabies.
You're not me,
And I'm not you.
We're as different as pickles and stew.
So from now on, Sam,
You go to the shelf,
And pick out the books you want,
Yourself."

And ever since then
We get along fine.
She reads her books;
I read mine.
And if we choose to converse together,
We smile—
And talk about the weather.

*"Sam at the Library" appears in *Jack and Jill*, copyright © 1967 by Curtis Publishing Company. Used by permission of Children's Better Health Institute, Benjamin Franklin Literary & Medical Society, Inc., Indianapolis, Indiana.

The Booktalk: Advertising the Game

Booktalks, once thought to be the domain of the librarian, are too important a tool to be left to the librarian alone. Booktalks are advertisements. They're come-ons. They invite the students to participate. When I stop by a student desk and say, "Last night I was thinking of you as I read.... It reminded me of that problem we were talking about. You see in this story ..." Thirty seconds later I'm on my way to another desk. I've just given what I call a mini-booktalk. Sometimes I'll read an exciting passage from a book or read just one short story from a volume, then place the book strategically where students will pick it up.

I also think that longer, more formal booktalks are important. In her video *Booktalking*, Joni Bodart (1986) offers these four simple rules:

1. Don't talk about a book you haven't read.
2. Don't talk about a book you don't like.
3. Don't tell the ending.
4. Don't tell everything about a book, just enough to make the audience want to read it.

For those who would like help with their booktalks, Bodart, in two volumes of *The New Booktalker* (1992, 1993), offers ready-to-use booktalks and practical booktalking guidelines. She also includes information on appropriate age levels for books, various books, and relevant informative articles.

I like to build my more formal booktalks around themes. Here are several examples.

For primary grades:

MONSTER THEME

Books:

I'm Coming to Get You! by Tony Ross (1984)

There's a Nightmare in My Closet by Mercer Mayer (1968)

Where the Wild Things Are by Maurice Sendak (1963)

The Very Worst Monster by Pat Hutchins (1985)

The Paper Bag Princess by Robert N. Munsch (1980)

In a Dark, Dark Room and Other Scary Stories by Alvin Schwartz (1984)

Props:

- Black bag that holds a monster
- Monster cookies
- Some scary music and a lighted candle

Sample Booktalk:

Are any of you afraid of the dark? Do monsters lurk in your closet or under your bed? I had a terrible tiger under my bed when I was little. I had to be ever so careful not to dangle my feet over the edge or he'd eat my toes. Other boys and girls besides you and me worry about monsters, and today I'd like to share their stories with you. When I've finished telling you about them, you'll find the books on the monster table in the back of the room. You can go look at them or check them out at the end of the day. First a little monster music and a candle. Now a poem by Alvin Schwartz. [When I tell the story, I change the final word—GHOST—to MONSTER.]

In a Dark, Dark Room

In a dark, dark wood,
there was a dark, dark house.
And in that dark, dark house,
there was a dark, dark room.
And in that dark, dark room,
there was a dark, dark chest.
And in that dark, dark chest,
there was a dark, dark shelf.
And on that dark, dark shelf,
there was a dark, dark box.
And in that dark, dark box,
there was—A GHOST!"

And that's just one of the many stories from Alvin Schwartz's book *In a Dark, Dark Room and Other Scary Stories* (1984, 34-40)*.

Sometimes we just think there might be a monster in our bedroom or in our closet. The boy in *There's a Nightmare in My Closet* finds out that there really is a real live nightmare in his closet and decides to take action. If he succeeds, what if there is more than one? What can a little boy do? You can find out for yourself by reading this book, *There's a Nightmare in My Closet*.

In *I'm Coming to Get You!* Tommy Brown is certain that a terrible space monster is coming to earth to Get Him! And it is true. The monster gobbles up whole planets, chews up mountains, and crushes the banana people, but he is still hungry. So he gets into his spaceship and flies to earth to get Tommy Brown. (Here is a picture of the monster attacking Tommy.) Does Tommy get away? Is the earth safe with the terrible monster lurking about? You'll have to finish the book on your own to find out.

---

*"In a Dark, Dark Room" appears in *In a Dark, Dark Room and Other Scary Stories* (New York: HarperCollins Publishers), copyright © 1984 by Alvin Schwartz, and is reprinted with permission.

The monster family in *The Very Worst Monster* is so excited (all except Hazel Monster, that is). Hazel has a new baby brother, and Hazel's parents are sure that when Billy Monster grows up, he is going to be the Worst Monster in the World. Hazel is crushed. Every time Billy does something naughty, his parents beam with pride. Hazel points out that she can do things that are just as naughty, but her parents ignore her. Finally Hazel does something that is so terrible, that is so awful, that her parents have to admit that she is indeed the Worst Monster in the World, and her little brother is only the Worst Baby Monster. To find out what she does, you'll have to finish the book on your own.

The dragon in *The Paper Bag Princess* burns the princess's castle, burns off all her clothes, and carries off her future husband, Prince Ronald. But she is a real princess! She puts on a paper bag and off she goes to rescue Prince Ronald from the horrible monster. Does she succeed in the rescue? How can one small princess defeat a dragon? You'll have to read the book to find out.

Max is so naughty that his mother calls him Wild Thing and sends him off to bed without any supper. That night Max sails away to *Where the Wild Things Are* and becomes King of the Wild Things. Even the King of the Wild Things can miss his family and get lonely for home, but can Max find his way home? Will the Wild Things let him leave? Even if he can get home, I wonder whether his mother will want a Wild Thing back? The book is over in the monster center if you'd like to find out.

Extension Activities:

Cooking: Have the cooking team make cookies to share with the class.

Monster Cookies*

Ingredients:

½ cup softened butter (one stick)

1 cup white sugar

1 cup brown sugar

3 eggs

1½ cups peanut butter

1½ tablespoons white syrup

1 teaspoon vanilla extract

2 teaspoons baking soda

4½ cups regular oatmeal

2 cups "M & M's"

½ cup chocolate chips

*The recipe for monster cookies is reprinted with permission from Joann Kitchens, Grand Forks, North Dakota, 1993.

Steps:

1. Cream butter in a large mixing bowl.
2. Stir in sugar and eggs. Mix well.
3. Add peanut butter, white syrup, and vanilla. Mix well.
4. Add oatmeal and baking soda. Mix well.
5. Mix in "M & M's" and chocolate chips carefully.
6. Lightly grease a baking sheet.
7. Bake at 375 degrees for 10-12 minutes or until cookies are slightly brown on the bottom. Do not overbake.
8. Take off of pan while hot and let them cool on paper towels.

Art:

- In the art center make monster masks. Have the students put them on and then dance the dance of the Wild Things to recorded music.
- Make a monster. Divide the children into teams of five. Give each team a scrap box of collage materials. Set the timer. A designated child on each team has two minutes to start making a monster by gluing materials on a piece of paper. At the end of two minutes, the child passes the monster to the next child, who spends two more minutes working on it. The play continues until all five children have each worked on the monster for two minutes.

Language Arts: Have students read monster poems as a choral reading or readers theatre or make puppets that will perform the readings.

For middle grades:

SURVIVAL THEME

Books: *Island of the Blue Dolphins* by Scott O'Dell (1960)

Lost in the Barrens by Farley Mowat (1956)

My Side of the Mountain by Jean George (1975)

Julie of the Wolves by Jean George Craighead (1972)

Sample Booktalk:

I often wondered whether I had what it would take to survive in the wilderness, but I never expected to be put to the test.

My brother, two other friends, and I decided to hike into the high mountains in southern Colorado to ski the glacial fields and camp for a few days. The early June day was clear and bright with no hint of what was to come. The hiking was difficult at best. The snow was still deep, up to 4 feet in places, with a hard crust on the surface. The warm days had weakened the surface, making it rotten in places. One moment I'd be walking with a good pace on the surface, and the next minute I'd drop through the fragile crust. The snow holes were deep, and it exhausted me to crawl out of hole after hole with a 40-pound pack on my back.

That's OK, I thought, at least we'll have the path broken for the trip back. I was comforted by the orange triangular forest service trail markers that showed clearly approximately 6 inches above the snow. It will be a lot easier coming back, I said to no one in particular. How wrong I was.

After 7 miles of exhausting hiking, we reached our camp at the base of the glacier. Skiing would have to wait until the next day—I couldn't walk another step.

We slept in two tents. When I awoke, it was still dark, but I felt unusually refreshed for one who had awakened before dawn. I got out my flashlight and looked at my watch. It was 10:30 in the morning. It had to be a mistake. I tried to push open the door to get out of the tent. I couldn't get it open. I pushed harder, moving a pile of snow at least 18 inches deep from in front of the tent. No wonder it was dark inside—only the outline of the tent was visible. The other tent, only 10 feet away, was invisible through the opaque veil of falling snow.

I woke up my fellow hikers and talked about what we should do. That's when we made our mistake. We decided to leave all of our equipment and go back to the car, 7 miles away. Only when we were a 100 yards from our camp, which now looked as if it had never existed, did we realize that the orange triangular markers were covered with the new snow and that there was no trace of our previous evening's trek. We wandered for hours, like people trapped in one of those round glass paperweights where the snow swirls and blinds as you shake it.

One of our party panicked and began to run wildly away from the group. As he was tackled, falling face first in the demonic fluff, the snow let up for the microsecond it took for us to see a mountain ridge. We had come around that mountain from the east to get to our camp. The car lay in a parking lot 2 or 3 miles from the far edge of the mountain. Then the curtain came down. We were once again enclosed in our viewless prison, but now we knew the way.

Time after time during that endless day, I fell into snow holes. Each time I crawled out, I'd wonder whether I had the strength to make my way out of the next one. At last we could see a hint of a blue Dodge Polaris buried in a nearby drift. I dropped through another snow hole and told my companions that I couldn't go any farther. Scott, one of the hikers, pulled me out, and within three minutes we were shoveling out the car with our arms and hands.

How had this happened? We hadn't heard the weather forecast. The snow gate into the mountains must have been closed only an hour after we passed through it. We had told no one where we were going. We would have been safe if we'd just stayed put at the campsite (we had food and warm clothing to last for many days). Yet, we had fled the safety of the camp and tried to find our way out through a terrible blizzard.

I guess I didn't have what it takes after all.

I became interested in how other people survive in life-threatening circumstances. The four books I'd like to share with you today answer the question in different ways.

Island of the Blue Dolphins is about a young girl named Karana who is left alone on an island in the Pacific. As she watches year after year for someone to return, she keeps herself alive by finding food, building shelter, making weapons, and fighting her enemy, the wild dogs. As I read the book, I asked myself whether I would have had such strength. How about you? Think about it as you read this book.

Sam isn't really running away from home. He is just tired of living in an apartment in New York with 11 other people. In *My Side of the Mountain*, Sam hitchhikes to his great-grandfather's land in the Catskill Mountains and survives alone in the hollowed-out base of a hemlock tree. Living in clothing made of animal skins, Sam looks less and less like a teenager and more like the "wild boy" people report seeing in the mountains. How long can he live like that? And who is Bando, the man that arrives with police sirens wailing in the distance? And what about the hunters? For answers, I'd recommend you read this book.

Julie isn't her real name. Her real name is Miyax and she is lost and alone on the North Slope of Alaska. Julie/Miyax in *Julie of the Wolves* survives because she is accepted by a wolf pack and they take care of her. Her real father is a hunter. What happens when her real father, the hunter, comes face to face with her wolf father, her protector? I highly recommend this moving novel to you.

Awasin and Jamie, their canoe destroyed by the fury of the rapids, are lost in the Canadian wilderness. In *Lost in the Barrens*, the boys know that there is no hope for rescue during the punishing winter ahead. Savage wolves and towering grizzly bears are no more a threat than starvation or death from the elements. Do the boys live through the winter? What other dangers does the frozen land hold? Read this book if you'd like to find the answers.

In addition to the theme of survival, another common thread runs through these novels. To live, all of the young people must somehow learn to relate to the wild animals. As you read, test yourself. Could you survive? I'll mention a few other books with similar themes: *The Sign of the Beaver* by Elizabeth George Speare, *The Game of Survival* by Dian Curtis Regan, *Call It Courage* by Armstrong Sperry, and *Hatchet* by Gary Paulsen.

■ ■ ■ ■ ■

Booktalks don't have to be fancy. They can last for 30 seconds or an hour. You can read a passage or do a character or plot summary. They can be planned or spontaneous.

Something interesting happened in my classroom when I started doing my booktalks. (We called it "Selling Books.") Soon I had four or five students each day who wanted to "sell" their books. I was pleased at the proprietary pride they showed as other students stood in line to sign up for *their* book.

Do Something Crazy

Come to school dressed like a character in one of the stories and let students guess who you are. One week later let them do the same. Take a thick paperback book and tear it into one-hour readings. That is especially effective if a student is complaining that all the books are too long. Wear an exotic stuffed bird on your shoulder all day long to advertise Arthur Yorinks's *Hey Al* (1986). Start on Wednesday placing signs in the room that say, "It will happen on Tuesday." Keep building up the suspense all week. On Tuesday read David Weisner's *Tuesday* (1991).

Provide Opportunities for Book Ownership

Remember what it felt like to have your very own basketball, baseball glove, ballet slippers, or hockey puck. It made you feel like you were a REAL athlete. Kids need to own books to feel like REAL readers. Again we have plenty of research that backs up the importance of book ownership (Lesesne 1991, 61; Atwell 1987; Callaway 1981, 214; Carlsen and Sherrill 1988). Carlsen and Sherrill (148) explain, "That which is precious and valuable is that which we want to own.... Writers tell of their pride in owning books, particularly during childhood. Books were so important that the writers kept the same volumes into adult life." That's why organizations like Reading Is Fundamental (RIF) got started—to get books into the hands of readers. (More information about RIF and how your school might participate appears in chapter 18.)

Students in numerous studies (e.g., Carlsen and Sherrill 1988; Callaway 1981; Berglund, Telfer, and Heimlich 1991) reflect fondly on the opportunity to join book clubs. These provide not only freedom of choice but the joys of ownership. Here are addresses:

The Book Plan
921 Washington Avenue
Brooklyn, NY 11238

Firefly Book Club
P.O. Box 485
Pleasantville, NY 10570

Parents Magazine Read-Aloud Book Club for
Little Listeners and Beginning Readers
Division of Parents Magazine Enterprises
52 Vanderbilt Avenue
New York, NY 10017

Scholastic Book Clubs [See-Saw, Lucky, Arrow]
2931 East McCarty Street
P.O. Box 7500
Jefferson City, MO 65102

Troll Book Clubs [grades K-1, 2-3, 4-6]
320 Route 17
Mahwah, NJ 07498

Trumpet Club
P.O. Box 604
Holmes, PA 19092

Weekly Reader Paperback Clubs
4343 Equity Drive
P.O. Box 16628
Columbus, OH 43272

Young America Book Club
1250 Fairwood Avenue
Columbus, OH 43216

Believe in Kids

"Believe in kids" may sound trite, but it's so important. How many times have I seen kids' eyes twinkle when I hugged them and said, "I knew you could do it." Every good coach has to make the players believe in themselves or they won't rise to their potential. Mrs. Adsit believed in me when I had given up on myself, and it made all the difference. Accept and celebrate children's differences, whether in the game of track, reading, or life.

Create Opportunities for Children to Respond, to Interact with Literature

It's not enough to provide books, time, and encouragement; teachers must build in the response. Atwell (1987, 164) says, "to respond, to engage in literacy talk with the teacher are crucial." Although independent reading is important, it is not enough. The context in which readers read must support and extend their interests beyond the SSR time. In chapters 4-12, we'll explore ways to elicit the response and extend reading to action.

It's hard to have a winning team without a good coach. Good coaches are role models; they know the kids, the books, and the plays. They surround kids with literature, give kids freedom of choice, and, most important, they believe in kids.

References

Anderson, Richard, Linda Fielding, and Paul Wilson. 1988. "Growth in Reading and How Children Spend Their Time Outside of School." *Reading Research Quarterly* (Summer): 285-303.

Anderson, Richard C., Elfrieda H. Hiebert, Judith A. Scott, and Ian A. G. Wilkinson. 1985. *Becoming a Nation of Readers: The Report of the Commission on Reading*. Champaign-Urbana, IL: Center for the Study of Reading.

Artley, A. S. 1975. "Good Teachers of Reading—Who Are They?" *The Reading Teacher* 29: 26-31.

Atwell, Nancie. 1987. *In the Middle: Writing, Reading, and Learning with Adolescents*. Portsmouth, NH: Heinemann.

Barchers, Suzanne I. 1990. *Creating and Managing the Literate Classroom*. Englewood, CO: Teacher Ideas Press.

Beers, G. K. 1990. "Choosing Not to Read: An Ethnographic Study of Seventh-Grade Aliterate Students." Ph.D. diss., University of Houston.

Berglund, Roberta L., Richard J. Telfer, and Joan E. Heimlich. 1991. "Developing a Love of Reading: What Helps, What Hurts." *Northern Illinois University Literacy Research Report No. 7* (July).

Bodart, Joni Richards. 1986. *Booktalking*. New York: H. W. Wilson. Video.

______. 1992, 1993. *The New Booktalker*. Englewood, CO: Libraries Unlimited.

Bruckerhoff, C. 1977. "What Do Students Say About Reading Instruction?" *Clearing House* 51: 104-107.

Callaway, Byron. 1981. "What Turns Children 'On' or 'Off' in Reading." *Reading Improvement* 18 (Fall): 214-217.

Carlsen, G. Robert, and Anne Sherrill. 1988. *Voices of Readers: How We Come to Love Books*. Champaign-Urbana, IL: National Council of Teachers of English.

Cochrane, Orin, Donna Cochrane, Sharon Scalena, and Ethel Buchanan. 1984. *Reading, Writing and Caring*. Winnipeg, Canada: Whole Language Consultants.

Durkin, D. 1983. *Teaching Them to Read*. 4th ed. Boston: Allyn & Bacon.

Estes, Thomas, and Julie Johnson. 1983. "Twelve Easy Ways to Make Readers Hate Reading (and One Difficult Way to Make Them Love It)." In *Motivating Children and Young Adults to Read*, vol. 2, edited by James L. Thomas and Ruth M. Loring. Phoenix, AZ: Oryx Press: 5-13.

Fader, Daniel N., and Elton B. McNeil. 1968. *Hooked on Books: Program and Proof*. New York: G. P. Putnam's Sons.

Gilliland, H. 1978. *A Practical Guide to Remedial Reading*. Columbus, OH: Charles E. Merrill.

Goodland, John I. 1984. *A Place Called School: Prospects for the Future*. New York: McGraw-Hill.

Goodman, Ken S. 1986. *What's Whole in Whole Language?* Portsmouth, NH: Heinemann.

———. 1973. "Unity in Reading." In *Theoretical Models and Processes of Reading*, 3d ed., edited by H. Singer and R. Ruddell. Newark, DE: International Reading Association.

Holbrook, Hilary Taylor. 1983. "Motivating Reluctant Readers: A Gentle Push." In *Motivating Children and Young Adults to Read*, vol. 2, edited by James L. Thomas and Ruth M. Loring. Phoenix, AZ: Oryx Press: 29-32.

Jett-Simpson, M. 1980. Students' Attitudes Toward Reading Motivational Activities. Paper presented at the 70th annual conference of the National Association of Teachers of English, Cincinnati: 5.

Karlin, R. 1971. *Teaching Elementary Reading*. New York: Harcourt Brace Jovanovich.

Krashen, Stephen. 1993. *The Power of Reading: Insights from the Research*. Englewood, CO: Libraries Unlimited.

Lesesne, Teri S. 1991. "Developing Lifetime Readers: Suggestions from Fifty Years of Research." *English Journal* 80 (October): 61-64.

Livaudes, M. F. 1985. "A Survey of Secondary (Grades 7-12) Students' Attitudes Toward Reading Motivational Activities." Ph.D. diss., University of Houston.

Lynch, Douglas J. 1988. "Reading Comprehension Under Listening, Silent, and Round Robin Reading Conditions as a Function of Text Difficulty." *Reading Improvement* 25 (Summer): 98-104.

Robertson, J. 1974. "Use Oral Reading Wisely." *Instructor* 83 (June): 29.

Smith, Frank, 1974. "12 Easy Ways to Make Reading Hard." In *Psycholinguistics and Reading*. New York: Holt, Rinehart & Winston.

Sullivan, Anne McCrary. 1991. "The Natural Reading Life: A High-School Anomaly." *English Journal* 80 (October): 40-46.

Thimmesch, Nick, ed. 1984. *Aliteracy: People Who Can Read but Won't*. Washington, DC: American Enterprise for Public Policy Research.

Trelease, Jim. 1989. *The New Read-Aloud Handbook*. 2d ed. New York: Penguin Books.

Literature Resources

George, Jean Craighead. 1975. *My Side of the Mountain*. New York: E. P. Dutton.

______. 1972. *Julie of the Wolves*. New York: Harper & Row.

Goble, Paul. 1984. *Buffalo Woman*. Scarsdale, NY: Bradbury Press.

Hemingway, Ernest. 1952. *The Old Man and the Sea*. New York: Scribner.

Hutchins, Pat. 1985. *The Very Worst Monster*. New York: Mulberry Books.

Kerr, M. E. 1972. *Dinky Hocker Shoots Smack*. New York: Harper & Row.

Mayer, Mercer. 1968. *There's a Nighmare in My Closet*. New York: Dial Press.

McCloskey, Robert. 1941. *Make Way for Ducklings*. New York: Viking.

Mowat, Farley. 1972. *A Whale for the Killing*. Boston: Little, Brown.

______. 1956. *Lost in the Barrens*. New York: Bantam Books.

Munsch, Robert N. 1980. *The Paper Bag Princess*. Toronto: Annick Press.

O'Dell, Scott. 1960. *Island of the Blue Dolphins*. New York: Dell.

Paulsen, Gary. 1987. *Hatchet*. New York: Viking Penguin.

Regan, Dian Curtis. 1989. *The Game of Survival*. New York: Avon Books.

Ross, Tony. 1984. *I'm Coming to Get You!* New York: Dial Books for Young Readers.

Schwartz, Alvin. 1984. *In a Dark, Dark Room and Other Scary Stories*. New York: Harper & Row.

Sendak, Maurice. 1963. *Where the Wild Things Are*. New York: Harper & Row.

Speare, Elizabeth George. 1984. *The Sign of the Beaver*. New York: Dell.

Sperry, Armstrong. 1940. *Call It Courage*. New York: Macmillan.

Weisner, David. 1991. *Tuesday*. New York: Clarion Books.

Yorinks, Arthur. 1986. *Hey Al*. New York: Farrar, Straus & Giroux.

3

Getting the Playing Field Just Right

Creating a Literacy Environment

You can't always tell the condition of a playing field by looking at it. The grass looks green and lush from the stands, but scrutiny at the players' level may reveal holes and knee-twisting lumps, residuals of the resident pocket gopher. Some fields are "long hitters'" fields, some aren't. Some are great for night play; others blind fielders at certain angles. Trouble is, you can't tell by looking—you have to play on the field to find out. Certainly you can tell whether the baseline is straight or whether you have the correct number of players, but the only way to really find out about a field is to play on it.

It's a lot like that with a literacy environment. You can't just look at an environment and know, "Yep, that's one for sure." You may have to live in it a while. Suzanne Barchers, in her book *Creating and Managing the Literate Classroom* (1990, 4), explains why that might be so: "No matter what the constraints regarding space, materials, supplies and student and/or administrative needs, creating a literate classroom is as much a state of mind as a state of being." Perhaps a literacy environment is more an ambiance, more an attitude than a "look." It may be hard to imagine that an eighth-grade classroom with desks bolted in rigid rows could be a literacy environment, but I've seen one. On the other hand, in a primary classroom with the same desk configuration, creating a literacy environment would be next to impossible. The following suggestions will help you create a literacy environment.

The Classroom

Attitude

The teacher in a literacy environment is a coach, a catalyst, a listener, a collaborator, a mentor, a model, a facilitator, an educator, and, most important, a part of the community of learners. The students in a literacy environment are motivated, self-directed, curious, cooperative, involved, challenged, and certainly a part of their community of learners. When we walk into the room, we sense a flexible, stimulating environment that fosters critical thinking, collaboration, sharing, creativity, risk taking, and cooperation. We sense what I call a "crinkle," an environment so alive as to be tangibly felt, an environment that invites "the response." Although we have a feeling of freedom in the room, on closer scrutiny we discover a finely tuned, highly effective structure.

Space

What does an ideal literacy classroom look like? Barchers (1990, 3-4), who created "the atmosphere of a library," says,

> A literate classroom has structure, although at first it may appear chaotic. It is full of books and materials.... If it is a primary classroom, everything has labels at the children's eye level. There are projects in progress and artwork or writing on every available wall, hanging from wires, and propped on shelves. There are areas that invite reading, writing, creating, contemplation, or isolation. There may be centers with materials for learning organized by subject matter or theme.

Lesley Mandel Morrow (1993), in her book *Literacy Development in the Early Years*, recommends dedicating at least one-fourth of the primary classroom space to what she calls a literacy center, which would contain a library corner, writing area, oral language area, and additional language arts materials. She suggests that the literacy center be the focal point of the room as a visible indication of the importance of literacy development. Well-designed classrooms not only increase the number of books children read (some researchers report up to a 50 percent increase in the number of books read), but they also increase the likelihood that children will engage in literacy activities during their free time.

Whether the teacher designs the entire room as a literacy center or devotes a portion of the classroom as Morrow suggests, certain things are essential to that right environment. Books are displayed where they can be easily reached. At least some of the books are presented "cover first" to entice a reader to take a look. The week's special book display may feature one author's books or several books about a similar topic. It's important to change the featured books each week or two to keep interest piqued.

Creative teachers have special places for independent reading—a claw-footed bathtub filled with cushions, bean bag chairs and a soft rug in front of a fake fireplace, a tepee with blankets and pillows, an artificial tree with a big trunk to lean against. Children have so little privacy in the typical school that even a painted oversized carton, a coat closet, or a quiet area partitioned with moveable bulletin boards may be a welcome addition.

Attractive wall displays, both commercial and student-produced, show poems, advertise books, suggest extension activities, give thoughtful or humorous quotes from books, and so on. The message board has pens, pencils, and paper and two messages waiting—one for the teacher and one for a student. Each student may be engaged in a different activity—writers here, readers there—journalizing, sharing, thinking.

The space is flexible to accommodate activities for individuals and groups of varying sizes. Table space for large projects such as bookbinding is available. Materials, supplies, and books are well organized and easily accessible to students. Established routines allow the students to negotiate the space without disturbing others. Areas can be "cornered off" for quiet reading and writing or for student collaborations. The whole environment invites children to get involved, to respond.

Materials

Both print and nonprint materials abound in a literacy environment. Materials will certainly vary according to the age level of the students and the type of projects currently underway. Print materials include:

Fiction and Nonfiction Books (Both Paperback and Hardcover)

- Wordless picture books
- Predictable books
- Big books
- Picture books
- Fiction representing different styles of writing, different cultures and topics
- Music books
- Self-help books
- Travel books
- Biographies
- Cookbooks
- How-to and craft books
- Informational trade books
- Research books (dictionaries at various reading levels, a thesaurus, encyclopedias, an atlas)
- Books written by students
- Joke and riddle books
- Cartoon books such as Calvin and Hobbes or Garfield
- Poetry

But I don't have a book budget, you say. You can't wait for a book budget, I say! Chapter 15, pages 184-185 includes recommendations for parents on how to build a home library. The same suggestions are appropriate for teachers. To review briefly, some book sources are garage sales, used bookstores, book club dividends, community book drives, thrift and resale shops, attics and basements, and library sales. So many wonderful children's books don't seem to go out of style. However, be sure to avoid books that may be sexist or racist or that may contain dated information. If the content of the book is good but its appearance is unattractive, have the kids make new book jackets. It's important to keep the books in good repair. Book repair presents an excellent service opportunity for older students or volunteers.

Ask your students to help you develop a circulation policy and system. Have them take turns managing book circulation and creating book displays. My book circulation policy and system left a great deal to be desired. By the end of the year my library had shrunk by at least a third, so during the last week of school we held amnesty week. Kids were asked to return books, no questions asked, and for every book they returned, they received a piece of candy. I'm sure purists are shuddering, but it worked. I got back lots of books that weren't even mine!

If you have the luxury of ordering classroom books, you will want to consult the bibliographies in appendix A, which list books containing thousands of book reviews. If possible, it helps to go to a bookstore, where you can examine the books firsthand. Take several students with you and get their opinions. Once I knew a book was popular, I'd strive to have at least five or six copies available so that students could have reading and response groups reflecting on the same work. I'd devote the dividends from the book clubs to this "set development."

Other Print Materials

- Sheet music
- Newspapers
- Magazines, both for children and adults
- Catalogs
- Pamphlets
- Appliance and driver manuals
- Government publications
- Posters
- Record covers
- Recipe cards
- How-to directions for classroom procedures
- Student mailboxes
- Message centers and bulletin boards

The materials listed above are available everywhere. The challenge is one of appropriate selection, not availability. One benefit of being an experienced teacher is that you can predict at least to some degree what the interests of your students might be, given your community. However, it wouldn't be teaching if there weren't surprises. A teacher told me that the only thing she could interest one of her students in was steam-powered tractors. By using government publications, collector's catalogs, and various pamphlets, she found out more about steam-powered tractors than she ever wanted to know.

Students can help you collect materials about topics that interest them. Writing for free or inexpensive material is an excellent activity with tangible results for the writers. Your librarian will have several resource books on where to write for free and inexpensive materials.

Nonprint Material

- Films and filmstrips
- Records and audiocassettes
- Pictures
- Artifacts to stimulate reading, writing, research

- Puppets
- Puppet theater
- Materials for centers and thematic units
- Materials for bookmaking
- Grandma's trunk for play production
- Art supplies for book extension activities
- Folders and personal spaces for children to maintain their records and their works-in-process
- Writing materials
- Maps
- Globes
- Specimens

As the curriculum unfolds during the year, the materials you use in your classroom will change. The nonprint materials should be viewed as conduits for making reading connections across curricular areas. They should be introduced and displayed to invite children to respond through reading and writing.

Much more could be said about the effects of the classroom environment upon literacy. If you'd like to explore the topic in more depth, Catherine Loughlin and Mavis Martin offer a concrete, practice-based book, *Supporting Literacy: Developing Effective Learning Environments* (1987), which not only looks at the physical environment of the classroom and its profound influence on behavior and the acquisition of literacy, but also describes in practical terms how classroom teachers can structure their classrooms for maximum literacy acquisition. In addition, Barchers (1990), writing from her experiences as a classroom teacher, describes the nuts and bolts of organizing a literate environment and explores reading, writing, and researching within its context in her book *Creating and Managing the Literate Classroom*.

The School Library

Although the role of the library and the librarian will be explored more fully in chapter 16, it needs mentioning here as we explore the literacy environment. Certainly the library media center provides the tone for the literacy environment for the entire school. I'd propose an "environmental checklist" to see whether the library media center and the librarian promote reading.

Appearance

Is it an environment that welcomes students? Is it colorful, clean, well lighted? Are there attractive book displays featuring special books? Are those displays changed on a regular basis? What do the signs tell us about the library? Are they warm—"Welcome to New Worlds"—or negative—"Silence," "No Gum

Chewing," "Do Not Touch"? Are there things other than books the students can enjoy, such as magazines, newspapers, tapes in a listening center, goldfish, puppets, thought-provoking posters, and works of art?

Scale

If this is a primary school media center, is the checkout desk big and formidable or easily reachable by a small child? Are the tables and desks of varying sizes so that kindergartners can be as comfortable as sixth-graders? Are the materials appropriate to a particular grade level shelved at the right height for browsing?

Personnel

Do the library personnel smile at the children when they walk in? Does the librarian move out from behind the desk to greet the children? Do the librarian's dress and demeanor welcome children or put them off? Can the children pick up clues that the librarian wants them to handle and check out books, or is the message "don't disrupt my lovely book warehouse"? Does the librarian move about helping children without waiting to be asked? Does the librarian plan special programs to create excitement about the library visit? Does the library extend its hours so that parents might visit the library with their children? Does the librarian go into classrooms to work with teachers and kids on information needs or instruct the students in library skills? Is the librarian on curriculum development teams?

Collection

If I were to go into the library and randomly select 20 books from the shelves, how many of them would have been purchased during the "great library era" of the late 1960s and early 1970s? Do I find books with dated information or books that are sexist or racist? Do I find books that reflect an awareness of social and cultural diversity? Are the books in good repair? Are there any books of students' writing? Are the books displayed attractively? Are there paperback books, newspapers, magazines, and other print materials?

Promotion

Does the librarian have promotional activities that stimulate interest in the library and in reading? Are the teachers, the administrators, the parents, and the community involved in library events? In chapter 16, we'll explore other issues related to the library's and the librarian's role in promoting reading.

The Feeling

Add all the above questions together and ask: Does the library feel like a nerve center or a warehouse? Do students feel welcome or do they feel like intruders? Is this an environment that promotes and invites children to respond to literature? Is this a literacy environment?

The playing field has to be right. Both the classroom and library have to be environments that invite the response. Teachers and librarians have to have resources, but more important they have to create an environment that says, "Come on in—a wonderful world awaits you here."

References

Barchers, Suzanne I. 1990. *Creating and Managing the Literate Classroom*. Englewood, CO: Teacher Ideas Press.

Loughlin, Catherine E., and Mavis D. Martin. 1987. *Supporting Literacy: Developing Effective Learning Environments*. New York: Teachers College Press.

Morrow, Lesley Mandel. 1993. *Literacy Development in the Early Years*. Boston: Allyn & Bacon.

4

Children as Sports Writers

Written Responses to Literature

Players play the game. Sports writers analyze it, think about it, and write about it. What were the plays that worked and why? Who were the stars and why? What were the strengths and weaknesses of the team and the team's strategies? What does the team need to do to prepare for next week's challenge?

Readers play the game, but like the sports writer, responding to the game in writing causes them to reflect, to think. Philip Egan (1989, 15) says, "Good readers are active in that they create coherence; that is, they discover how the different parts of the text make sense when considered together.... The best way to teach students to read ... is to have them write about it ... in a way that invites them to create coherence." In this chapter we'll explore several ways to help create that coherence and extend reading through writing.

The Response Journal

Many teachers and researchers strongly promote the use of journals to encourage "deeper" reading (Atwell 1987; Barchers 1990; Spencer 1991; Short and Pierce 1990). The response journal—also called dialogue journal, literature log, and response log—is based on the belief that if students are passive before a text, they will engage it at a superficial level. Nancie Atwell (1987, 165) says that in the years she has corresponded with students through their dialogue journals, she has found that students move far beyond plot summaries into speculation on the authors' process as writers, to seeing connections between books and their lives, and to comparisons between their own writing and the published author's work.

The response journalizing process is simple. Each student has a spiral notebook just for reading responses. As the students read, they write down thoughts, quotes, observations, or questions; place their journals in their teacher's box; and the teacher responds. At first, students may produce only plot summaries, but with prompting, probing questions from the teacher, they will move inside the text. (You have to move them or you'll die of boredom. Kids' reactions are fascinating; plot summaries you can get off the inside cover.)

Suzanne Barchers (1990, 74)* used a literature log (see fig. 4.1) with her elementary students. In one writing, you may wish your students to focus on only one or two of the items listed; however, the log suggests a wide range of ideas for responses. Teachers might use the log with their own modifications, such as adding a "why" after certain questions.

The question most often answered among Atwell's eighth-grade students is "What do you think of the writing, of how this author has written?" Atwell (1987, 178) says, "Answering this question takes kids inside the text where they can actively engage, evaluating and analyzing rather than synopsizing the plot."

---

*The literature log and other material from Suzanne I. Barchers, *Creating and Managing the Literate Classroom* (Englewood, CO: Teacher Ideas Press, 1990), copyright © 1990 by Suzanne I. Barchers, is reprinted with permission.

Fig. 4.1. Example of a literature log.

Name: ____________________

Date: ____________________

Title: ____________________

Author: ____________________

The best part was ____________________

____

The worst part was ____________________

____

The main problem was ____________________

____

____

The problem was solved when ____________________

____

____

Powerful words were ____________________

Words I didn't understand were ____________________

My favorite character was ____________________

My least favorite character was ____________________

An important character was ____________________

I didn't understand ____________________

I laughed when ____________________

I cried when ____________________

I celebrated when ____________________

I will never forget ____________________

I would recommend this book to ____________________ because ____________________

____

____

Does it take a lot of time to read and respond to entries? Atwell, as she reflects on her work with students in reading workshops, says (194) that reading the kids' letters gave her more pleasure and delight than she'd ever realized from grading book reports, worksheets, and quizzes. And keeping up with 75 correspondents took no more time and was much more satisfying.

Think of questions that will take your students deeper into the text—questions like:

- What have you liked or not liked about this book and why?
- How does this book relate to your experience?
- What have you noticed as you've read this book?
- What has surprised you, disappointed you, challenged you, upset you, made you sad, made you angry about this book, and why?
- What has this book meant to you and why?
- What do you wonder about as you read this book?
- What questions do you have about this book that I can help with?

Atwell also encourages her students to write to each other about their reading. This seems to me to be an excellent way to encourage and demonstrate for students a model for literary discourse beyond the classroom. Atwell (189-190) reports that students most frequently ask each other, "How did you feel when...?" and ask for book recommendations from their correspondents.

Patricia Spencer (1991, 68),* in her article "Recovering Innocence: Growing Up Reading," tells about a slightly different approach she uses with high school students. The last six minutes of class each day are devoted to mandatory journal writing. "Without overwhelming requirements for journalizing, students maintain a positive outlook and expect to benefit from the experience of interacting with the text in writing. Pleasure is preserved, but thoughtful response is also expected." Students may choose their own journal topic or explore one of Spencer's prompts:

- Literary letters—Write a letter to someone who might like your book; write a letter to someone who would probably dislike your book; write a letter to the author
- Write a dialogue in which you talk directly with a character
- Write a newspaper headline/article for an event in your book
- How does the author portray female characters?
- Where/how/why does the author use repetition? (ideas/description/whatever)
- Describe contrasting characters presented in the book

*The list of prompts is reprinted with permission from Patricia Sylvester Spencer, "Recovering Innocence: Growing Up Reading," *English Journal* 80 (October 1991).

- What is the significance of the title? Can you think of a better one?
- What is the point of view? What are possible changes/effects?
- What makes a book challenging?
- What author investigation/research is necessary to write a book?
- Character motivation. What do characters want? Why? What are they willing to do to get it?
- How does this book rate in terms of your all-time favorite book? Explain
- Write a diary entry for a character
- Draw a symbol for some aspect of your book. Respond, explain
- Respond to a previous entry on this book

A Potpourri of Extension Ideas for Elementary and Middle School Children

Patterned writing. Have students read *The Jolly Postman* (Ahlberg and Ahlberg 1986) and write similar letters involving their favorite characters. For example:

- Rapunzul writes to a ladder company special ordering an unusually long ladder.
- Prince Charming writes to a detective agency to help him find Cinderella.
- Cinderella writes an ad for her scrubbing and cleaning company.
- The troll writes to complain to the goats about his insomnia and their incessant trip, trap, tripping.
- Little Red Riding Hood writes a complaint letter to the doctor who prescribed her glasses.

Have the students read *Fortunately* (Charlip 1964) or *Alexander and the Terrible, Horrible, No Good, Very Bad Day* (Viorst 1972) and write about their own misadventures, or read *Brown Bear, Brown Bear* (Martin 1970) using the classroom or a room in their home as a model.

Character letter exchange. Have students write to each other as characters in a novel might. For example, have Marty Preston in *Shiloh* (Naylor 1991) write a letter to his mom explaining how he feels about Shiloh and asking her for her help.

Job wanted. Ask students to write a job-wanted ad for the main character in a book or story they have recently read. For example *Maniac Magee* (Spinelli 1990) might write:

> Homeless boy seeks a job requiring speed, skill in negotiating, and daring. Not afraid to take risks. Would consider a reading/tutoring job in exchange for live-in situation. All replies will be kept confidential. References furnished upon request. If interested, reply in writing to Box 751 by a week from Friday. Otherwise, I may be moving on.

Illustrate and bind original books. Circulate student-produced books in the classroom and, if possible, around the school. Bookbinding instructions are included in appendix B.

Write reviews of children's books. The school newspaper or the community paper may have a book review section. Students could develop different themes for different issues, such as science fiction, biographies, scary or humorous books. The principal might put the reviews in the principal's biweekly newsletter.

Write to an author. The letter could include why the student liked the author's books. Students could ask questions they thought of when they were reading the book, or questions about how the author goes about writing the books, or questions about the writer personally. If students can't get the author's home address at the library, they can write to the publisher and ask that the letter be forwarded.

Write to a friend. Suggest students write to a friend telling them why they think their friend would like the book they just finished reading. Remind them to include the title and the author so their friend can find it in the library.

Write a character journal. As students read a book, or after they have finished it, they could pretend they are the main character and keep a diary or log representing their experiences. For example, they could imagine that they are Tuck, Karana, Charlotte, or Maniac Magee.

Compare the video or TV version of a book with the written version. Sometimes as students read a book, they imagine things quite differently from the way the filmmaker portrays them. Sometimes filmmakers even change the setting or the ending. Have students use a chart (fig. 4.2) to compare what they thought as they read the book with how it was portrayed in the video or TV version.

Write ads or publisher's blurbs for books. Have students sell the book in as colorful and precise terms as possible. Try different ads for different audiences. For example, try a travel ad for *Island of the Blue Dolphins* (O'Dell 1960), or a "protection of an endangered species" ad for *Julie of the Wolves* (George 1972).

Fig. 4.2. Chart for comparing book with film version of same story.

NAME OF BOOK	
Book	TV or Video
Main Character (Name) Appearance	**Main Character (Name)** Appearance
Voice	Voice
Characteristics	Characteristics
Setting: Location and Time	Setting: Location and Time
Major Conflict in Story	Major Conflict in Story
Ending	Ending

Write headlines for books. Have students create special headlines for books they've just finished and post them on a "Read All About It" bulletin board. Have students try to guess the names of the headlined books. For example, for primary grades, "Woman Receives Strange Gift from Son" (*Crictor*, Ungerer 1958) or Lion Escapes from the Zoo" (*The Happy Lion*, Fatio 1954) or "Miraculous Broom Discovered" (*The Widow's Broom*, Van Allsburg 1992). Older children might write "Boy Uncovers Cruelty to Dog" (*Shiloh*, Naylor 1991) or "Brave Girl Saves Family from Certain Death" (*Number the Stars*, Lowry 1989) or "Worms, Hot Sauce and Other Gourmet Delights" (*How to Eat Fried Worms*, Rockwell 1973).

Write new endings for books by including a character from another book. For example, what if Encyclopedia Brown joined Meg, Calvin, and Charles Wallace in *A Wrinkle in Time* (L'Engle 1962)? What if *Harriet, the Spy* (Fitzhugh 1964) lived next door to the boys from *How to Eat Fried Worms*?

Make lists. Some children love to make lists. Have them create an unusual word book from their reading—books, newspapers, magazines, and so on. After they have accumulated a page of weird or unusual words, have them incorporate 10 of them into a story.

Create a new adventure for a favorite character in a book. For example, the boys in *How to Eat Fried Worms* might open a "gourmet" restaurant with unusual foods aimed at grossing out the kids in the neighborhood, or Marty Preston and Shiloh might see something strange in the woods near their house and go to investigate.

Write classified ads for fairy tale characters or favorite book characters. For example:

> Found: One glass slipper, only worn once. Will the owner please contact Prince Charming at 682 Castle Drive. Owner must be able to prove rightful ownership.
>
> For Sale: One gingerbread house on Dark Woods Lane. Has an unusually large oven and a nice enclosed space for outdoor pets. To make an appointment to see this charming house, please call the H. and G. Baking Company at 786-0961. Ask for G.
>
> Wanted: A nice quiet bridge with no goats within 40 miles. Must be able to accommodate sleeping quarters for a gentle, soft-spoken Troll beneath. Prefer a woods on one side and a meadow on the other but purchaser will negotiate. Send pictures and specifics to Box 95 at Troll Tripping Hollow.

Think about the stories you've read and create names of businesses for your own professional building. Figure 4.3, a Frank & Ernest cartoon, might inspire students to create names for their own professional building.

Fig. 4.3. Names of make-believe businesses from "Frank & Ernest."

FRANK & ERNEST® by Bob Thaves

"Frank & Ernest" is reprinted by permission of UFS, Inc.

Read several myths, then write your own. Creation myths abound in every culture. Ask students to read several from the books on creation myths listed in the bibliography, or read the stories that follow. Have the children write a new episode to each myth or introduce a new character who might change the direction of the story. Students could also take the myth from one culture and place it in another, writing a new myth patterned after the original tale. Notice how the story "How the Sioux Came to Be" reads very much like the great flood described in the Bible.

HOW THE SIOUX CAME TO BE

from *Stories of the Northern Plains*
(Pelton 1991)

In the time before people recorded time, a time when animals and humans were more closely related than they are today, The Great Spirit, Wakan Tankan, looked down upon his people and he was angry. The people of the earth lived only for themselves. They took from the earth and gave nothing back. They no longer followed the sacred ways.

I will have a better people, he thought. He brought the lightning and the rain fell in rivers of tears. As the waters rose higher and higher, he sent the water monster to fight the people.

Only a few people survived the monster's vengeance. Those people found one hill that was not covered with water, and to its safety they retreated. But there was no sanctuary from the anger of Wakan Tankan. The Great Spirit sent the winds, and the winds brought the waves. The water swept over the hill, tumbling the rocks and pinnacles down upon the people crushing them like fragile seashells. The water took the life of all but one.

A young woman who, unlike the others, followed the sacred teachings of her people, climbed a hill seeking refuge. A great spotted eagle took pity on her and grabbed her in with his powerful talons carrying her to safety in the top of a tree that stood on the highest pinnacle in the Black Hills. From her sanctuary, she wept as she watched the destruction of her people.

The Great Spirit willed that the Eagle and the woman become husband and wife. In time the woman bore twins, a boy and a girl. After the waters subsided, the great eagle carried the mother and the children down to earth.

Then Wakan Tankan warned, "You must remember these sacred teachings. During the flood, the blood of your ancestors mixed with the waters and the silt of the earth. When the waters receded, the blood and the silt turned into red pipestone that lies to the east. The pipestone quarry is the sacred grave of the ancient ones. From this rock, you will make the sacred ceremonial pipe. The breath and the power of the ancient ones flowed through it. It is a living thing."

He concluded by saying, "Tell your children and your children's children that you are the descendants of the eagle, the most powerful and wisest of all the birds. You are pure and from you shall come a great nation. Now let the new order begin." The children grew and had children and those children had children and from them, a new order was born, The Lakota.

■ ■ ■ ■ ■

RAVEN BRINGS THE LIGHT

from *Images of a People: Tlingit Myths and Legends*
(Pelton and DiGennaro 1992)

Long ago, so many years ago that, even among the elders, none can remember this time, there was no light in the world. People found their way from place to place by listening carefully to the sounds their footsteps made as they picked their way along a trail. They noticed the soft feel of pine needles beneath their feet and listened to the sigh of wind in the hemlock trees as they reached a certain point in their journey. With their fingers the people carved grooves in the trees along a path. In this way they could remember where to turn going to the spring for water or to the house of a friend. The light from the sun, the moon, and the stars was held captive by an old man, who lived at the head of the Nass River. No one, not even his beloved daughter, was allowed to take the light from the boxes where he had hidden it. So his daughter, like all the other people, had to grope her way to the spring to find water for cooking.

Raven, the trickster, was tired of living in darkness. He could not see the beauty of the world around him, and in his vanity, he felt sad that no one could see and admire his great beauty and his magnificent plumage. Raven was determined to find a way to bring light into the world from its hiding place in the old man's house.

First, Raven turned himself into a speck of dirt and hid in the basket the old man's daughter used to collect fresh water. He thought that in this way he could trick her into swallowing him.

As the girl dipped her basket into the spring, however, she murmured to herself, "I don't remember if I cleaned this basket yesterday. I had better throw this water away and collect some more." So Raven was dashed to the ground with the water, where his feelings, as well as his feathers, were very much ruffled.

Next, Raven changed himself into a single hemlock needle and attached himself to a branch along the path where the old man's daughter groped her way to the spring each day. As her fingers brushed against the bough where Raven was attached, the hemlock needle broke loose and drifted down into the young girl's basket. This time, as she dipped her basket into the spring, the hemlock needle floated gently on the surface of the water, where it remained as she carried it home.

When the girl paused for a drink of the cool water from her basket, the Raven-turned-hemlock-needle slipped unnoticed down her throat into her belly, where it began to grow into a boy-child.

The time came for her to deliver, and a hole was dug in which she would give birth in the usual Tlingit manner. Although the birthing place was comfortably lined with soft furs, the baby would not come forth, for he did not want to be born on these fine furs. His grandfather had the furs removed and soft moss put in their place, and then the baby was born.

The baby's eyes darted all around, trying to pierce the darkness. Somewhere beneath night's heavy black blanket were the boxes containing the light. His soft baby croon, like the bubbly warble that Raven can make, enchanted his grandfather, who delighted in holding the child. But the baby could also wail with the hoarse, raucous cry of Raven. During these times the grandfather was beside himself trying to quiet the young boy.

As the baby grew he began to crawl and to explore the house where he lived with his mother and grandfather. The grandfather, like all grandfathers before him and since, indulged his young grandchild. He made rattles for the boy from dried deer hooves, which he fastened to a stick. This amused the Raven-child for a time, until he discovered the light-boxes hid in the corner. The child pointed at the boxes and wailed piteously until his grandfather could not stand the awful sound any longer.

"Give my grandson what he is crying for!" insisted the old man to his daughter. "Give him that small box in the corner."

So the Raven-child was given the smallest of the boxes, which contained the stars. He chortled and crooned his melodious Raven cry as he rolled the stars about on the floor. Suddenly, he tossed them high in the air, through the smokehole. The stars continued heavenward, scattering themselves about the sky, where they remain until this day. Then the boy began to cry again, louder and harsher than before, all the while pointing to the boxes that were hidden away.

"Let him play with the moon, then," said the grandfather, holding his hands over his ears to shut out the racket. He handed the medium-sized box to the child to open. The boy was delighted, rolling and bouncing the beautiful, luminous ball around and around the house. He played catch with his mother, his black eyes dancing with mischief as they were illuminated by the silvery light. All at once he bounced the moon hard against the floor. It flew high over his mother's head and out of the smokehole, coming to rest at last in the topmost branches of a tall spruce tree.

Raven-child's gurgles of delight soon turned to hideous wails of dismay as he begged once more for the remaining prize in the corner. There was nothing his grandfather or mother could do to console him except to give him the last and largest of the boxes.

When the boy opened this box, which contained the daylight, he gave the Raven cry "Ga." Then, changing himself into his true raven form, he flew through the smokehole with the light. The grandfather and his daughter had just enough time to catch a glimpse of Raven in his magnificent plumage before he was gone, streaking across the sky with the light that he had released from the box.

As for the daughter, she was delighted that she no longer had to grope her way to the spring for water. And after that, she always looked in her basket for any stray hemlock needles before she drank.

■ ■ ■ ■ ■

Read several pourquoi ("how and why") stories, then write your own for a classroom book. Pourquoi stories, closely related to myths, explain the how and why of physical or cultural phenomena. Animal pourquoi tales explain how animals came to have various characteristics. A good way to get started is to use the following formula:

"Why the (*name of the animal*) has (*a particular feature*).

The following two examples of pourquoi stories were written by students Kyle Archbold and Jon White Owl.

WHY HOUSES HAVE CHIMNEYS*
by
Kyle Archbold
(Written while a third-grade student in
Enderlin, North Dakota)

A long time ago houses did not have chimneys and so it would get hot and stuffy and people usually spent their days outside. There was a boy named Dennis and he loved bubble gum, so he went around town blowing bubbles with his gum. One day he made a bet with his friends that he could blow the biggest bubble out of gum, so he ate 10 pounds of gum and blew a bubble and he went up, up, up and up. He fell down, down, down, and down and right through the roof of his house and made a hole. He was all right because he landed on his couch and all the smoke went out of the roof and led to the modern chimney today.

■ ■ ■ ■ ■

WHY THE PHEASANT IS SO HANDSOME**
by
Jon White Owl, Sioux
Fort Peck, Montana
(Written while a seventh-grade student
at Wahpeton Indian School)

When the Great Spirit was choosing the form and colors of the pheasant, the male spoke up and said, "I am the man so I should have the beautiful body." Then the Great Spirit asked the female, "Do you agree with what he said?" She agreed. She was smarter than he. She chose to be brown and gray, all the ugly colors. Then the Great Spirit made the first people. When they got hungry they went hunting. They could see the male right away, but the female blended right in with everything. The lesson of this legend is not to choose everything right away or you might end up like the male pheasant.

■ ■ ■ ■ ■

*"Why Houses Have Chimneys" is reprinted with permission from Kyle Archbold and his parents, Dennis and Carmen Archbold.

**"Why the Pheasant Is So Handsome" is reprinted with permission from Jon White Owl and his guardian, Violet Martell.

Read several legends, then write a classroom book. Ask students to go to the library and read several legends or tall tales. They can either place the hero or heroine in a new setting with new adventures, friends, or problems, or they can create their own legends. The following story comes from *Every Child a Storyteller* (Kinghorn and Pelton 1991, 39). It shows how a legendary character can be placed in a new setting.

PAUL BUNYAN AND THE BLIZZARD OF 1892

by

Mary Helen Pelton

The temperature had been hovering around ninety-seven degrees below zero for six weeks. Even Paul and the boys couldn't go out in weather like that. The big lumbermen were getting right cranky and mean from being cooped up like a bunch of angleworms in a bait can.

Sam Redeye was particularly cantankerous. "Mighty Luke, you are breathing too loud; a fellow can't hear himself think."

"What do you mean too loud, you ugly frog. If I looked as bad as you, I wouldn't care if I ever breathed again," hollered Mighty. Mighty didn't even have time to blink. A huge pillow hit him square in the face and burst in an explosion of goose down. Mighty hurled a pillow back at Redeye knocking off his hat and his pipe.

Before you knew it all the boys had picked up pillows and were pounding the daylights out of each other. Pillows were exploding like fireworks on the Fourth of July. Goose feathers were flying everywhere. Just then a huge wind came up and picked up the feathers turning them into huge snowflakes. The Great Blizzard of 1892 began.

Within three days those goose down snowflakes covered the state we now call Minnesota with twenty-five feet of snow and with it the temperature rose to a warm two below zero.

As soon as the blizzard stopped, the boys started digging out Babe, the Blue Ox, and the other livestock. If it hadn't been for the Big Thaw they'd be digging still. But then, that's another story.

■ ■ ■ ■ ■

The seventh-grade students at Wahpeton Indian School in Wahpeton, North Dakota, wrote a book called "Indian Legends." Two of the stories follow.

LEGEND OF THE SPIDER GIRL*
by
Jon White Owl, Sioux
Fort Peck, Montana
(Written while a seventh-grade student at
Wahpeton Indian School)

A long time ago a Navaho girl loved to weave. From early morning to late at night she weaved and weaved. She did nothing but weave. Sometimes she would weave all night. Her parents would tell her to do something like water the sheep. She just kept on weaving. One day an old medicine man called everybody to a council in the middle of the village. Then he told the people to start to get ready for a sacred ceremony. Then he came to the girl and told her to get something special for the ceremony. She said she would do it right away. Then she started back to her living place. She said to herself, "The ceremony won't be until tomorrow." So she started to weave. She kept on weaving. Pretty soon she fell asleep. When she awoke the ceremony had already started. She went to it. When the medicine man saw the girl he asked where the stuff was she was supposed to get. Then she told him what had happened. The Great Spirit was so mad at her, he turned her into a spider. From this day on, the spider does nothing but weave.

■ ■ ■ ■ ■

THE BEAT OF THE DRUM**
by
Prairie Rose Greyeagle, Sioux
Fort Yates, North Dakota
As told to her by her uncle, Allan White
(Written while a student at Wahpeton Indian School)

Many people believe that the beat of the drum at a pow wow is the heart beat of every dancer, expressing how they feel by dancing. Here is the story.

Long, long ago, when people first started to roam the earth, Old Man Coyote was very old and was very sick. He needed medicine badly, but there was no medicine man around to hold a ceremony for him.

Soon a young warrior, by the name of Iyan Hokshi, Stone Boy, came along and saw that Coyote was old and dying. Coyote

*"Legend of the Spider Girl" is reprinted with permission from Jon White Owl and his guardian, Violet Martell.

**"The Beat of the Drum" is reprinted with permission from Prairie Rose Greyeagle and her mother, Jennifer Jacobsen.

told him he was afraid to die, so Stone Boy held a ceremony for him.

Stone Boy told Coyote to stay in the lodge and not to come out until he said so. For three days and three nights, Stone Boy kept a bonfire going and beat on a drum. After the ceremony was fulfilled, the beat of the drum became Coyote's heart beat. That is why he is alive to this day.

In many stories and legends, Coyote is always the enemy. But as Stone Boy was growing up, his mother always told him to love his enemies even at times when they made him very, very angry. This is why, whenever Coyote becomes very sick, Stone Boy beats on the drum to keep him alive.

■ ■ ■ ■ ■

Read several poetry books and write poems in the style of the poet. Another possibility is to read about poetry forms such as quatrains, haiku, limericks, cinquains, tanka, and couplets and have students write poems in one of these forms. An excellent source for ideas is *Super Kids Publishing Company* (Robertson and Barry 1990).* The authors also suggest other poetry ideas, including vertical poems (see fig. 4.4).

Fig. 4.4. Example of a vertical poem.

Vertical

To start a vertical poem, first choose a word describing an idea. Then, on the left hand side of your paper, write the chosen word vertically, one letter per line. Now write the poem, each line beginning with the letter written there and also describing or giving information about the chosen word.

Running

Racing to get
Under the wire
Never looking back
Never faltering
Inch by inch
Nearing the finish
Going at full speed.

about *Make Way for Ducklings* by Robert McCloskey

Mallards
Always searching,
Looking for a nest.
Lay their eggs in the park
And burst with pride.
Responsible now for so many
Ducklings,
So content!

*The vertical poem from Deborah Robertson and Patricia Barry, *Super Kids Publishing Company* (Englewood, CO: Teacher Ideas Press, 1990), copyright © 1990 by Libraries Unlimited, is reprinted with permission.

Desktop Publishing

Many of the writing ideas mentioned in this chapter can be made more manageable through the use of computers. Even young children can be taught to use computers to enhance their work. In their book *From Scribblers to Scribes: Young Writers Use the Computer*, Katzer and Crnkovich (1991, xii)* say, "Computers give students and teachers neatly printed copies of their work with a minimum of effort. They allow young writers to address the higher cognitive skills of composition, revision, and editing without the problems associated with forming letters. The teacher's job is made easier because student work can be easily compiled into impressive final products." Later in the book (76-77, 118), the authors discuss the advantages of publishing with computers.

1. *Motivation*. Computers motivate children to publish. They can produce their own work that looks "like a real book."

2. *Ease of correction of errors*. The creative work of writing is fun, but the editing and correcting can be laborious for little hands as they copy and recopy. The computer makes it easy to correct errors and make changes in graphics and text.

3. *Increased output*. Katzer and Crnkovich found that young children write more because of the motivation, ease, and flexibility that computers provide.

4. *Print, fonts, and features*. With computers, children can add interest by varying the size of print (even creating their own big books) and by designing their own special published pieces using different fonts.

5. *Graphics*. Not only can students illustrate their writing using the computer, they also have access to the graphics that come with various computer programs.

6. *Quick and easy duplication*. The computer and printer allow for copies that are as clear and sharp as the original.

7. *Easy storage*. No longer is it necessary to save hard copies of children's work in classroom file cabinets. Children's work can be saved on a disk and stored in small boxes.

8. *Multisensory development*. The computer allows young children to learn the shapes, names, and sounds of the letters in two or three modalities. The keyboard provides tactile support as the letters are pressed. The left-to-right and top-to-bottom orientation in reading is reinforced as the words appear on the computer screen. If a talking-text word processor is used, auditory reinforcement is also provided.

---

*Excerpt from *From Scribblers to Scribes* by Sonia Katzer and Christine A. Crnkovich. Copyright © 1991 Libraries Unlimited, Englewood, CO.

Certainly writing and reading can occur without the help of the computer, but computers provide one more way to get kids and print together. They can help children feel like real writers as they share their very professional-looking books with others or see them displayed on classroom and library shelves.

The ideas for reading and writing connections are seemingly endless. Certainly the response journal takes kids deeper into the text, making them true participants in the meaning-making process, and the many desktop publishing ideas can extend children's reading in fun and creative ways.

After all, it's not just the sports players who have fun. Sports writers first enjoy watiching the game. Later they also have the pleasure of thinking about the game and exploring its meaning in new and creative ways, just as readers do.

References

Atwell, Nancie. 1987. *In the Middle: Writing, Reading, and Learning with Adolescents*. Portsmouth, NH: Heinemann.

Barchers, Suzanne I. 1990. *Creating and Managing the Literate Classroom*. Englewood, CO: Teacher Ideas Press.

Egan, Philip J. 1989. "Frequent Short Writing: Motivating the Passive Reader." *College Teaching* 37 (Winter): 15-16.

Katzer, Sonia, and Christine A. Crnkovich. 1991. *From Scribblers to Scribes: Young Writers Use the Computer*. Englewood, CO: Teacher Ideas Press.

Kinghorn, Harriet R., and Mary Helen Pelton. 1991. *Every Child a Storyteller*. Englewood, CO: Teacher Ideas Press.

Pelton, Mary Helen, and Jacqueline DiGennaro. 1992. *Images of a People: Tlingit Myths and Legends*. Englewood, CO: Libraries Unlimited.

Robertson, Deborah, and Patricia Barry. 1990. *Super Kids Publishing Company*. Englewood, CO: Teacher Ideas Press.

Short, Kathy Gnagey, and Kathryn Mitchell Pierce, eds. 1990. *Talking About Books: Creating Literate Communities*. Portsmouth, NH: Heinemann.

Spencer, Patricia Sylvester. 1991. "Recovering Innocence: Growing Up Reading." *English Journal* 80 (October): 65-69.

Literature Resources

Ahlberg, Janet, and Allan Ahlberg. 1986. *The Jolly Postman or Other People's Letters*. Boston: Little, Brown.

Charlip, Remy. 1964. *Fortunately*. New York: Four Winds Press.

Fatio, Louise. 1954. *The Happy Lion*. New York: Scholastic.

Fitzhugh, Louise. 1964. *Harriet, the Spy*. New York: Harper & Row.

George, Jean Craighead. 1972. *Julie of the Wolves*. New York: Harper & Row.

L'Engle, Madeleine. 1962. *A Wrinkle in Time*. New York: Dell.

Lowry, Lois. 1989. *Number the Stars*. Boston: Houghton Mifflin.

Martin, Bill. 1970. *Brown Bear, Brown Bear, What Do You See?* New York: Holt, Rinehart & Winston.

Naylor, Phyllis Reynolds. 1991. *Shiloh*. New York: Macmillan.

O'Dell, Scott. 1960. *Island of the Blue Dolphins*. New York: Dell.

Pelton, Mary Helen. 1991. *Stories of the Northern Plains*. Grand Forks, ND: Storyteller of the Northern Plains. Audiotape.

Rockwell, Thomas. 1973. *How to Eat Fried Worms*. New York: Franklin Watts.

Spinelli, Jerry. 1990. *Maniac Magee*. New York: HarperTrophy.

Ungerer, Tomi. 1958. *Crictor*. Harper & Row.

Van Allsburg, Chris. 1992. *The Widow's Broom*. Boston: Houghton Mifflin.

Viorst, Judith. 1972. *Alexander and the Terrible, Horrible, No Good, Very Bad Day*. New York: Atheneum.

5

Children as Announcers

Using Drama and Storytelling

Announcers must pay close attention to the game and certainly must understand the game at more than a superficial level. If they don't, their play-by-play account of the game will be neither accurate nor interesting.

Readers who want to interpret literature for audiences through drama or storytelling face the same challenges. Drama and storytelling demand that children understand the internal logic and meaning of a text so that they can help the audience "be in the text," much like a radio announcer takes you "into the game." As Terry Johnson and Daphne Louis (1987, 143) say in *Literacy Through Literature*, "Any form of dramatization is a comprehension exercise par excellence. The demands placed on a reader taking cold printed text and turning it into a convincing simulation of reality, replete with the cadences of living language, movement, gesture, costume, setting and timing, go far beyond anything demanded by comprehension questions." Johnson and Louis distinguish drama and theater by saying, "Drama encompasses everyone in the room; there is no stage and no audience. Theatre, on the other hand, involves active actors and a passive audience. We believe drama has immediate and direct educational benefits; the educational value of theatre is less direct" (143). We'll explore both drama and theater as ways to engage children in the interpretation of literature and to stimulate reading through storytelling, readers theatre, choral reading, puppetry, radio scripts, and drama.

Storytelling

The road that intertwines storytelling and reading can begin at two points. A storyteller can share a story that comes from a book. The listeners will clamor to read the story on their own or will look for other stories by the same author or on the same topic. It works! I've seen it happen hundreds of times. The second access point connecting storytelling and reading occurs when the child becomes the storyteller. Children are engaged in reading as they look for appropriate "telling" stories and must think deeply about the subtleties of the story to convey it meaningfully to an audience.

The storytelling process is the same for children and adults. We'll explore in more detail how storytelling connects to reading, how to select stories for telling, how to learn and present stories, and how to make stories come alive.

How Storytelling Connects to Reading

Human beings are storytelling animals. Since the days of the ancients, storytelling has fired the imagination of listeners throughout the world. The stories were told to entertain, to pass on the traditions of the tribe or the culture, to teach values, to celebrate triumphs, to offer solace, to connect with listeners through the shared experience of story, to offer caution, and to express fears. Today we tell stories for the same reasons; however, reading experts also regard storytelling as an important step toward children's literacy for the following reasons:

Storytelling gives children a sense of how stories work. In their book *Stories in the Classroom*, Bob Barton and David Booth (1990, 15) say, "When young children listen to stories, they develop the sense of narrative that will be the core of their thinking and languaging processes. The story continuum that will last for a lifetime begins in the earliest years, and continues forever. Children who are provided with a rich story environment—both in hearing stories and in talking about them—will grow as thinkers and storyers." Without having to be directly "taught," children recognize that stories have a beginning (which introduces the characters, the setting, and the problem), a middle (which develops the theme), a climax, and a conclusion. They also develop a sense for the language and detail that bring the story to life.

Storytelling helps build vocabulary. Most people's listening vocabulary is much larger than their speaking or reading vocabulary. The context in which the words are spoken gives clues to the meaning of unfamiliar words. For example, first-graders might not be able to read the word *gnash* or *rumpus* found in *Where the Wild Things Are* (Sendak 1963); however, as the storyteller gnashes his or her teeth and describes the wild rumpus of the Wild Things, the meaning becomes very clear.

Storytelling stimulates creative imagination as children visualize the story. Good storytellers create pictures with words. I was telling stories to some of the favorite children in my life when one said, "But Tia, I want to see the pictures."

I replied, "This story has the most beautiful pictures of any book you've ever seen, but the pictures are all in your head and no one can see them except you. Close your eyes tight and see if you can see them."

First his little eyes were squeezed shut and an intense look of searching came across his face, then came the most wondrous of replies, "Oh WOW!" Later his mother told me that after that day he wanted her to put away the book so he could see the pictures in his head. I'm not sure how she felt about having to brush up on her storytelling skills.

Storytelling whets children's appetites for more stories so that they will turn to books. In a booklet entitled *What Works: Research About Teaching and Learning*, published by the U.S. Department of Education (1987, 23), the authors say, "Storytelling can ignite the imaginations of children, giving them a taste of where books can take them. The excitement of storytelling can make reading and learning fun and can instill in children a sense of wonder about life and learning."

Storytelling makes literature more accessible for students who will read a story on their own. Often children who have seen a TV program or a movie based on a book or heard a booktalk about a book will want to read the book or story on their own. Storytelling works the same way. These activities provide a "prereading" activity that stimulates interest and helps the child have a context for unfamiliar vocabulary.

Even as an adult, storytelling performances have drawn me to literature. We were required to read *Beowulf* in high school, but it obviously didn't have much of an impact, because when I saw *Beowulf* on a storytelling program, I thought we were going to have a rousing tale of werewolves. The storyteller made the tale of Beowulf live for me as my reading it had never done. I shrank in horror at the approach of Grindel. I "saw" the destruction of the people. The story lived for me in the voice of the teller and I couldn't wait to read it again on my own.

How to Pick Good Telling Stories

Among storytellers there is an expression, "Storytellers don't pick stories, stories pick storytellers." In other words, stories that work for one teller won't necessarily work for another. However, good telling stories have a few basic characteristics that are worthy of note. In *Every Child a Storyteller* (Kinghorn and Pelton 1991, 16-17) Harriet Kinghorn and I advise that a good tellable tale should have the following:

1. One central plot uncluttered with secondary plots. Each incident must follow logically one from the other, creating clear and vivid pictures in the mind of the listener. Stories with flashbacks or long descriptive passages that interfere with the flow of the story should be avoided.

2. A variety of sensory and visual images. The story should create a "movie of the mind" as it is shared with the audience. The language should be beautiful, descriptive, and colorful.

3. A limited number of characters.

4. Colorful characters who are interesting and believable or, in the case of the traditional fairy tale, who clearly represent qualities such as greed, beauty, and goodness.

5. Emotional appeal, courage, love, laughter, suspense, excitement, sentiment, and plenty of action.

6. A strong introduction that motivates the audience to listen. It should also set the time and place, create the tension in the story, and establish the mood. If the story is good but the introduction is weak ... construct an opening that grabs attention, sets the theme and mood, and leads swiftly into action.

7. A satisfying conclusion.

The best place to look for stories is in the folktale section (Dewey Decimal System #398) of your library. Folktales come from the oral tradition and are therefore ideal for retelling. In addition to having all the qualities of good tellable tales as listed above, they are usually short, easy to learn, and work best when told in the storyteller's own words.

How to Learn and Present Stories

In describing the best methods for learning and presenting stories, I again refer to our book *Every Child a Storyteller* (26):

> Stories should *not* be memorized, rather they should be learned. The teller takes the story into his or her heart and gives it back as a gift to the audience. The story is shared through the teller's own words except for repetitious phrases, rhymes and poems, and beginning and ending sentences. If the story is memorized, it may lose its spontaneity and freshness in retelling. Interruptions can thrown the teller off course. Fortunately, learning and presenting stories is much easier than one might imagine....
>
> 1. Find ... a simple story that you truly enjoy.
>
> 2. Read the story several times, both silently and orally.
>
> 3. Put the story away and visualize the story. Make a movie in your mind imagining the characters, setting, and action.
>
> 4. Think through the sequence of events. Make a story map or outline of the story.
>
> 5. Think through the characterization of each person in the story. How will you distinguish one from another? Do you need to add dialogue? Is there extraneous detail that doesn't add to the story?
>
> 6. How will you begin and end the story? Are there any of the author's phrases that you want to be sure to use?
>
> 7. Read the story again. Then, using the outline or story map, tell the story out loud without an audience.
>
> 8. Put the map or outline down and say it again out loud. If you get stuck, refer back to the outline or the map.
>
> 9. Practice one more time, alone. You may wish to tape yourself and review the tape, listening for gaps in the story.
>
> Then tell your story—you are a storyteller.

How to Make Stories Come Alive

Many of the suggestions on pages 23-24 on how to read aloud apply just as well to storytelling as to story reading. Here are a few more tips especially for tellers.

Use colorful words. Your language must be rich and descriptive so that kids can visualize the story as you go along. Don't avoid unfamiliar words or phrases, or phrases peculiar to one part of the country. I'm convinced the main reason my northern listeners enjoy the Appalachian Jack Tales is the rich descriptions that are so much a part of the language of so-called mountain people—phrases like "looked like death eating a cracker" or "waked up dead in the mornin'."

Change your voice. The teller can distinguish between the characters by changing the voice tone for each character. The teller shouldn't have to say "John said," "the Ghost screamed," and so forth, once the voice of the character is established. Remember to use your voice for dramatic effect by speeding up and slowing down and by raising and lowering your voice.

Use props for variety. My favorite props are flannel boards and puppets. I particularly enjoy using a flannel board for a familiar story such as "The Three Little Pigs" and asking the children to join with me as I tell the story. Children can create their own flannel board stories and puppets to tell their favorite stories. What a wonderful way to check for understanding that doesn't involve worksheets. Puppets will be discussed later in this chapter.

Children as Storytellers

Once children have heard a few stories told, they won't have to be cajoled into telling them—they'll want to join in. The same principles of finding, preparing, and presenting stories apply to both adults and children. In *Every Child a Storyteller*, we have included many ideas for children to use literature such as fables and parables, folktales, fairy tales, nursery rhymes, legends, myths, pourquoi (how and why) stories, children's literature, factual material, and urban legends as storytelling sources. Again, as children search for, read, and retell stories, we are inviting them to participate with literature.

Readers Theatre

Readers theatre is not a play. There are no sets, no costumes, no memorized lines. Readers theatre is an interpretative reading that gives students a chance to bring characters to life through voice, simple gesture, and facial expression while feeling safe with a text in hand. As the performers entertain with dramatic reading style, the listeners create their own vivid mental images of the story. Although it may be nice to perform for an audience, Nellie McCaslin (1984, 265), in *Creative Drama in the Classroom*, notes,

> Readers theatre does not require an audience beyond the classroom; indeed, the primary values are derived from the selection and interpretation of the material and the proactive in reading aloud. Inasmuch as the result is so often worth sharing, this type of presentation is recommended for the opportunity it offers those engaged in it, an opportunity bearing much pleasure and no problems of production detail and lengthy rehearsals.

Whether the theatre is done for an audience or not, the process is the same. A piece of literature is selected and prepared for readers theatre. "He said," "she said," and the like are taken out, and descriptive material is given to the role of the narrator. Care should be taken to find selections that include as much dialogue and as little description as possible. In the beginning, the narrator introduces the characters and the performers. The narrator should also give any needed information about preceding events and identify the setting of the scene to be presented. The characters should address each other by name until identities are clearly established. To add interest to the stage, the performers may sit on platforms, stools, chairs, ladders, or benches. At the end, the narrator may wish to close with some summary lines tying the scene to the entire work (if the scene is part of a larger work); however, care should be taken not to tell so much that it spoils the ending for potential readers.

Children can create readers theatre from folktales, original variations on folktales, history, poetry, biographies, or letters, or they might use scenes from favorite books. In *Readers Theatre for Children* (Laughlin and Latrobe 1990) and *Readers Theatre for Young Adults* (Latrobe and Laughlin 1989),* the authors offer excellent advice on how to select and prepare readers to participate in readers theatre and how to select and adapt literary works. They also include presentation and scripting techniques. In addition to offering scripts based on stories from the classics, they also show how to work with contemporary literature to develop powerful scenes for readers theatre. An example is provided in figure 5.1, page 80.

---

*The readers theatre script for Paul Zindel's *The Pigman* appears in Kathy Howard Latrobe and Mildred Knight Laughlin's *Readers Theatre for Young Adults* (Englewood, CO: Teacher Ideas Press, 1989), copyright © 1989 by Libraries Unlimited, and is reprinted with permission.

Fig. 5.1. Example of a scene for readers theatre.

THE PIGMAN
Paul Zindel

The following scene from Paul Zindel's *The Pigman* is taken from chapter 5 when John and Lorraine go to Mr. Pignati's house to collect the money.

SUGGESTED STAGING

The narrator stands at a lectern. John and Lorraine are seated in straight chairs; Mr. Pignati is seated in an armchair.

John X   Lorraine X   Mr. Pignati X

Narrator X

NARRATOR'S OPENING LINES

We shall share a scene from *The Pigman* by Paul Zindel. The characters are Lorraine and John, two high school sophomore friends who feel lonely and neglected by their parents, read by ________ and ________; and Mr. Pignati, a lonely old man, read by ________. I, ________, am the narrator.

Lorraine and John have telephoned Mr. Pignati to trick him into giving them ten dollars for a supposed charity. They are embarrassed at their deception, but John needs money so they go to Mr. Pignati's house to collect the money. They have picked his number at random from the phone book, so they have never met him. He ushers them into the living room and asks them to sit down. He seems very happy to see them.

SUGGESTIONS FOR SCRIPTING

1. Begin by having Mr. Pignati say he just got back from the zoo.
2. Be sure to give John's and Lorraine's readers clues to their changing moods—laughter, nervousness, kindness, impatience, and embarrassment.
3. Mr. Pignati's moods change from happiness at their arrival to excitement in the game and depression as they prepare to leave.
4. End the scene when Lorraine hesitantly says they have not seen his pigs.

NARRATOR'S CLOSING LINES

Mr. Pignati shows them a room full of glass, clay, and marble pigs of all sizes and colors. He tells them he began his wife's pig collection before they were married to remind her of him because his name is Pignati. Lorraine and John leave, and the next day they go to the zoo with Mr. Pignati. A strange friendship develops with this lonely old man who is trying to forget his wife's death. Although it ends in tragedy, Mr. Pignati gives them a new realization about life.

■ ■ ■ ■ ■

Choral Reading

Choral reading may be one of the oldest forms of drama. McCaslin (1984, 230) says, "Evidences of choral speaking have been found in the religious ceremonies and festivals of primitive peoples.... In the early twentieth century, however, it was recognized as one of the most effective methods of teaching the language arts and improving speech habits."

One of the values of choral reading is that it can be used successfully, regardless of space or class size. It works just as well for a group of 20 as it does for 50. When I work with children and adults in choral reading, one of my favorite sources is *The Random House Book of Poetry for Children* (Prelutsky, 1983). Although poetry works very well with this medium, other literary works can also be used effectively. For example, when I'm working with church groups, we use the Bible or the Torah. In her book *Fun with Choral Speaking*, Rose Marie Anthony (1990) describes various types of poems appropriate for choral speaking and includes numerous samples of each—from nursery rhymes and nonsense verse to aesthetic verse and humor. Beginners will find her specific guidelines on how to interpret and deliver some of the selections particularly helpful.

The procedure for choral reading is simple:

1. Have children read the passage silently and think about the meaning. Discuss the text to ensure that they have a clear understanding of the literature. Without a clear understanding it will be difficult for them to convey the feeling and tone of the work in their reading.

2. Discuss unfamiliar words and phrases and review the pronunciation of new words and unfamiliar names.

3. Divide the voices into groups: boys and girls, high and low, solo and chorus, dark and light, or any way that works well with the text. The drama is created by blending words and sentences; have children think of themselves as an orchestra producing beautiful music. Although in the beginning stages I generally "script" the passages, as the group becomes more experienced they can easily take over this function and do it very creatively and effectively.

4. Discuss where the students will read loudly or softly, where they will speed up or slow down, where they will pause, and so on.

5. Assign parts. You are ready to begin.

Puppets and Masks

Puppets

Children are wonderfully creative. All you have to do is give them a box of assorted materials for making puppets and they'll do things you wouldn't have dreamed of. Figure 5.2 will give you some ideas of what to include in your box.

Fig. 5.2. Suggestions of materials for making and decorating puppets.

For Making Puppets		
Styrofoam balls	rubber balls	gloves
paper plates	socks	corks
popsicle sticks	clothespins	cardboard
boxes	felt squares	old stuffed animals
wooden spoons	old fabric	old nylon stockings
egg cartons	milk cartons	paper bags

For Decorating Puppets		
ribbons	yarn	sequins
craft pom-poms	wallpaper scraps	carpet scraps
noodles	pipe cleaners	feathers
thread	lace	rickrack
fabric scraps	seeds	buttons
straw	cotton	string
cardboard tubes	fake fur	plastic craft eyes

In their book *Storytelling with Puppets*, Connie Champlin and Nancy Renfro (1985) not only offer many excellent suggestions for puppet construction, but also include a good bibliography of other books dealing with the same subject. As grown-ups we may need books for ideas, but children won't need much prompting. When selecting stories that work well for puppets, Champlin and Renfro (17-18) suggest that you look for simple and strong action, strong lead characters, and a minimum number of characters, props, and visuals.

Once children have decided on the story, develop the script, emphasizing dialogue, characterization, and mime/action. Other elements such as music, lighting, and background sets can be added.

As a warm-up activity I like to help children and adults learn how to show emotion with their puppets. I call out emotions like sad, proud, frightened, happy, and penitent and have the puppeteers show their puppets reacting with those emotions. One of the best ways for puppeteers to see what the audience sees is to practice with their puppet while looking in a mirror. I also provide coaching tips such as "have the puppet face the audience even when talking to the other puppet characters" and "move only the puppet who is 'talking.'"

I also enjoy working with comic strips as a warm-up activity. For years I have saved comic strips where the joke is in the language and not in the picture. Children select a comic strip and choose a puppet from the classroom collection (or make a puppet) to play each of the comic-strip characters. Puppeteers introduce the characters and the context of the story, and then, using the puppets, "perform" the comic-strip story, speaking the characters' parts. The result is quick, easy, and delightful.

Although we often think of puppets as something for young children, middle and high school kids can enjoy them, too. In her book *Teaching and Dramatizing Greek Myths*, Josephine Davidson (1989)* presents 14 plays dramatizing Greek myths. She also includes directions for making hand puppets from papier-mâché and directions for building a sturdy folding puppet theater. I have created the puppets and constructed the theater, and I can say with certainty that older children love it. I selected the play "Pyramus and Thisbe" (see fig. 5.3, pp. 84-86) to perform for my audiences. Not only is it an example of a classical Greek myth, but it is also an excellent introduction to *Romeo and Juliet* and *West Side Story*.

A puppet theater or puppet stage adds "class" to a performance, but a decorated refrigerator box or a table turned on its side works almost as well. In the appendix of her book, Davidson includes the directions for a sturdy wooden puppet theater. I originally had my puppet theater constructed according to her directions, but, unfortunately, I could not get it into my car. I therefore had to modify it to make the legs removable. If your puppet theater needs to be transportable, as mine does, you may want to consider this modification before construction. If, however, you are building it for long-term classroom use, you should be very happy with the design.

(Text continues on page 86.)

*The script for *Pyramus and Thisbe* appears in Josephine Davidson, *Teaching and Dramatizing Greek Myths* (Englewood, CO: Teacher Ideas Press, 1989), copyright © 1989 by Libraries Unlimited, and is reprinted with permission.

Fig. 5.3. Example of a play based on a classical myth that can be performed with puppets.

PYRAMUS AND THISBE

The Play

Cast of Characters
In Order of Appearance

Narrator
Pyramus, youth living in Babylon
Thisbe, the girl next door

Narrator: Have you ever wondered why mulberries are red? The change from white berries to red berries came about because of the love that two young neighbors had for each other. They lived in Babylon in what we would call a duplex or townhouse. Throughout their childhood they were playmates and as teenagers they found themselves in love. Their parents were much against a marriage, so they had to be content to talk to each other through a chink in the wall.

SCENE 1. A room with a wall from upstage center to downstage center.

Pyramus is on one side of wall and Thisbe on the other.

[curtain]

Pyramus: [he knocks gently on wall] Thisbe, can you hear me?

Thisbe: Yes, Pyramus, I can hear you.

Pyramus: If only our parents would let us mingle with one another. I could see no harm in our enjoying each other's company.

Thisbe: I want with all my heart to see you.

Pyramus: Perhaps if we explained to them that we would have a chaperon, they would be receptive to the idea.

Thisbe: My father refuses to let me have any friends much less a boy next door.

Pyramus: Do you have a trusted nurse that might arrange something for us?

Thisbe: Yes, I have a trusted nurse. My father trusts her and she is devoted to him.

Pyramus: Well, thank the wall that allows us to communicate with one another. Of course, if it were not for this wall, I could take you in my arms and kiss you.

Thisbe: But at least the wall lets us speak to one another. [kissing the wall and talking to it] Thank you wall. Thank you for taking this kiss to Pyramus.

Pyramus: Now wall, transport this kiss to Thisbe.

Thisbe: I received your kiss, dear Pyramus. Now you take another kiss of mine. I will smother you with kisses, my beloved. [kisses the wall many times]

Pyramus: Dear Thisbe, sweet dreams. I will talk to you in the morning.

Thisbe: Wait, Pyramus. Do not go yet. I cannot live like this. I wish to feel your strong arms around me. Please, let us find a way to be together.

Pyramus: We could steal away. Perhaps we can meet out in the country, beyond the city walls.

Thisbe: But how shall we do this?

Pyramus: Tomorrow, wait until after the sun sets. Then go out the gates just before they are closed for the night.

Thisbe: Yes, oh, yes, this is a marvelous idea. But where shall we meet?

Pyramus: At the tomb of Ninus. There is by the tomb, a tall mulberry tree full of snow white berries, and nearby a running creek.

Thisbe: I will be there. About three hours after the sun sets, when the moon is out, I will be at the tomb.

Pyramus: Wall, take my kisses to Thisbe. It will be the last time you have to transport my kisses as the next time I kiss Thisbe I will take her in my arms. I love you, Thisbe.

Thisbe: I love you. Sweet wall, take my kisses to Pyramus.

[curtain]

SCENE 2. By the tomb of Ninus, that next night.

Thisbe: [enters from left] Pyramus, are you here? Do you hear me? [to audience] He must not have arrived as yet. I'm really not afraid, I'll wait quietly for him. [growls from offstage] But what is it that I hear? The sounds seem to come from behind the mulberry tree. [louder sounds] Who is it? What do you want? Gods on Olympus, help me. It is a lioness, dripping with blood. I must get away. [Thisbe exits left quickly, dropping her cloak in front of the tomb of Ninus]

(Figure 5.3 continues on page 86.)

Fig. 5.3—*Continued*

Narrator: Thisbe got away. However, the lioness took Thisbe's cloak in her mouth and shook it vigorously before dropping it and disappearing into the woods. Needless to say, this caused problems.

Pyramus: [enters from left] Thisbe, are you here? [sees the cloak] Apollo save me. It cannot be. But it must be. I allowed my own sweet loved one to come here alone. It is I who killed her. [picks up the cloak and kisses it over and over, while he walks over to the mulberry tree] Now I shall die, too. [he pulls his sword and sinks it into his breast]

Thisbe: [enters from left] Pyramus, have you come? I cannot seem to see. [she sneaks around, sees something on the ground, shudders, and then comes closer for a look] Pyramus, Pyramus, speak to me. [throws herself next to him and holds him in her arms kissing him] It is I, your Thisbe, your dearest. [he opens his eyes, sees her, and dies]

Thisbe: [picks up her cloak and holds it to herself] Your love for me has killed you. Death could be the only thing that could keep us apart. Not the wall. Not our parents. And I will not allow death to keep us apart.

Narrator: Thisbe plunged the same sword that killed her intended husband into her own heart. Ever since, the mulberry tree, drenched with blood of the two young lovers, blossoms forth with red berries.

[curtain]

■ ■ ■ ■ ■

Masks

The use of masks is closely related to the art of puppetry. Sometimes wearing a mask helps to stimulate children's imagination and free them from inhibitions. The children project their feelings and ideas through the mask while remaining "hidden," just as they can hide behind a puppet.

The teacher may wish to give some background information on the use of masks before mask-making projects begin. McCaslin (1984, 140) explains that in ancient times people believed that by putting on the face of another, they gained power over that person. They also believed that "they could release the wearer's personality by concealing it; and they became symbols of universal awareness of gods or a creative force in the universe." The ancient Greeks used masks to project the actors' features and amplify their voices. In the huge amphitheaters, where performances took place, the masks helped Greek actors appear larger than life. In commedia dell'arte, the Italian traveling theater of the sixteenth and seventeenth centuries used masks to represent stock characters. McCaslin (141) says, "The covering of the face seemed to have an effect on the actor's body, making it freer and more expressive."

Masks play an important part in most cultures. Children may enjoy researching the use of masks in various cultures, including Native American cultures. My interest in masks led me to one of my favorite "mask stories," a wonderful African tale, *Who's in Rabbit's House?* (Aardema 1977). The masks in the illustrations can be adapted for classroom performances.

Masks may cover the entire head, the face, or just the upper part of the face. Talking through a mask requires practice, so the half-mask may be best for beginners. Like puppets, masks can be made from a wide variety of materials.

Paper bags. For young children this may be the easiest and most inexpensive type of mask. Holes can be cut for the eyes and mouth. The mask is then ready for decoration. Anything can be used—buttons, feathers, paint, crayons, chalk, cloth, jewelry, and so forth.

Cardboard boxes. Although it is hard to find boxes in the appropriate sizes and shapes, they can be very effective with stylized characters such as robots.

Paper plates. Masks made of paper plates work well for middle grade kids because of their shape, toughness, and availability. McCaslin (143) describes how to make paper plate masks three dimensional:

> Cut two slits about two inches deep and about two inches apart on the edge of the plate. By overlapping the sides adjacent to each slit and stapling them back together again, a chin is formed, making the mask fit on the child's face.... The holes for the eyes, mouth, and nose must be cut in the appropriate places. A nose that protrudes from the face can be made of construction paper and pasted on the plate, further adding to the three-dimensional quality.

Papier-mâché. When I am making a few masks or puppets, I prefer to use CelluClay, a commercially prepared instant papier-mâché product. When mixed with water and kneaded, it turns into an easy-to-use claylike product. This would probably be too expensive for an entire class, so I've included directions for traditional papier-mâché.

Materials:

- Wheat paste (wallpaper paste) mixed according to package directions
- Strips of torn paper approximately 1 by 10 inches
- Form or mold (large balloon, chicken wire with cheesecloth, or wig form)
- Cold cream or oil
- Razor blade or mat knife

Steps:

1. Grease the mold.
2. Apply paper strips that have been dipped in the paste diagonally in bandage fashion across the face, overlapping wherever possible. Two layers are usually enough.
3. Soak smaller pieces of paper in the paste, squeeze out the moisture, and apply them for eyebrows, nose, lips, etc.
4. Allow the face to dry for at least two days. If the masks are thick or the room humidity is high, it may take longer.
5. When the form is completely dry, use a mat knife or razor blade to cut out eye and mouth holes. If the child has made a whole head mask, trim the bottom so the mask will fit over the child's head and rest on the shoulders.
6. The dry head of a mask can then be painted or decorated. You may wish to spray it with a plastic protective spray to enhance its durability.
7. Fasten the face mask with elastic across the back of the child's head.
8. The child's hair can be covered with a wig, scarf, hat, or fake fur to complete the disguise.

Radio Drama

I would be hard pressed to improve on Jerry Flack's excellent suggestions regarding radio drama. The following guidelines for creating radio mystery dramas are from his book *Mystery and Detection* (1990, 85-87).*

Creating Radio Mystery Dramas

After students have listened to old-time radio tapes of mysteries, allow them to create their own radio broadcasts. Recreating or simulating the "Golden Age" of radio with an audio broadcast is a project which affords students great latitude and practice in the exercise of creativity and problem solving. The agenda for such a project may include the following checkpoints:

1. *Determine the subject matter*. Will the students create an original drama for the broadcast or will they use a published mystery? If the published mystery is chosen, stories for all ages abound. Elementary school children may want to use a mystery like James Howe's *The*

*"Creating Radio Mystery Dramas" and other material from Jerry Flack, *Mystery and Detection* (Englewood, CO: Teacher Ideas Press, 1990), copyright © 1990 by Libraries Unlimited, is reprinted with permission.

Celery Stalks at Midnight. Middle school students might read a chapter from Ellen Raskin's *The Westing Game*, while high school students might make use of classic tales by Poe and Doyle. Of course, decisions on length will determine whether a cutting from a longer story or novel, or a short story is used.

2. *Decide how the broadcast will be made*. Will the radio drama be a live broadcast or will it be taped? Taped dramas are much more forgiving of student errors and can be listened to again and again, but live broadcasts more closely approximate the true flavor of the environment of the old-time radio days. Many of the other decisions will be affected by this one.

3. *Write a script*. Unless actual copies of a radio mystery script are used, students will have to revise existing works or create new mysteries using a radio script format. Copyright permissions may be needed. The library media specialist can be especially helpful in finding the answer to this question. Script writing involves cutting out all the "he said" and "she said" explication, eliminating unnecessary narration, frequently shortening the text, and providing cues for both actors and sound effects personnel. Students who have not previously written in the script format will find this experience another new and useful challenge.

4. *Choose roles*. The most important roles may be the sound effects persons. In addition to actors and crew, a producer is needed to supervise the total production, including time schedules and budgets. Of course, advertisers have to be contacted and commercials written as well. Incidentally, separate actors are not necessary for the commercials. In radio days actors often stepped out of character for sixty seconds to tell listeners of the joys of buying war bonds, a particular cigarette, cereal, or detergent.

The sound effects crew has some real, but fun, problem solving ahead. Remind students that no pictures will be available to their audience. If a carnival scene is called for in the script, the sound effects crew must convincingly create the impression of one via auditory stimuli. The following are just a few of the many sounds which may be called for in a script:

the creaking of stairs	the squeak of a door hinge
a ringing telephone	eerie whistling sounds
echoes	muffled cries
galloping horses	a house aflame
footsteps	a window being broken
rain on a roof	

Experimentation and problem solving occur as students try different techniques of sound effects production. One of the author's students, for example, discovered that cellophane cookie container dividers, when crinkled, emit a sound like a crackling fire. Some research in the school library media center or at the public library may aid experimentation. If students do not find books on sound effects, they may be able to locate books about radio production with chapters on sound effects.

Of course, music needs to be part of the radio play. The sound effects and engineering team need to select appropriate music carefully for the various mood passages that require a musical interlude.

A decision about advanced taping of some sound effects and music must be made. Even in the case of dramas where the rest of the broadcast is live, musical backgrounds and sound effects may be prerecorded.

5. *Rehearsal*. After the sound effects crew and the actors have rehearsed separately, at least one joint rehearsal with a complete, uninterrupted reading should be held.

6. *The audience*. Part of the producer's job is to find a listening audience. If a large class is involved there may be as many as two or three groups creating radio dramas. The groups can serve as audiences for one another. With the convenience and sophistication of tape equipment and public address systems, it is not difficult even for younger students to broadcast a radio drama into other classrooms in the school. Sixth grade students, for example, can create a radio drama of a James Howe story and become the storytelling entertainment for third grade classes. One ninth grade class can select a story by Edgar Allan Poe, found in their ninth-grade literature anthology, dramatize and broadcast it into all ninth grade English classrooms. Many larger school systems have their own radio studios and broadcast frequencies, and may be willing to publicly air the drama. If students create an unusually well-polished radio drama, teachers and the producer may want to contact a local affiliate of National Public Radio to see if a broadcast is possible there. If students know their work will ultimately be shared with many people, the levels of quality and productivity increase dramatically.

It may be profitable, during the creative process, to show students a short segment of Woody Allen's 1987 movie *Radio Days*. The film, available in VHS format, contains wonderful scenes of "live" radio broadcasts complete with sound effects technicians.

Creative Dramatics

In play creation, I have worked with children, using both commercially prepared scripts and scripts the children have written; we have also created and performed plays without scripts. Because most readers have probably had experience with the first two play forms, I'd like to focus on the "play without script," which for me has been the most fun, the most successful, and by far the most satisfying.

Let me describe our church production of *The Littlest Angel* by Charles Tazewell (1946). We had only two rehearsals, each two hours long, so we had to be efficient:

1. I read the story aloud, and then the children who could read, read it to themselves.

2. We talked through the story and pantomimed parts of it. For example, how did the Littlest Angel feel when he got to heaven? How could you show that with your body? What would his voice sound like? How would you feel if you saw the Littlest Angel about to jump off a cloud when you knew he couldn't fly? Show it in your face. What would you do when he hit the ground? We talked through the whole story. We felt it. We experienced it.

3. We blocked out scenes from the story that we wanted to portray and the children volunteered for parts. (We had about 50 baby angels ages 3-5 for our angel choir and about 25 other children ages 5-12 for speaking parts.) I'll never forget a 10-year-old, raising her hand and asking, "Could God be a woman?" "Certainly," I replied. And she became God.

4. I was the narrator. If we had had more time to prepare, a child would have been the narrator. As the narrator, I introduced the story and, between scenes, provided the transitions. For example, as a transition I said, "And then the Littlest Angel presented himself to the Understanding Angel." Then children would act out the scene, keeping in mind the story line and the discussion we had had about character and mood. The children coached each other to make our drama more effective.

5. We discussed costumes, how to make the stage look more heavenly, how we could make the gift rise into the "heavens," and how we could create a moving, meaningful ending.

6. We practiced two Saturday mornings and performed the following Sunday. The children created such a moving story that I could hear the audience sniffling in the background.

I like this approach to drama for several reasons. No lines have to be memorized. The play really "belongs" to the children. Whether the children have to do the play once or a hundred times, each performance is fresh, new, and alive. Children have to know and feel the story to be able to perform it, which may not be required in plays for which roles are memorized.

Two footnotes concerning the performance. First, I don't recommend using a fog machine to make heaven seen ethereal. I was halfway through my introduction when the fog started creeping under the closed curtain, making the audience twitch in their seats, particularly when they heard 50 baby angels coughing and gasping backstage. And second, by all means cast your characters creatively and then be prepared. One of the grandfatherly types must have mused for at least five minutes after the close of the performances: "Mabel, did you see that, God was a woman ... a woman, Mabel, God, a woman ... never seen anything like that before. Yep, sure enough, God was a woman."

Although the creative dramatic activity discussed above was created for a public performance, it is just as effective as a class activity. Lee Galda (1982) found that children who "played a story," that is, reenacted it for their own pleasure, had significantly higher recall than those who either discussed the same story or drew a picture of it.

Other Ideas

Broadcast a book review. Have children select a favorite book and prepare a review either for a radio audience or for broadcast over the school intercom system. Not only does this activity require a careful reading of the book to be presented, but it also challenges children's ingenuity in planning sound effects and background music.

Create tapes of books. Older children can prepare tapes of stories to be used in conjunction with books for the younger children's listening center. Or they can create games using tapes. For example, they could tape favorite quotes or descriptive passages from a number of books or make a "which character said this?" tape and place it in the classroom listening center (with an answer key) for other children to enjoy during their free time.

Create a character. Children can pantomime an event or a character from a story. The other children can guess who or what the performers represent.

Create a movie of a book. Children can draw a series of pictures on a long sheet of paper that fastens to rollers. As the rollers turn, the pictures move into view. A storyteller could narrate the story.

Create a videotape of the book. The children can videotape a scene from a book performed by classmates, or they can record the students' creative booktalks. Videotaped commercials for favorite books are also very popular among students.

Perform monologues. Older children in particular enjoy researching a historical character and performing a monologue spoken in the voice of that character.

Create a rap. Children may enjoy writing and then performing their own original rap. Orin Cochrane (1988) has written the delightful *Cinderella Chant*, and Ethel Buchanan (1990) has a lively "Three Little Pigs" rap that could serve as a stimulus for children to produce original work.

The possibilities of combining literature and dramatization are limited only by creativity and time. The impact of the connection is powerful. As Johnson and Louis (1987, 148) reflect, "To say that dramatization helps to develop comprehension is a colossal understatement.... [It] is the final word in comprehension." Not only that, but the activities we've described give children an opportunity to get actively involved with literature in creative and stimulating ways.

References

Anthony, Rose Marie. 1990. *Fun with Choral Speaking*. Englewood, CO: Libraries Unlimited.

Barton, Bob, and David Booth. 1990. *Stories in the Classroom: Storytelling, Reading Aloud and Roleplaying with Children*. Portsmouth, NH: Heinemann.

Champlin, Connie, and Nancy Renfro. 1985. *Storytelling with Puppets*. Chicago: American Library Association.

Davidson, Josephine. 1989. *Teaching and Dramatizing Greek Myths*. Englewood, CO: Teacher Ideas Press.

Flack, Jerry D. 1990. *Mystery and Detection*. Englewood, CO: Teacher Ideas Press.

Galda, Lee. 1982. "Playing About a Story: Its Impact on Comprehension." *The Reading Teacher* 36, no. 1: 52-55.

Johnson, Terry D., and Daphne R. Louis. 1987. *Literacy Through Literature*. Portsmouth, NH: Heinemann.

Kinghorn, Harriet R., and Mary Helen Pelton. 1991. *Every Child a Storyteller*. Englewood, CO: Teacher Ideas Press.

Latrobe, Kathy Howard, and Mildred Knight Laughlin. 1989. *Readers Theatre for Young Adults*. Englewood, CO: Teacher Ideas Press.

Laughlin, Mildred Knight, and Kathy Howard Latrobe. 1990. *Readers Theatre for Children*. Englewood, CO: Teacher Ideas Press.

McCaslin, Nellie. 1984. *Creative Drama in the Classroom*. 4th ed. New York: Longman.

U.S. Department of Education. 1987. *What Works: Research About Teaching and Learning*. 2d ed. Washington, DC: U.S. Government Printing Office.

Literature Resources

Aardema, Verna, 1977. *Who's in Rabbit's House?* New York: Dial Press.

Buchanan, Ethel. 1990. *Three Little Pigs*. Steinbach, Canada: Derksen.

Cochrane, Orin. 1988. *Cinderella Chant*. Steinbach, Canada: Derksen.

Prelutsky, Jack, selector. 1983. *The Random House Book of Poetry for Children: A Treasury of 572 Poems for Today's Child*. New York: Random House.

Sendak, Maurice. 1963. *Where the Wild Things Are*. New York: Harper & Row.

Tazewell, Charles. 1946. *The Littlest Angel*. Nashville, TN: Ideals.

6

Children as Publicists

Using Art and Book Reviews

Where would sports be without publicists? Without the press, without television and radio coverage, without people talking about the sport, we'd have a hard time sustaining interest. We wouldn't know what games were being played or when, where, and by whom. And somehow sports are meant to be shared, whether in playing or in discussing the game afterward. Reading isn't so very different. Through creative book-related art activities and many other different kinds of book-sharing activities, children can relive their enjoyment of books, publicize books to others, and sustain their interest through active participation with books.

Art

Probably the most widely used classroom activity for connecting art with books is "now boys and girls, draw your favorite part of the book." Even as a kid I found that rather uninteresting, so I made sure my favorite parts were night scenes. Sports can be like that, too. My sport of choice is jogging, but if a teacher asked me to draw my favorite part of that activity I'd draw a picture of myself in the shower. I'd definitely come up with more interesting pictures if the teacher asked me to draw a picture of the most ferocious dog that ever chased me or to draw the time I almost got run over by a truck. So here are a few ideas to engage your publicists in creative work.

Book Illustration

As we think about book illustration activities, we want to challenge children with an activity that requires a close and careful rereading or interpretation of the text. A primary teacher may wish to read a book without showing the accompanying illustrations. Children can then create their own illustrations and later compare them with the artist's interpretation. Terry Johnson and Daphne Louis (1987, 55) recommend that

> Folktales are ... a rich source for illustration. We either read stories that have no illustrations or do not show the pictures of illustrated versions. The wicked queen before her magic mirror, the tormented huntsman, the tangled forest catching Snow White's clothes, the house of the dwarves and Snow White's funeral all provide colorful possibilities for the children's imagination. Having made their own illustrations and encountering some of the problems involved in translating verbal information into visual, they examine the beautiful pictures in the many available editions with a high degree of concentration.

Johnson and Louis also offer an excellent suggestion for a class book production project. First the teacher breaks a story or folktale into parts. Then the teacher prepares a job card for each incident, each card containing a direct quotation from the story and a simple written direction (see fig. 6.1).

Fig. 6.1. Example of a job card for book illustration activity.

> Job Card
>
> Draw Rapunzel as she throws her hair down from the tower to the waiting witch. "The tower stood deep in the darkest part of the woods. It had neither staircase nor doors, and only a little window quite high up on the wall. Rapunzel had splendid long hair, as fine as spun gold. As soon as she heard the voice of the witch, she unfastened her plaits and twisted them round a hook by the window and they fell to the hideous witch below."

The children work in teams of two, each with a job card and art materials. The picture should include all the details mentioned in the quotation on the card. When all the illustrations are completed, they are combined with the appropriate text and bound together for the school library. Older children can use this same method to create big books for primary classrooms.

Job cards can be used to illustrate parts of a story. Figure 6.2 is a job card for Madeleine L'Engle's *A Wrinkle in Time* (1962, 173-174).*

Fig. 6.2. Example of a job card for illustrating a scene from *A Wrinkle in Time*.

> Job Card
>
> Draw the scene in the chapter "Absolute Zero" where Calvin, Mr. Murry, and Meg are approached by three figures: "On Uriel there had been the magnificent creatures. On Camazotz the inhabitants had at least resembled people. What were these three strange things approaching? They were the same dull gray color as the flowers. If they hadn't walked upright they would have seemed like animals. They moved directly toward the three human beings. They had four arms and far more than five fingers to each hand, and the fingers were not fingers, but long waving tentacles. They had heads, and they had faces. But where the faces of the creatures on Uriel had seemed far more than human faces, these seemed far less. Where the features would normally be there were several indentations, and in place of ears and hair were more tentacles. They were tall, Meg realized as they came closer, far taller than any man. They had no eyes. Just soft indentations."

For the children to be able to draw the scene accurately, they will have to go back to the story for more visual clues, such as: What do Meg, Calvin, and Mr. Murry look like? What color is their hair? Do they wear glasses? How old are Meg and Calvin? What are they wearing? Where are they in this scene? What does the land around them look like? What time of the day is it? Children can then help each other by doing a point-by-point comparison between the picture and the text. In creating the job cards, the teacher may wish to list specific information children should include in the picture.

Book Advertisements

When children enjoy a book, they will be able to think of many art-related advertisements for the book that will encourage others to read it.

Book jackets. Many excellent books sit on the library shelf because they are visually unappealing. Have children examine eye-catching book jackets at the library and at the bookstore and read the intriguing story summaries on the inside cover. Then have them create new book jackets for books they have read and enjoyed. They may even want to go as far as researching some interesting facts about the author and then including a short author biography on the back inside flap. Perhaps the librarian can show the children how to encase the jackets in plastic to make them more durable.

Bookmarkers. Children can make a bookmarker that will stay with a particular book, be given as a gift, or provide the bookmarker's creator with a lasting memento of an enjoyable reading experience. I brought in my collection of bookmarkers, and we discussed which ones were most visually appealing and which ones were the most likely to stimulate someone to read the books for which they were made. Then the children created their own markers. The markers will be more durable if they are laminated.

Posters. The children may wish to write to book companies requesting book advertising posters so they can analyze which designs work and which ones do not. Posters can be created with paint, crayons, magic markers, paper sculpture, ink, cutout pictures, and fabric. Tangible objects can be used to create either flat or three-dimensional advertisements. Johnson and Louis (1987) also suggest variations on the advertising poster:

- A missing person poster, e.g., Sylvester in *Sylvester and the Magic Pebble* (Steig, 1969) or Mr. Murry in *A Wrinkle in Time*
- A wanted poster, e.g., IT in *A Wrinkle in Time*
- A greatest hero, e.g., *Maniac Magee* (Spinelli 1990)
- A Wall of Fame, e.g., a poster of Minna Shaw in *The Widow's Broom* (Van Allsburg 1992)

Any poster can be made into a sandwich board, which could be worn during lunch or recess times to advertise books.

T-shirts. Have a T-shirt day. Kids work with a washed T-shirt, fabric markers, and imagination to create a T-shirt designed to advertise a favorite book. Kids may wish to draw a picture with the title on the front and a quote or another picture on the back. If a project with real T-shirts isn't possible, children could draw paper cutouts of life-size T-shirts and design them as they would real T-shirts. The teacher could then hang a laundry line to display the creations.

Other advertising ideas. Have kids make laminated placemats, book banks (to save money to buy books) made from tennis ball tubes or other tubelike cans, or jigsaw puzzles to advertise their books.

Other Ideas for Book Sharing Through Art

Mobiles. Using coat hangers, dowels, or wires, children can create story mobiles by suspending objects related to the story or drawings of scenes from the story. Children could also hang favorite quotes from the story on the mobile, making sure the shapes containing the writing are visually interesting and related to the story. Children might prefer doing "character mobiles." These work well when hung vertically, with the head of the main character at the top, the title and book author next, and then quotes, descriptions, or scenes. Children could also create theme book mobiles with the titles of books and pictures hanging from the main theme. For example, for a monster theme, an octopus could be placed at the top, with tentacles extending below; a minimobile of other monster books could then be suspended from each of the tentacles.

Timelines. Have children draw a large colorful timeline of the events in a chosen book. They could also show other events that were taking place in the world during the same period. This activity not only helps children see the logical sequence of the story, but also helps them place the story in the context of world events.

Maps. Like timelines, this is a deceptively simple activity that actually demands a very high level of understanding of the text. Johnson and Louis (1987, 63) say, "Creating a map on which the action occurs often helps the writer to sustain the internal logic of the story." The teacher may wish to show books that contain literary maps of the world of the book. The maps in *Winnie-the-Pooh* (Milne 1926) and *The Hobbit* (Tolkien 1966) are good examples.

I ask my storytelling students to draw maps of their stories. Not only does it cut down on the time needed to learn the story, but it also helps the reader/teller "see" the story at a glance. I introduce mapping by having the class work together on a map of a familiar story, for example, "Little Red Riding Hood." After working together, the students then design their own maps of the stories they plan to present. For best results, the same procedure (doing a map together as a class before students create their own) should be followed for other map making.

Storybook characters out of clay, papier-mâché, or any other three-dimensional material. Children can create storybook characters out of almost any three-dimensional material and then dress the three-dimensional figure appropriately.

When I was in third grade, I remember carving a little one-legged Pooh bear out of a big chunk of Ivory soap. I chose to leave my bear undressed as befits a bear. In *The Legend of the Bluebonnet* (dePaola 1983), the little girl's prize possession was a warrior doll made from buckskin. The leggings were beaded, and the doll wore a belt of polished bone. The eyes, nose, and mouth were painted on with the juice of berries. In its hair were brilliant blue feathers. Materials for costumes need not be more elaborate than construction paper or crepe paper, though more elaborate costuming can be created with scrap pieces of cloth, leather, fake fur, lace, or anything else that will add authenticity to the character.

A still life that displays objects representing a story. The kids could collect objects connected with a story and display them in a still life in the reading center. Each week a different book could be featured. For example, for *Sir Gawain and the Loathly Lady* (Hastings 1985) the objects might be a coat of arms, a king's crown, King Arthur's empty scabbard, and a large question mark made from pipe cleaners, tagboard, wire, or the like. For *The Legend of the Bluebonnet*, the objects might be a drum, a replica of She Who Is Alone's doll, a picture of the bluebonnets, and a map of Texas.

Life-size figures of favorite characters. Kids can work together in teams to trace their own bodies on large sheets of paper and then add details to turn the silhouettes into favorite book characters. The teacher can hang the drawings around the room or in the hall. The full-size characters can also be placed in students' classroom seats, and the class can have a Character Day or Character Evening. Other classes or parents can be invited to the class to meet the "new" class members. This would be a great opportunity for kids to do mini-booktalks as they introduce their characters to the visitors. Once my class called the event "Meet My New Best Friend" and had the other kids guess the identity of their character.

Graffiti walls. Isn't there a little child in each of us who always wanted to color on the walls? Here is the opportunity for kids to fulfill that fantasy. Hang up huge sheets of paper around the room or in the hallway. Give kids markers, chalk, crayons, or paint and have them draw pictures or write quotes from their favorite books. It's a good idea to tell them about the planned activity several weeks in advance so they can start looking for great quotes in their reading. Several years ago when I was redoing my house, I invited all my small friends over to draw on my walls before the wallpaper was stripped. A side benefit was that after a while the kids became more interested in the stripping than in the drawing, so I suggested they "go for it." Within two days all the wallpaper in the house was stripped from 2 feet down.

Thumbnail sketches. Have each child cut a large thumbnail out of paper, place it on the bulletin board titled "Thumbnail Sketches." Children can decorate the thumbnails with either drawings or written notes identifying their books.

Murals or montages. Closely associated with the graffiti wall is the mural or montage. Whereas the graffiti wall is more "free form," with quotes and pictures usually unrelated, the mural or montage is a sequence of scenes from a story. Different teams of kids could be responsible for different scenes.

Biography cube. After reading a biography, have the children create a cube from construction paper and draw a scene from the person's life on each side of the cube. The surfaces of the cube should be large enough to accommodate the drawing: 4 by 4 inches works well. Kids could also research the lives of favorite authors and create cubes with scenes from their lives.

Dioramas. A diorama displays a scene in three-dimensional form. A shoe box or any sturdy box will work well. The scene can be viewed from a hole in the end of the box, or one side of the box can be left open, with the other three sides forming the scene. Children will think of endless ways to depict rocks, snow, fences, trees, water, flowers, buildings, animals, and people.

Rebuses. Children are fascinated with rebus, or picture-writing, puzzles. Picture writing is an ancient art practiced by many people, from the ancient Egyptians to Native Americans. I was fascinated when visiting the Smithsonian Institution to study the picture writing on a Lakota buffalo skin called a winter count. The pictures told the poignant story of smallpox and drought, of birth and death. Children can create their own winter count either by making up their own symbols or by studying those listed in books on the topic. I have children cut a buffalo-shaped "skin" out of brown paper, crumple it, wet it thoroughly, then lay it out flat to dry. After the paper is dry, children draw their stories in picture writing, drawing symbols with crayon or magic marker. Several books are suggested in the bibliography.

Rebuses for Readers (Martin, Kelly, and Grabow 1992)* presents more than 100 literary rebuses challenging readers to decipher the titles, authors, characters, and settings. Figure 6.3, page 102, provides a rebus for C. S. Lewis's *The Lion, the Witch, and the Wardrobe*. After practicing decoding sample rebuses, children can create their own rebuses to challenge friends.

Studying the Art of Children's Books

Not only can children enjoy the stories and the art in picture books, they can also study and replicate the artist's techniques. They can read the picture book and research the art form used in the illustrations and then create their own stories using the same illustration technique. For example, after studying the sponge painting techniques in *Swimmy* (Lionni 1963), kids can create their own sponge paintings. They may even want to write some new adventures for Swimmy to go with their sponge painting. *Super Kids Publishing Company* (Robertson and Barry 1990)** includes directions for a number of art techniques and references to books that reflect the technique (see fig. 6.4, pp. 103-104).

(Text continues on page 105.)

---

*The rebus in figure 6.3 appears in Pat Martin, Joanne Kelly, and Kay Grabow, *Rebuses for Readers* (Englewood, CO: Teacher Ideas Press, 1992), copyright © 1992 by Libraries Unlimited, and is reprinted with permission.

**"Wallpaper Layered Cut-outs" and "Tissue Overlay" in figure 6.4 appear in Deborah Robertson and Patricia Barry, *Super Kids Publishing Company* (Englewood, CO: Teacher Ideas Press, 1990), copyright© 1990 by Libraries Unlimited, and are reprinted with permission.

Fig. 6.3. Example of a literary rebus.

Fig. 6.4. Examples of art techniques.

Pat Barry
"Sam"

Wallpaper Layered Cut-outs

1. Choose plainly patterned floral wallpaper pieces of pleasing, complementary colors.

2. Cut out differing sizes of flowers, leaves, etc.

3. Layer pieces on top of one another to give a 3-D effect.

4. For an extra effect, use the same wallpaper for your book pages, and write your story in the blank areas between the flowers.

Treasures to share:

Let's Make Rabbits by Leo Lionni
New York: Pantheon Books, 1982.

Alexander and the Wind-up Mouse by Leo Lionni
New York: Pantheon Books, 1969.

Peter's Chair by Ezra Jack Keats
New York: Harper & Row, 1967.

The Girl Who Loved the Wind by Jane Yolen
New York: Thomas Y. Crowell Company, 1972.

(Figure 6.4 continues on page 104.)

Fig. 6.4—*Continued*

Tissue Overlay

1. Choose tissue colors for your illustration.
2. *Tear* tissue pieces to desired shapes.
3. Lay tissue pieces down on illustration paper.
4. Use a mixture of one (1) part white glue to three (3) parts water and brush *over* the tissue to seal it to the paper.
5. Gentle rubbing with the glue mixture will cause colors to bleed or blend, causing a soft, dreamlike effect.

Treasures to share:

The Very Hungry Caterpillar by Eric Carle
Cleveland: World Publishing Company, 1970.

1,2,3 to the Zoo by Eric Carle
Cleveland: World Publishing Company, 1968.

Pat Barry
"Cannas"

Book Sharing Through Book Reviews

Although we intuitively know the power of books as a basis for social interchange, educators have often overlooked the unique opportunities that books provide for socialization. Children, like adults, enjoy sharing their favorite authors and favorite books. In their study of reading autobiographies of students, Robert Carlsen and Anne Sherrill (1988, 148-149) observe, "Many of these autobiographies indicate that reading is a social as well as a solitary phenomenon.... Reading material can become a part of human interaction: not just an interaction between author and reader but between the readers themselves.... Again and again, our respondents tell of their need to talk about their reading." I couldn't agree more. Few things give me as much pleasure as discussing a good book with a friend. It's important to capitalize on the socialization function of book sharing. We also must recognize that middle school and high school readers often give more credence to the recommendations of peers than to those of a parent, teacher, or librarian. In the next chapter we'll discuss cooperative learning activities for book sharing, but let's look now at creative book reviews as a sharing activity.

"Selling" books. As I mentioned in an earlier chapter, I gave mini-booktalks every day in my classroom and usually ended with, "Does anyone want to buy this book?" One day one of the students asked whether he could "sell" his book. The next day five students asked to "sell" their books. The students were thrilled when other kids lined up to borrow their books, and it became a regular part of our week. The students followed my example of a mini-booktalk, with the booktalk not lasting more than three to four minutes and always ending with "Does anyone want to buy this book?"

Star-rated books. Have the children review several copies of the movie review section of their newspaper and notice the rating system. In our local paper, movies are rated as follows:

****Excellent

***Good

**Fair

*Poor

No star—not even worth considering

After each rating, a very brief plot summary and a comment justifying the rating is given. After children read the book, give them a big index card to record their ratings and set up a book review card file. Children can refer to the peer book reviews to get recommendations for future reading. As children read the book, they can add their own ratings to the card, so each story could eventually have many reviewers. Teachers may wish to develop a rating chart for the bulletin board.

Critics' choice. This cumulative book review is a variation on the previous idea, but in this case the books aren't rated. After reading a book, the children record their reaction and place the review in a file marked with the book title. The students have an opportunity to compare their reactions with previously recorded reviews.

Critics circle. After several children have read the same book, have them make notes of their opinions of the book. For example, was the book well written or poorly written, did it have believable characters, was the ending disappointing or satisfying, was the plot fast-moving or did it drag? The opinions should be backed up with examples from the book. Appoint one child as moderator and let the discussion begin. I remember kids continuing their debates during recess, on the playground, and over lunch—I thought I was listening to a graduate English class.

Newbery club. Carlene Aborn (1979) in her article "The Newberys: Getting Them to Read (It Isn't Easy)" came up with this variation on the critics circle. She noted that few of the John Newbery Medal winners were checked out of the library. These books had received the most coveted award in the field of children's literature, yet children weren't reading them; to elicit interest in these books, she created the Newbery Award Club. Participation in the club was voluntary, and the guidelines were simple:

1. Students received criteria for judging a book, questions to consider when reading a book, and an annotated list of the Newberys.

2. For each book read, students turned in a card containing a brief annotation, a critical opinion, and a discussion of *why* they reached a favorable or unfavorable conclusion. A student who read at least two chapters of a book and didn't like it was not required to finish it.

3. When students had read at least 10 Newbery award books, they would become members of the Newbery Award Club and receive buttons and membership cards.

4. A chart of Newbery books was made, and as each student finished a book, the student would initial the chart by the name of the book.

The students particularly enjoyed meeting in small groups to discuss a book they had all read. At the end of the year, the students created a yarn-on-burlap tapestry. For each Newbery book they designed a symbol, drew it on the burlap, and stitched it in bright colors. In the center of the tapestry was a facsimile of the John Newbery Medal.

Children who work as publicists through art and creative book review activities are sure not only to understand their books so they can interpret them, but also to find pleasure in stimulating others to read the books they are advertising.

References

Aborn, Carlene. 1979. "The Newberys: Getting Them to Read (It Isn't Easy)." In *Motivating Children and Young Adults to Read*, vol. 1, edited by James L. Thomas and Ruth M. Loring. Phoenix, AZ: Oryx Press.

Carlsen, G. Robert, and Anne Sherrill. 1988. *Voices of Readers: How We Come to Love Books*. Champaign-Urbana, IL: National Council of Teachers of English.

Johnson, Terry D., and Daphne R. Louis. 1987. *Literacy Through Literature*. Portsmouth, NH: Heinemann.

Martin, Pat, Joanne Kelly, and Kay Grabow. 1992. *Rebuses for Readers*. Englewood, CO: Teacher Ideas Press.

Robertson, Deborah, and Patricia Barry. 1990. *Super Kids Publishing Company*. Englewood, CO: Teacher Ideas Press.

Literature Resources

dePaola, Tomie. 1983. *The Legend of the Bluebonnet*. New York: G. P. Putnam's Sons.

Hastings, Selina. 1985. *Sir Gawain and the Loathly Lady*. New York: Lothrop, Lee & Shepard.

L'Engle, Madeleine. 1962. *A Wrinkle in Time*. New York: Dell.

Lionni, Leo. 1963. *Swimmy*. New York: Pantheon Books.

Milne, A. A. 1926. *Winnie-the-Pooh*. New York: E. P. Dutton.

Spinelli, Jerry. 1990. *Maniac Magee*. New York: HarperTrophy.

Steig, William. 1969. *Sylvester and the Magic Pebble*. New York: Scholastic.

Tolkien, J. R. R. 1966. *The Hobbit*. New York: Ballantine Books.

Van Allsburg, Chris. 1992. *The Widow's Broom*. Boston: Houghton Mifflin.

7

Building the Team

Cooperative Learning Activities

Most sports are played in teams, even individual sports like track, swimming, and gymnastics. Teamwork means cooperation. It means working toward a goal, valuing each player's contribution, capitalizing on individual differences, and seeing other players' points of view.

Teamwork and cooperation can be just as important in the classroom as they are on the playing field. By using the wisdom gained from three national educational trends—cooperative learning, heterogeneous grouping, and literature-based instruction—we can create a reading environment that builds on teamwork and cooperation and ensures that reading will NOT be a spectator sport.

Cooperative Learning: The Model

Although it is beyond the scope of this book to provide a detailed analysis of cooperative learning strategies, I have included an overview of the essential elements of cooperative learning and have referred the reader to additional sources for a more in-depth study. The gurus of cooperative learning, D. W. Johnson and R. T. Johnson (1987), outline the five basic elements in a cooperative learning model:

1. Positive interdependence
2. Face-to-face interaction
3. Individual accountability
4. Interpersonal and small group skills
5. Group processing

In the cooperative learning model, students are actively involved in their learning through discussion and group work. Children learn from the different perspectives and thought processes of other group members. Working in cooperative groups can improve students' achievement, self-esteem, attitudes toward others, and social skills.

Teachers need to structure the groups so students understand how they need each other and that they're individually accountable for contributing to the group's work. Social skills such as encouraging each other to participate, communicating effectively, and disagreeing with ideas, not people, need to be stressed. Students also need to be taught how to "process" or "debrief" at the end of every cooperative group project. Students share with each other what they did well in their group work and set goals for what they would do better next time. For study in the area of cooperative learning, I would recommend Johnson and Johnson (1987, 1989), Johnson, Johnson, and Holubec (1986), and Totten (1991).

Cooperative Learning and Literature: One Model

In their book *Literature Circles: Cooperative Learning for Grades 3-8*, Mimi Neamen and Mary Strong (1992)* demonstrate how to use cooperative learning strategies as a means for students to collectively build an understanding of a particular novel. Students work on an equal basis, regardless of reading ability, to contribute to a final project. Students are assessed not only on group participation and meeting deadlines but also on the quality and appropriateness of their contribution.

First we'll explore Neamen and Strong's cooperative learning model as it relates to the study and sharing of literature. Then we'll look at an example from their book.

Selection of novels. The teacher selects the novels to be read by the class and prepares a project list for each novel. The teacher explains how much total time will be allotted for the reading and the projects.

Group assignment. The teacher does a short booktalk on each book and students decide which book they'd like to study. Kids draw numbers to determine the order in which they will choose their groups. For example, for a class of 25 students, the teacher would want to select six novels and have 5 slots available in each group, thereby offering 30 slots. The extra five slots ensure that the last student, number 25, will also have some group choice. When the five slots in one group are filled, the student must choose a different group.

Beginning of group work. The kids assemble in their groups and the novels are passed out. The checker and facilitator are appointed for the first day (these responsibilities rotate daily). Each group is given a folder containing the following items:

- Listing of group members
- Daily checklist so the group facilitator can record the number of pages read by each group member and the daily grade for group participation
- Rules for group work

  Give everyone a fair turn.

  Give reasons for ideas.

  Give different ideas.
- Description of group projects

*Neamen and Strong's cooperative learning model and project sheet appear in Mimi Neamen and Mary Strong, *Literature Circles: Cooperative Learning for Grades 3-8* (Englewood, CO: Teacher Ideas Press, 1992), copyright © 1992 by Mimi Neamen and Mary Strong, and are reprinted with permission.

Beginning work. The group decides how many pages should be read each day to complete the book and the projects in the allotted time. Students decide whether class time will be spent reading, working on projects, or a combination of both.

Group projects. The information provided about the projects should be self-explanatory. The group decides how they will accomplish the tasks. Some groups do all the projects together; others divide the work among group members. They work together in class, after school, and on weekends. Neamen and Strong feel that it is very important for the students to make these choices and take responsibility for their decisions. Students also have the option of creating a project on their own that will demonstrate their knowledge of the novel.

Presenting the work. On the appointed day, the groups present their projects to the whole group.

Evaluating the group. To assess individuals' participation in the daily group activities, each student is asked to honestly and conscientiously fill out a checklist each day for every other group member. Then by referring to the daily checklists, each student completes a midproject and a final group evaluation form. Neamen and Strong suggest that students consider these questions when evaluating individual contributions. Did the student do an equal share of the work (or extra)? Was the student a good group member? Was the student dependable? Was the reading and the individual contribution completed on time? Did the person contribute ideas to the group? Was the work done neatly and with pride? After grading the person, students tell why they think the person earned the grade they recommend. Neamen and Strong (1992, 5) observe, "Students often perceive their contributions very differently from how others perceive them. There is always a marked difference in the quality of group interaction and sharing the day after the midpoint evaluation."

In *Literature Circles*, Neamen and Strong include cooperative learning project sheets for 28 novels and six picture books (see fig. 7.1, pp. 113-115, for one example). Although they list important vocabulary words for each book, they report that often they don't use the list directly.

(Text continues on page 115.)

Fig. 7.1. Example of cooperative learning project sheet.

THE DOOR IN THE WALL

Marguerite de Angeli

Scholastic, 1949

The beautiful language of the text carries the reader along on Robin's journey to Castle Lindsay to meet his father, who is fighting the Scots in the north, and his mother, who is travelling with the queen. Brother Luke teaches Robin to be strong in spite of his useless legs so that he is ready and able to take advantage when "the door in the wall" appears. English life in the Middle Ages is authentically described.

Vocabulary

mailed (page 7)	shire reeve (page 9)	putrid (page 9)
porridge (page 10)	victuals (page 11)	hospice (page 12)
plague (page 15)	cloister (page 15)	pallets (page 15)
friar (page 16)	jennet (page 17)	breviary (page 18)
monasteries (page 19)	scriptorium (page 23)	parchment (page 23)
tonsured (page 31)	missal (page 38)	galled (page 51)
pasty (page 52)	abbot (page 64)	heath (page 73)
turret (page 78)	fripperies (page 84)	portcullis (page 85)
bailey (page 85)	priory (page 100)	sacristan (page 104)
coif (page 117)		

(Figure 7.1 continues on page 114.)

Fig. 7.1—*Continued*

Making a Map

The United Kingdom (U.K.) consists of England, Scotland, Wales, and Northern Ireland. Go to the library and consult an atlas. Locate London, England, where the book begins. Then find the Welsh border (between Wales and England), near which was Castle Lindsay. Make a map showing the United Kingdom. Locate and label the places mentioned above. Your map may be traced or drawn freehand, or you may choose to present this part of the world in a more creative and innovative way.

Charting Life in the Middle Ages

This book takes place during the Middle Ages. You have learned much from your reading about life in this time period. For example, foods, methods of transportation, styles of dress, kinds of shelter, types of occupations, recreational activities, and dangers encountered while travelling are mentioned throughout the book. Go to the library and find supplemental information about everyday life in the Middle Ages. Take notes on your research. Using these notes and information from the book, arrange everything you have learned in categories. Compare each aspect of life in the Middle Ages to life today. For example, one category might be transportation. In the Middle Ages people travelled by boat, horse, or wagon or on foot. Today people travel by boat, plane, train, motorcycle, or bicycle or on foot. Present your information. Draw pictures or cut pictures from magazines to enhance your presentation.

Creating a Book of Illuminations

In the Middle Ages parchment was used for writings rather than paper. To keep from wasting any space on the parchment, the monks did not skip to the next page to start a new chapter. Instead, they showed where a new chapter began by making the first letter of the first word in a chapter very large and fancy. These elaborate letters were often made with gold leaf, and they were called illuminations. Make a book of illuminations using the first letters of the names of at least five of the characters in the book On each page write a sentence about one character, beginning with the character's name. (See page 23 in the text.) Illustrate the page on which the sentence appears. Make a cover or a title page and a table of contents for your book. Put all of your pages together in book form.

Designing Your Coat-of-Arms

A coat-of-arms is a pictorial representation of a family's ancestry, occupation, and station in life. During the Middle Ages families of importance used coats-of-arms to identify themselves in many ways. The design was frequently embroidered on cloth or publicly displayed in other ways. On page 114 in the text, coats-of-arms appear on flags. Create a book of heraldry that consists of coats-of-arms designed by at least three group members. These coats-of-arms should represent their family characteristics. They may be drawn, painted, stitched, or done in any other original manner. They should be organized in a book of heraldry to present to the class.

Building a Castle

Castle Lindsay and the surrounding countryside is shown on pages 122 and 123. Construct a castle using Castle Lindsay as a model. You may use cardboard (paper-towel rolls, toilet-paper rolls, plastic-wrap rolls), sugar cubes, blocks, or any material of your choice. Make your castle on some kind of platform so it can be moved. Detail the surrounding countryside on the platform. The following book is a good resource:

Macaulay, David. *Castle*. Boston: Houghton Mifflin, 1977.

Designing Your Own Project

If you can think of another project that will clearly demonstrate your knowledge of the book, you may substitute it for one of the other projects mentioned above. Talk with your teacher about this.

■ ■ ■ ■ ■

Collaborative Activities

To have "pure" cooperative learning groups, students need to be trained appropriately to be effective evaluators and group participants. Some teachers enjoy using group activities as an alternative to individual work but are not interested in formally training students to use the cooperative learning process on an ongoing basis. The following are ideas for group projects to supplement those suggested in other chapters.

Buddy System

More and more schools are pairing younger children with older ones for a wide variety of activities, for example, pairing first- with fourth-graders, second- with fifth-graders, and third- with sixth-graders. Wilder School in Grand Forks, North Dakota, has a "Buddy in a Bean Bag Chair" program, where older children can be excused at various times during the month to read to their buddy or have their little buddy read to them in a bean bag chair outside the classroom door.

Older buddies make "big books"; put on puppet plays, radio programs, and skits; and write stories with their buddies. They accompany the younger children to the library, on field trips, through the school carnival, or to special school reading events. The buddy system is rewarding not only for the younger children, who thrive on the additional attention, but also for older students, who feel valued and important.

Fairy Tales: They're Positively Criminal

In his book *Mystery and Detection*, Jerry Flack (1990, 55) describes a delightful group activity exploring the "crimes" in fairy tales:

> Have your students ever pondered the crimes committed in fairy tales? Murder, kidnapping, larceny, child abuse and abandonment, vagrancy, malicious and willful destruction of property, false identities and impersonations with intent to do great bodily harm. The list goes on and on! Why, a law school primer could be written about the crimes committed in Little Red Riding Hood alone! And, what are we to make of the legal wranglings which might emanate from the Rumpelstiltskin child custody dispute?
>
> Ask students to examine a classic fairy tale, carefully noting all the crimes for which characters could at least be under suspicion or indicted. Then, direct students to find one of the cases which begs for a trial. Allow students to have fun examining the evidence and arguments for all sides involved. Some students can be on the prosecution team and build a case against the big bad wolf, for example, while those in the legal activist society and Save the Wolf environment group can join forces to work out his defense. The remaining class members can be jurors, witnesses, and reporters covering the trial for Black Forest TV Station or the Grimm Newspaper Syndicate. A resident cartoonist can draw wonderful cartoons of a poor, pitiful wolf taking the stand in his own defense, or of a shy, frightened girl in red cloak recounting that horrible afternoon in the forest when her grandmother sprouted a hairy upper lip.
>
> Crime can be fun when it is housed within the context of fairy tales, and considerable creativity and good humor can flow in the classroom.

Compare a Tale

In another activity using fairy tales, each group is assigned a different fairy tale. Group members find a different version of the tale and discuss the similarities and differences in the versions. *World Folktales: A Treasury of Over Sixty of the World's Best-Loved Folktales* (Clarkson and Cross 1980) contains an excellent index that cross-references stories. A local or school librarian also has several cross-referencing indexes.

Pro and Con Panel

A book is chosen and the author is represented by a class member. An impartial chairperson is appointed to ensure that the discussion is well balanced.

Students who have read the book volunteer to serve on the panel on either side. Pro and con sides might be:

- Liked or disliked the book
- Thought the book was realistic or not realistic
- Agreed with the main character's perspective or disagreed
- Liked or disliked the ending
- Liked the writing style or didn't like it

The "author" can add his or her perspective to the discussion.

Panel Discussions of All Types

Panel discussions of various kinds are possible even when no two members of the panel have read the same book.

Themes. Students each read a book by a different author but on a common theme such as survival. The books mentioned in chapter 2 might be a start. Students explore such questions as: How did the main characters get into difficulty? What perils did they face? What did they do to survive? How did they "escape" the perils? What would the students do if they were in a similar situation?

Solutions. Students compare stories with one another, reacting to the kind of solution presented in each story—did it involve magic, accident, or purposeful effort on the part of a character or characters? Did the students feel that they would have handled the problem in the same way if they'd been there? Why or why not?

Importance of setting. Students discuss various stories they have read, thinking about the importance of the setting to the story. For example, could *Island of the Blue Dolphins* (O'Dell 1960) have taken place in the Caribbean? How about New York City? Why or why not? How would the setting have changed the story? Could *Shiloh* (Naylor 1991) or *Maniac Magee* (Spinelli 1990) have taken place in Boston, the Everglades, or the Outback of Australia? Why or why not?

Importance of historical context. Students read various stories and discuss the importance of the historical context to the stories. Could *The Witch of Blackbird Pond* (Speare 1958) have taken place in a contemporary Amish village? Why or why not? How about *Johnny Tremain* (Forbes 1967)? Could the story have occurred in a different time?

Characterization. Students read different stories and discuss how the author develops character. Which characters are well developed? How can you tell? Are there characters in the books that are inconsistent, not well developed? Do you think the author did it on purpose? Why or why not? How would the students change or add to the character development?

In cooperative and collaborative reading activities, formally structured or not, make sure that kids are "in the game." It is virtually impossible to be a member of a team and not participate. Spectators watch. Team members play.

References

Flack, Jerry D. 1990. *Mystery and Detection*. Englewood, CO: Teacher Ideas Press.

Johnson, D. W., and R. T. Johnson. 1989. *Cooperation and Competition: Theory and Research*. Edina, MN: Interaction.

———. 1987. *Learning Together and Alone: Cooperation, Competition and Individualization*. 2d ed. Englewood Cliffs, NJ: Prentice-Hall.

Johnson, D. W., R. T. Johnson, and E. Holubec. 1986. *Circles of Learning: Cooperation in the Classroom*. Rev. ed. Edina, MN: Interaction.

Neamen, Mimi, and Mary Strong. 1992. *Literature Circles: Cooperative Learning for Grades 3-8*. Englewood, CO: Teacher Ideas Press.

Totten, Samuel, et al. 1991. *Cooperative Learning: A Guide to Research*. New York: Garland.

Literature Resources

Clarkson, Atelia, and Gilbert B. Cross. 1980. *World Folktales: A Treasury of Over Sixty of the World's Best-Loved Folktales*. New York: Scribner.

Forbes, Esther. 1967. *Johnny Tremain*. New York: Coward, McCann & Geoghegan.

Naylor, Phyllis Reynolds. 1991. *Shiloh*. New York: Macmillan.

O'Dell, Scott. 1960. *Island of the Blue Dolphins*. New York: Dell.

Speare, Elizabeth George. 1958. *The Witch of Blackbird Pond*. Boston: Houghton Mifflin.

Spinelli, Jerry. 1990. *Maniac Magee*. New York: HarperTrophy.

8

Putting the Game in Context

Reading Across the Curriculum Through Thematic Units

Kids practice batting, running, catching, and pitching. They study strategy, assess their opponents' strengths and weaknesses, and finally put it all together for the big game. Reading is like that, too. Although reading for reading's sake is rewarding, just as batting for batting's sake is rewarding, reading takes on a new dimension when placed in a larger context, when it is a vehicle for something bigger. Reading and literature can be the core of the program or the basis upon which all other curricular areas are built. In this chapter we'll explore how to create thematic units that bring together all curriculum areas for the "big game."

One Model for Planning and Organizing an Integrated Program

Winship School in Grand Forks, North Dakota, has a dynamic multigrade, integrated program. The fifth- and sixth-grade teachers, along with a teacher of the learning disabled, have developed a theme-based program that integrates the study of reading, social studies, science, writing, and art.

The four teachers began with a problem. How could they provide a quality learning experience for the students in the one combined fifth- and sixth-grade classroom? As the teacher split her time between two levels, how could the two-year curriculum be adequately covered? Didn't the teacher lose vital "time on task" as she taught one grade level, temporarily neglecting the other?

After visiting several other schools and reading extensively, the teachers decided to create a theme-based integrated curriculum. In a two-year period the fifth- and sixth-grade curriculum would be covered.

They debated: Should the curriculum be literature-based or should the curriculum be approached through a different discipline? They decided that the entry point for their integrated curriculum would be social studies, although the integration would work just as well for any curriculum "window," be it literature, science, writing, or art.

After a brief orientation unit, the students and the staff began their two-year journey around the theme Discovery and Survival, which tracked human progress through time. During the first year, six periods in history were explored, beginning with humans' first recorded history and concluding with the Middle Ages. In the second year, the study progressed through modern times.

In a 1993 personal interview, the staff—Nan Campbell, Jeanne Erickson, Terry Hager, and Cheryl Hoekstra—described implementing the program. They worked for two weeks during the summer to get ready for the transition, although that was just the beginning of their research and preparation. For each of the six blocks, one teacher would take responsibility for one of the areas (social studies, writing, art, science, or reading), locating and readying resources and materials, planning for student interaction, preparing the lesson plans, and making arrangements for special events such as field trips or guest speakers. "It is a tremendous advantage to have four of us working on this," reflected Hoekstra; "it would be a real challenge to do all the planning and preparation alone."

Nan Campbell, the teacher of the learning disabled, used to remove her students from the classroom to provide services. Now she is an important part of the team and works with kids in the classroom. She states, "Although all the children are excited about learning in ways the teachers couldn't have imagined, the average and below average learners may have benefitted the most." They are now active learners. They've learned to respond. Campbell continued, "I think of one learning-disabled fifth-grade student who was able to pick up the sixth-grade textbook and read it fluently—all because we had built so much background. He brought knowledge and understanding to his reading in ways we could never do in our formerly segmented curriculum."

Hoekstra said, "It's amazing to see the metacognition—the kids know what they know, totally confident in their knowledge. The students have deep conversations about the topics they are studying. It's so exciting to see all students responding." At first the children asked whether they were studying reading or social studies, then they began to understand the interrelatedness of all their studies. Hoekstra reports, "Textbooks have become the least important of our resources."

Erickson points out two other important features of their program, which speak to involving children as part of the educational team. The first is deemphasizing grades and focusing instead on student learning. Teachers and students use the portfolio as a way of tracking student progress. Students and parents are encouraged to help select the artifacts that will be included in the portfolio. A second important change is that children are encouraged to attend the parent-teacher conference. "It's one of the most beneficial things I've ever done," Erickson reports. In one sense, the children conduct the conference. They review their portfolio and share what they've learned with their parents and also report on what they plan to learn in the upcoming months.

The team also noted that communication is vital both internally with the staff and externally with the parents. The team of teachers, paraprofessionals, and student teachers meets for at least an hour once a week to review plans for the upcoming week. The team involved the parents at the beginning of the year so that they would understand the philosophy of the program. Even though the parents had been informed about the program ahead of time, one parent of a learning disabled child began expressing some objection to the program during the parent-teacher conference. The child immediately sprang to the defense, "But it is so much fun and I'm learning so much." Then the child proceeded to prove it as they reviewed the portfolio together.

Paperback books are also an integral part of the program. The team received $1,000 to purchase additional paperbacks that related to the curriculum.

The integrated program has much to recommend it, no matter what the grade level. By working with the library media specialists, teachers can bring together materials for an in-depth study of a topic that can lead to authentic discussions and deep understanding. The children in this type of program move beyond the superficial factual knowledge available through textbook study. Plus, the children are actively involved in their own learning.

Although the teachers at Winship School used social studies as their base, the integrated program works equally well when centered on other subjects.

Literature as the Center

In *Picture Books: Integrated Teaching of Reading, Writing, Listening, Speaking, Viewing, and Thinking*, author Joyce Armstrong Carroll (1991, 3)* says, "I found that integrating writing, speaking, viewing, and thinking was easily accomplished through reading books and that teachers enjoyed calling the related activities and artifacts 'jackdaws.'" Carroll has used 28 picture books as an entry point for work in other curricular areas. For example, she shows how *The Furry News: How to Make a Newspaper* (Leedy 1990) can be integrated with writing, library research, science, mathematics, language arts, social studies, and art (see fig. 8.1).

Fig. 8.1. Example of how a picture book can be integrated with many subjects.

Title: *The Furry News: How to Make a Newspaper*. Holiday House, 1990.

Author: Loreen Leedy

Grade level: 3-6

Jackdaw: A newspaper (try to obtain different kinds, issues, and sizes).

Summary: Several animals work hard to write, edit, and print their own newspaper.

READING/WRITING CONNECTIONS

1. Distribute the newspapers. Ask the students what section they would read first and discuss why.
2. Call attention to the newspaper's physical characteristics: size, number of columns per page, pictures, lead story, number of pages, and use of color, if any.
3. Before reading the book, invite students to decide what part of the newspaper they would like to work on while you read.
4. After the reading, get a sampling of what students would like to work on, but tell them that first they will all be reporters.
5. Divide students into pairs. Give each reporter five minutes to interview his or her partner about a favorite activity or hobby. Then allow ten minutes for reporters to write up a brief feature article to present to the class.

*"Jackdaw 23" in figure 8.1 appears in Joyce Armstrong Carroll, *Picture Books: Integrated Teaching of Reading, Writing, Listening, Speaking, Viewing, and Thinking* (Englewood, CO: Teacher Ideas Press, 1991), copyright © 1991 by Libraries Unlimited, and is reprinted with permission.

—EXTENSIONS—

VOCABULARY/SPELLING

Students become familiar with all the newspaper terms in the glossary.

LIBRARY CONNECTIONS

1. Visit the newspaper section of a large library and count how many different newspapers they handle each day.
2. Research newspapers in the United States. Write for samples.
3. Research the "Code of Ethics" for journalists.
4. Show the parts of the book, especially noting the glossary. Discuss the function of the glossary.

SCIENCE CONNECTIONS

1. Weather: Students, working in groups, become "experts" on aspects of the weather:
   - *Group one*—Graphs the city or town's high and low temperatures for a week or a month.
   - *Group two*—Graphs the state's high and low temperatures for a week or a month.
   - *Group three*—Graphs the high and low temperatures for the United States for a week or a month.
   - *Group four*—Clips out the newspaper's forecast, then assesses its accuracy each day.
2. Habitats: Students work in three groups—the Ocean group, the Fresh Water group, or the Land group—to find articles related to life in their assigned areas.
3. Plants and animals: Students work in either the Plant group or the Animal group to find newspaper articles related to plants and their uses or animals and their uses.

MATHEMATICS CONNECTIONS

1. Working with measurements: Find an article or an ad with measurements. For example, an article on the sports page may talk about yards gained or lost in a game. Convert those measurements to other units, such as inches or feet.
2. Basing problems on real ads: Using an ad for carpet or tile, measure the floor of the classroom in order to figure out how much carpet or tile to buy and how much it would cost.

LANGUAGE ARTS CONNECTIONS

1. Word choice/diction: Students work in one of three groups—the Noun group, the Verb group, or the Adjective group—to find a good example of "their" words. They share their example and why they think it is a good example of word choice. (You can rotate students so that all students eventually get into each different group.)

(Figure 8.1 continues on page 124.)

Fig. 8.1—*Continued*

2. Write an article using the Reporter's Formula: Who? What? When? Where? Why? How?
3. Interview someone for a feature article that will be published in the newspaper.
4. Find ads that spell brand names in unconventional ways, such as *SAVX*. Discuss acronyms.
5. Use advice columns and letters to the editor to reteach letter-writing.
6. Have students act as proofreaders and search for mistakes in the newspaper.

SOCIAL STUDIES CONNECTIONS

1. Clip maps out of newspapers and compare to those in encyclopedias and textbooks.
2. Discuss propaganda devices such as bandwagon, slogans, repetition, loaded words, powerful images, and emotional appeals. Discuss how these can affect prejudices.

ART CONNECTIONS

Make a collage of newspaper headlines, editorial cartoons, or pictures.

PUBLISHING

Let students write, edit, and publish their own class newspaper, using the model of the animals in *The Furry News*. Follow the directions given on the two-page spread entitled "Making Your Own Newspaper for Your Family, Neighborhood or School." Display these newspapers on a bulletin board captioned "WE KNOW HOW TO MAKE A NEWSPAPER"; cut the caption's letters out of a newspaper.

■ ■ ■ ■ ■

Anthony D. Fredericks (1992, 37-38),* in *The Integrated Curriculum*, shows how to integrate popular children's books throughout the curriculum. Fredericks says, "Students are provided with a multitude of ways to extend their comprehension of all subjects through the wide and wonderful world of literature.... When students are provided with opportunities to examine, process, and utilize literature in subjects such as reading/language arts, science/health, art, mathematics, music, social studies, and physical education, their growth as learners is tremendously enhanced." Fredericks suggests that students get involved in the planning by using the concept of bookwebbing. The steps are simple. A web such as the one shown in figure 8.2 is drawn on the board. The title of the book is placed in the center and students discuss some of the events, characters, and settings from the book. Then students brainstorm ideas related to each curricular area and select activities they wish to pursue.

---

*The web in figure 8.2 appears in Anthony D. Fredericks, *The Integrated Curriculum* (Englewood, CO: Teacher Ideas Press, 1992), copyright © 1992 by Anthony D. Fredericks, and is reprinted with permission.

Fig. 8.2. Example of a web for bookwebbing.

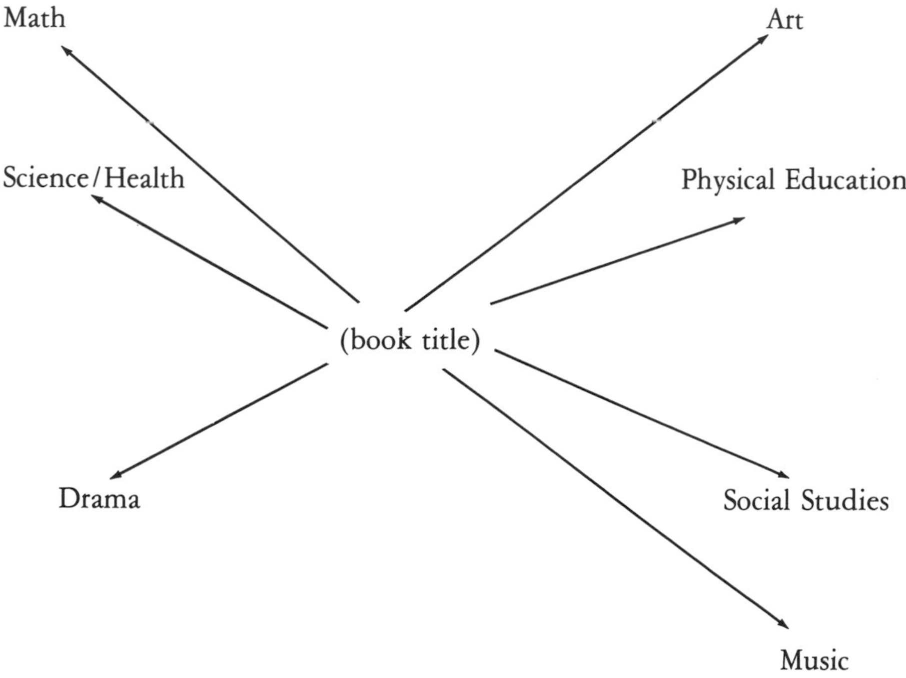

A Science-Literature Partnership

Glenn McGlathery and Norma Livo in *Who's Endangered on Noah's Ark?* (1992)* provide excellent examples of integrating literature and science. They present a tapestry of animal folklore, scientific information, news articles, classroom activities, and bibliographies. It's easy to see how their units could include other curricular areas as well. For example, the unit on wolves begins with the folklore "The Wolf and the Seven Kids" and goes on to discuss how the wolf has been presented in folklore. The authors describe the species; provide information about its behavior, habitat, and historical range; explain why it is endangered; and outline the attempts to save it. A sample of the activities is presented in figure 8.3, page 126.

*Used by permission of Glenn McGlathery and Norma J. Livo.

Fig. 8.3. Example of an activity for integrating literature and science.

WOLF ACTIVITIES

Wolves as Stereotypes

- Brainstorm all the things you think or feel when the word *wolf* is mentioned. If your reaction is mostly negative, reflect and discuss why this might be.
- Bring in pictures of wolves. Are there stereotypes? How is the stereotyping of wolves similar to those of other peoples or of different countries and cultures?
- What other animals are stereotyped? (For example, pigs and turkeys.) Why have they been stereotyped? Write a story stereotyping another animal.
- Brainstorm positive aspects of wolves. Research the literature for additional positive aspects of wolves.
- Create posters or bumper stickers with slogans that encourage positive feelings toward wolves.
- Brainstorm remedies to the stereotyping of wolves. Get together in small groups and discuss what you can do to eliminate the stereotyping.

Wolves and the Environment

- Discuss how animals adapt to new environments and the possible consequences of not adapting.
- Research wolf tracks. Make a transparency of the tracks. Discuss how wolves hide or escape from their predators.
- Discuss preparations wolves make for winter. Illustrate their preparations on a poster.
- Keep an imaginary journal of the life of a wolf for five days.
- Make a concentration game with cards of pictures of animals on half the cards and their habitats on the other half.

Wolves as an Endangered Species

- Brainstorm the things you think have contributed to wolves' becoming endangered.
- Research the laws in your state concerning killing wolves. How have these laws changed?
- Research why wolfhounds were developed.
- Collect newspaper and magazine articles about the studies or research done on wolves or their reintroduction into former habitats. Use this information for a bulletin board on wolves.
- Relate the similarities and differences of what is hapening to the wolf today and what has happened in the past. (Refer to current newspaper and magazine articles and books like *The Last Wolf of Ireland*.)

The whole language philosophy of teaching is based on the successful integration of literature throughout the curriculum. Fredericks (1992, 9) says, "Literature provides the vehicle by which children can travel to all parts of the elementary curriculum, observing and appreciating the scenery along the way." Reading is no longer a stand-alone activity, just as batting is not a stand-alone activity. Both are an integral part of playing the game.

References

Campbell, Nan, Jeanne Erikson, Terry Hager, and Cheryl Hoekstra. 1993. Interview with author. Grand Forks, North Dakota, January 14.

Carroll, Joyce Armstrong. 1991. *Picture Books: Integrated Teaching of Reading, Writing, Listening, Speaking, Viewing, and Thinking*. Englewood, CO: Teacher Ideas Press.

Fredericks, Anthony D. 1992. *The Integrated Curriculum*. Englewood, CO: Teacher Ideas Press.

McGlathery, Glenn, and Norma J. Livo. 1992. *Who's Endangered on Noah's Ark?: Literary and Scientific Activities for Teachers and Parents*. Englewood, CO: Teacher Ideas Press.

Literature Resources

Leedy, Loreen. 1990. *The Furry News: How to Make a Newspaper*. New York: Holiday House.

9

Working in the Weight Room

Heading for the Reading Centers

Players, of course, play the game. They also work out in the weight room, warm up in the bull pen, and run laps to get in shape and stay in shape for the game. Reading centers can help kids "work out," giving them an opportunity to practice and hone their skills. More important, reading centers require a response, and that, after all, is what this book is all about.

So What's a Center?

A classroom can have one learning center or many. The centers can be fun places for reading activities when other work is done, or they can be central to the curriculum of the classroom. Kids can visit them if they want to, teachers may assign students a number of center activities each week, or the centers may be so core to the curriculum that work there almost becomes the curriculum. Teachers must decide how learning centers fit into their philosophy, objectives, and class structure.

Here's how they work. At the centers kids learn independently, either by themselves or in small groups. Tasks are clearly defined by the teacher, with the materials, books, artifacts, and directions in place. The teacher should be available to troubleshoot, not direct. The idea is to have kids working on their own.

Ideas for Centers

When creating centers, teachers and kids are limited only by their imaginations and creativity. Here are some ideas to help you get started.

Catalog Center

Save the catalogs that flood the mail, catalogs featuring clothing, electronics, sporting equipment, needlecraft, coins, and other products. Sample activities might include filling out a sample order form, spending a given amount of money on sports gear/clothes/holiday gifts, and comparing prices and features of given products. Students could write an advertisement for the most expensive or the most unusual item in a particular catalog.

Mystery Center

In his book *Mystery and Detection*, Jerry Flack (1990) describes a center where mystery and intrigue are the central focus. Video stores might provide movie posters of Sherlock Holmes or Agatha Christie to help set the tone. The center may have mystery games like Parker Brothers' Clue or How to Host a Murder. Magazines like *The Armchair Detective* and catalogs from mystery stores should be available for perusal. In addition to appropriate mystery fiction, the center might include biographies of famous mystery writers and real-life detectives (e.g., Allan Pinkerton) and books about famous crimes, notorious criminals, police procedures such as fingerprinting, and the like. Activities might include checking for fingerprints, solving mysteries described on "unsolved mystery cards" developed by the teacher or class members, or writing a mystery story containing objects found in one of the "evidence bags."

Sports Center

Books, short stories, magazines, newspaper articles, filmstrips, videos, charts of sports teams and their current rankings, scrapbooks of local teams' game results, and local team mementos can be displayed in a sports center. Activities might include researching the background of favorite players and creating scrapbooks about them, or keeping statistics charts (e.g., fastest runner in the 440, most goals in a season, most home runs, longest pass, most passes completed, best golf score by a favorite player, best batting average, etc.).

Author Center

An author center set up to promote one author would display an author photograph, books by that author, and biographical information about the author. In her book *An Author a Month (for Pennies)*, Sharron McElmeel (1988)* provides a picture, biographical information, a bibliography, and recommended activities for twelve authors. See figure 9.1, pages 132-133, for a sample of the activities she suggests for author and illustrator Chris Van Allsburg.

Hobby Center

Have students bring in their hobbies and any related reading. They could develop audiotapes describing their hobbies and activity cards that would encourage fellow students to try the hobbies, too. Sometimes writing clear directions is the most difficult writing students will attempt. Two examples of directions students might try writing are for tying a fishing fly and making paper sculpture jewelry; materials might be made available for the other students to try the two activities.

---

*The author center ideas in figure 9.1 appear in Sharron L. McElmeel, *An Author a Month (for Pennies)* (Englewood, CO: Libraries Unlimited, 1988), copyright © 1988 by Sharron L. McElmeel, and are reprinted with permission.

Fig. 9.1. Example of information and activities for an author center.

CHRIS VAN ALLSBURG

Titles written and illustrated by Chris Van Allsburg.

Ben's Dream. (Houghton-Mifflin, 1982).

The Garden of Abdul Gasazi. (Houghton-Mifflin, 1979).

Jumanji. (Houghton-Mifflin, 1981).

The Mysteries of Harris Burdick. (Houghton-Mifflin, 1984).

The Polar Express. (Houghton-Mifflin, 1985).

The Stranger. (Houghton-Mifflin, 1986).

The Wreck of the Zephyr. (Houghton-Mifflin, 1983).

The Z Was Zapped. (Houghton-Mifflin, 1987).

The author poster pages can provide a focus for the author corner featuring Chris Van Allsburg. Houghton-Mifflin has made available posters of several Van Allsburg books. Those posters or book jackets will add more interest to your author corner or bulletin board.

Begin the unit by sharing some background information about Chris Van Allsburg. Explain that some people regard Van Allsburg's illustrations as quirky; discuss what this means. The humor in his stories is often subtle and sophisticated. You may want to share one or more of his books by using a filmstrip cassette version of one of his books. Random House has five of the Van Allsburg titles in nonprint format: *Ben's Dream*, *The Garden of Abdul Gasazi*, *Jumanji*, *The Polar Express*, and *The Wreck of the Zephyr*.

Activities

1. Write stories to accompany the titles and illustrations in *The Mysteries of Harris Burdick*.

2. Make a board game "Jumanji." Be sure to include the events that Van Allsburg includes in his book *Jumanji*.

3. Write a story of your trip on the Polar Express.

4. Read any of the Van Allsburg titles and discuss information that you think Van Allsburg did not reveal or discuss the events that you think might occur next. These discussions might be followed by journal writing.

5. Design a birthday card to send to Van Allsburg for his June 18th birthday, or send him a one-half birthday card on December 18th.

6. Van Allsburg's sculpture has been exhibited at the Whitney Museum of American Art, the Shiller-Wapner Gallery, the Alan Stone Gallery, and the Museum of Modern Art, all in New York City. Find out more information about these galleries. Visitors' brochures could be designed. Make sure enough information is included so that visits to the galleries could actually be scheduled if someone were to go to New York City.

7. In the Van Allsburgs' home is a sculpture of a white dog with one eye circled with a black spot. The sculpture is entitled: "Brancusi's Dog." This dog is used in various forms in Van Allsburg's books. Go on a dog hunt finding this dog in Van Allsburg's books. In *Jumanji* the dog is a pull toy on wheels, in *The Polar Express* the dog is a hand puppet propped on a bed post, and the dog appears as a dog beside his master in *The Garden of Abdul Gasazi*.

8. Explain what is happening to each of the letters of the alphabet in *The Z Was Zapped*.

■ ■ ■ ■ ■

Cooking Up U.S. History Center

At the history center, the teacher would have a display featuring artifacts and books from the time period being studied. The center would also have recipes and the ingredients so that students could make homemade foods or products from that period in history. Suzanne Barchers and Patricia Marden (1991)* have written an excellent book, *Cooking Up U.S. History*, that integrates the study of history with the foods or handmade products of a particular time period. Each chapter includes authentic recipes with clear step-by-step directions, "library links" (research ideas), and an annotated bibliography. For example, if the class is studying the colonial period, students might go to the history center to make nut ink and hand soap (see fig. 9.2, pages 134-135). For the westward expansion period, students might make sourdough starter and sourdough biscuits (see fig. 9.3, pages 135-136).

Magic Center

At the magic center, books on magic are displayed. Appropriate posters, videos, and catalogs from magic stores might add interest. The center would contain activity cards and necessary supplies to practice magic tricks. The teacher or a student demonstrates several tricks to stimulate interest. Students then visit the center, follow activity card directions that go with the available materials, and practice their skills. A list of books on magic is included in the bibliography.

(Text continues on page 136.)

---

*Recipes appear in Suzanne I. Barchers and Patricia C. Marden, *Cooking Up U.S. History: Recipes and Research to Share with Children* (Englewood, CO: Teacher Ideas Press, 1991), copyright © 1991 by Suzanne I. Barchers and Patricia C. Marden, and are reprinted with permission.

Fig. 9.2. Examples of items to make in history centers.

NUT INK

Ingredients

6 whole walnut shells
¾ cup water
½ teaspoon vinegar
½ teaspoon salt

Steps

1. Crush the empty shells by wrapping them in a rag and smashing them with a hammer.
2. Put the crushed shells in a pan and add the water.
3. Bring the water to a boil.
4. Turn the heat down and let the water simmer for about 45 minutes, until it turns dark brown.
5. Let the mixture cool. Pour it through a strainer into a jar.
6. Add the vinegar and salt to the ink.
7. Use nut ink with quill or wooden pens.

Library Link: Colonists also made their own paper. Find out how this was done. Find examples of contemporary artists who have returned to the art of making paper. (Ask your art teacher for help.) Consider making paper for an extra project.

HAND SOAP

Caution: Lye use requires adult supervision. Lye flakes are poisonous and can burn skin. If lye touches skin, immediately flood area with water. Do *not* use an aluminum pan. Soap making may produce smoke and irritating fumes.

Ingredients

32 ounces olive oil
14 ounces vegetable shortening
6 ounces lye flakes
16 ounces water

Equipment

Newspapers
Rubber gloves
Cooking thermometer
Shoe box or shallow pan

Steps

1. Cover table with newspaper. Wear rubber gloves.
2. Put oil and shortening in a large glass or stainless steel pot (not aluminum).
3. Heat mixture on lowest setting. Stir with wooden spoon.
4. In a small glass or stainless steel pot, dissolve lye flakes in 16 ounces of water.
5. Use a cooking thermometer to see that the mixtures in both pans reach 96 degrees. Lye and water mixture will get hotter; let it cool down to 96 degrees.
6. Slowly pour lye mixture into oil mixture, stirring constantly.
7. Stir until thick, about 15 minutes.

8. Line a shoe box or shallow pan with waxed paper or plastic wrap.
9. Pour soap mixture into box or pan.
10. Let soap harden for 24 hours.
11. Cut the soap brick into smaller pieces.
12. Allow soap to sit for at least 2 weeks before using it.

Library Link: The colonists used all available resources to survive. Ashes were used to make lye, and nuts and berries were used for ink. Use the library to find other examples of how the colonists utilized and conserved materials.

■ ■ ■ ■ ■

Fig. 9.3. Examples of recipes to use in history centers.

SOURDOUGH STARTER

Ingredients

½ teaspoon active dry yeast
½ cup very warm water
¾ cups flour
2 cups warm water (110 to 115 degrees)
2½ cups flour

Steps

1. Put first 3 ingredients in a large glass jar.
2. Stir well with a *wooden* spoon.
3. Let mixture sit uncovered for 5 to 6 days or until it bubbles and smells sour. Stir mixture each day.
4. When the mixture is ready, store in the refrigerator.

When you are ready to make biscuits, pancakes, or bread:

1. At least 10 hours before, add rest of the ingredients to the starter.
2. Mix until lumpy.
3. Let the mixture sit out until you are ready to proceed.
4. Remove 1 cup for the next starter and store in refrigerator.
5. Use remainder of starter for your recipe.

Library Link: Why was a Canadian or Alaskan prospector called a *sourdough*? What were the staples of the prospector's diet?

(Figure 9.3 continues on page 136.)

Fig. 9.3—*Continued*

SOURDOUGH BISCUITS

Ingredients

¾ cup sourdough starter (see preceding recipe)
1 cup milk
3 cups flour
½ teaspoon salt
1 tablespoon sugar
½ teaspoon baking soda

Steps

1. Use warm, bubbly starter. Put it in a large bowl.
2. Add milk to starter.
3. Mix the flour, salt, sugar, and baking soda in another bowl.
4. Stir the flour mixture into the starter mixture.
5. Put dough onto a floured cloth or piece of waxed paper.
6. Roll dough out with a floured rolling pin until it is about ½ inch thick.
7. Cut biscuits out with a 2-inch floured cutter.
8. Place biscuits on a well greased cookie sheet.
9. Cover biscuits with a slightly damp linen towel and put in a warm place to rise.
10. Let biscuits rise for about 30 minutes.
11. Bake biscuits at 375 degrees until slightly brown, about 10 to 15 minutes.

Makes 15.

Library Link: Find the origins of sourdough.

■ ■ ■ ■ ■

Listening and Viewing Center

In a listening and viewing center, students can listen to stories on tapes made by classmates or reading buddies; as they do so, they can follow along by silently reading the same book. When making tapes, some students add sound effects, complete with a little bell that tells the reader when to turn the page. High-quality commercial tapes, such as those produced by Windham Hill, are also available. In addition, short video programs advertising a favorite book could be made by students and viewed in the listening and viewing center.

Publishing Center

In their wonderful book *Super Kids Publishing Company*, Deborah Robertson and Patricia Barry (1990, 5) explore five learning centers that provide "multi-faceted, sequentially designed, example-laden activities for each stage in the composing process." Students are taken through the writing process, through the printing and binding process, and then to the final center, called "The Apples of Our Eyes," where students present their completed books to the library.

Everyday Materials Center

Display a telephone book, a map, a TV guide, automotive and appliance brochures, a driver's manual, and other such materials. Activities could be developed for each type of material. For example, create a scavenger hunt using the telephone book, asking where to go or whom to call to get a tattoo? To get the cat groomed? To order seed for the parakeet? To get a driver's license renewed? To order a cake for a birthday party? To get a Halloween costume?

Weight rooms, bull pens, and reading centers aren't all there is to the game, but they can help players "work out" and give them an opportunity to improve their skills in challenging and unique ways.

References

Barchers, Suzanne I., and Patricia C. Marden. 1991. *Cooking Up U.S. History: Recipes and Research to Share with Children*. Englewood, CO: Teacher Ideas Press.

Flack, Jerry D. 1990. *Mystery and Detection*. Englewood, CO: Teacher Ideas Press.

McElmeel, Sharron L. 1988. *An Author a Month (for Pennies)*. Englewood, CO: Libraries Unlimited.

Robertson, Deborah, and Patricia Barry. 1990. *Super Kids Publishing Company*. Englewood, CO: Teacher Ideas Press.

10

Reviewing the Play-by-Play

Making TV Work for You

For years I have railed against TV as reading's Enemy Number One. TV hasn't withered and died under my draconian diatribes. In fact, kids are watching more of it than ever. Most researchers agree that children watch between three and four hours of TV per day. Jim Trelease (1989, 4) says, "Add to that the number of hours spent watching videos and the average kindergarten graduate has already spent nearly 16,000 hours watching television—more time than it takes to obtain a bachelor's degree."

I am, above all, a practical person, so if we can't beat it, we'd better figure out ways to use it. The more I thought about it, the more sense it made. Kids watch sports on TV and out they go to have a game of their own, spectators no more. Certainly it could work the same way for reading.

I remember watching *Dr. Zhivago* my senior year in college and not having a clue as to what was going on. Throughout high school and college we never got beyond the American Civil War. Had the film been about fifteenth-century explorers, I probably could have written the script, because I'm sure we covered them every year up to seventh grade. *Dr. Zhivago* made me feel that there was so much more I needed to know. I spent the year reading Russian history (both fiction and nonfiction) from that period. Interesting, I thought, and all because I watched a movie.

Another time when I watched a movie and felt I needed to understand the characters better than the filmmaker had depicted them, I bought the book. On another occasion I remember my students charging in to check out *Brian's Song* after it had played on TV. I noticed, too, that the book clubs were aware of TV's power to "advertise," because they would occasionally offer books with TV tie-ins. Trelease (1989, 121) describes the power of "Reading Rainbow," the award-winning PBS series on children's books. "Conceived by producer Twila Liggett as a way to encourage reading during the summer vacations, the series' sixty shows boast a unique power. Once a book is spotlighted on the show, libraries and bookstores report an immediate positive response among children and their parents. It is not unusual for a book that normally sells 1,200 copies to sell 20,000 after appearing on 'Reading Rainbow.'"

Programs That Bring Books to Life

In the pamphlet "TV and Reading," the Reading Is Fundamental organization (1991)* suggests other programs that bring books to life and encourage reading:

> **CBS Storybreak**—This series of animated programs is designed to bring children's books to television and children back to books. Hosted by Bob Keeshan ("Captain Kangaroo"). Saturday mornings.

ABC Weekend Specials—Aimed at elementary school-age youngsters, shows are based on popular children's and teenage books. Some shows are live action, others animated. Saturday.

Reading Rainbow (PBS)—The aim of this highly acclaimed series is to excite children's interest in reading. Each show features one book and reviews several others. Hosted by LeVar Burton. Monday through Friday.

Wonder Works (WQED)—Most programs in this distinguished series of dramatic specials for families are based on notable works in children's literature. Check local listings.

Long Ago and Far Away (PBS)—This award-winning series features animated versions of classic and contemporary children's books, folktales, and fairy tales. Weekly programs recall the magic of storytelling and inspire a love of reading.

Read More About It (CBS)—One-minute messages, produced with assistance from the Library of Congress, suggest books offering additional information on subjects featured in CBS shows and encourage viewers to visit their local libraries.

CBS Reading Connections

While researching this book, I came upon several good examples of ways to bring kids, books, television, and action together. The following programs are offered by CBS; check the other networks for similar programs.

CBS Television Reading Program. The CBS Television Reading Program is a nationwide script-reading program designed to tap children's interest in and enthusiasm for TV to help improve their reading skills and their motivation for additional reading, learning, and creative thinking. Since the program started in 1977, more than 40 million students have become involved.

Students participating in the Reading Program receive matched-to-broadcast scripts of upcoming CBS Television Network primetime programs. Titles that have been included in the program are "All Quiet on the Western Front," "A Christmas Carol," "The George McKenna Story," "The Secret Garden," and "This Is America, Charlie Brown." Several of the programs were available in both English and Spanish.

Prior to broadcast, the students should read the scripts in the classroom. They may also refer to the script while watching the broadcast at home with their families. Participating teachers receive comprehensive guides that they use to initiate classroom reading, writing, and creative projects stemming from their intensive work with the scripts.

The guide contains not only ideas for reading and reading extension but also activities and questions that help students become more discriminating TV viewers. The guide begins by setting the stage with a plot synopsis and a cast of characters. Then it follows with suggestions for script study and critical viewing. For example, the guide points out filming techniques and asks the students to analyze camera angles and movement shots, the use of lighting effects to enhance dramatic effect, and the use of visual, auditory, and contextual transitions.

The study guide for "O Pioneers" suggests that students compare the original novel *O Pioneers* by Willa Cather with the broadcast adaptation by Robert W. Lenski. Then the guide moves on to vocabulary; an analysis of mood and language; a look at plot, characters, setting, theme, and literary devices; and, finally, enrichment activities. Also included is an excellent resource list of both fiction and nonfiction books with short summaries.

Because this is a decentralized project, not all affiliates may participate in the program. The local station's role is pivotal in setting up a local project. Corporate sponsors or foundations need to be found to underwrite the cost of the scripts, and, of course, the program must be endorsed by key policymaking educators. For more information about this program, call your local CBS affiliate or write to:

CBS Television Reading Program
Educational and Community Services
CBS/Broadcast Group
51 West 52nd Street
New York, NY 10019

CBS Schoolbreak Special. This CBS program presents original contemporary dramas involving conflicts and dilemmas often faced by today's youth. The one-hour dramas for preteens and adolescents provide opportunities for teachers, parents, and students to explore the many timely issues they address, including gangs, date rape, saving the environment, dealing with alcoholic parents, freedom of speech, compulsive gambling, homosexuality, and family mental illness. The broadcasts of all CBS Schoolbreak Specials are closed captioned for hearing-impaired viewers.

CBS provides a guide for teachers to use as a catalyst for discussion, research projects, additional reading, and other classroom activities. Information for each program includes a synopsis, discussion topics, suggested activities, and additional resources. For additional information, write to:

Kidsnet
Suite 208
6856 Eastern Avenue, NW
Washington, DC 20012

PBS "Ghostwriter"

The Program

The mystery/adventure series "Ghostwriter" premiered on October 4, 1992, on PBS. The program, a creation of the Children's Television Workshop (CTW), is underwritten by a $5 million grant from NIKE, Inc., and receives support from the Corporation for Public Broadcasting, The John D. and Catherine T. MacArthur Foundation, The Pew Charitable Trusts, the U.S. Department of Education, the Mary Reynolds Babcock Foundation, and PBS viewers.

CTW's promotional literature describes the series as follows: "Ghostwriter mixes the beat of contemporary music videos, the compelling imagery and energy of today's most popular movies and television and the fictional tradition of child detectives to show seven- to ten-year-olds that reading and writing are relevant, rewarding and just plain fun."

The creators of "Ghostwriter" have three goals for the project: to motivate children to enjoy and value reading and writing, to demonstrate effective reading and writing strategies, and to provide children with compelling opportunities to read and write. Set against an urban backdrop, the show features a multiethnic cast of three boys and three girls who set out to solve neighborhood mysteries with the help of an intriguing ghost who can communicate only through reading and writing. Ghostwriter's message can show up anywhere—from a computer screen to a classroom blackboard to a manhole cover. The key to solving each mystery is discovered through some type of literacy activity.

The Outreach

To complement the show, CTW has developed a variety of print and outreach activities to provide children with opportunities to read and write. Twenty million copies of a full-color *Ghostwriter* minimagazine (8 to 16 pages) will be supplied free to participating schools, youth-serving organizations, and public television stations. A newspaper feature with word games, puzzles, and children's writing is being developed, and a series of 12 paperbacks based on the characters in the "Ghostwriter" team was published during the 1992-1993 season by Bantam Doubleday Dell and will be for sale in bookstores and through the Trumpet Book Club.

More than 350,000 sets of teacher materials are in the process of being distributed. "Ghostwriter" is also working in conjunction with five national youth-serving organizations: the Boys and Girls Clubs of America, the 4-H Youth Development Education, Girls Incorporated, Girl Scouts of the U.S.A., and the YMCA to provide ideas for after-school activities related to the program.

For additional information, call your local PBS station or contact

Children's Television Workshop
"Ghostwriter"
One Lincoln Plaza
New York, NY 10023
(212) 595-3456

or

NIKE Public Affairs
One Bowerman Drive
Beaverton, OR 97005-6453

Discriminating Viewing

In the preface to *Visual Messages: Integrating Imagery into Instruction*, David Considine and Gail Haley (1992) suggest that by integrating media literacy into the existing curriculum, media and visual literacy can strengthen traditional print literacy. The book is rich with material on critical viewing and critical thinking applications. Through an examination of such topics as stereotyping, sexuality, violence, advertising, tobacco, alcohol, diets, political campaigns, the news, and film as literature, students are led to think, to assess, to expand their thinking, and perhaps to read more about the subject.

With all apologies to Considine and Haley, I'd still prefer that kids read and interact with print rather than be passive in front of the television set. However, if we can teach them to discriminate, to interact with the material, to connect viewing to thinking, I'd be willing to abandon my soapbox for at least an hour a day.

I know it can work. Children can and do become discriminating movie and TV viewers. I remember my students, having read *Sounder*, were outraged at the film version. "They got it all wrong," my students protested. "That's not the way the house looked. The movie totally missed the father's character." And horror of horrors, "They changed the ending!" How powerful are the pictures authors create in our minds. My students, two to one, preferred their imagined pictures of a story to anything a filmmaker produced. They had learned the power of the imagination.

Teachers can't fight the "one-eyed monster" (as a student called TV in Robert Carlsen and Anne Sherrill's 1988 book) alone. We have access to children only five hours a day. Parents and teachers have to work together. Like coaches, we can teach the kids all we know about baseball, but if all the kids do is watch it on TV, they'll never be players. Television is here to stay, but we have to limit it and teach kids how to view it discriminatingly. Appendix C contains additional television resources, including addresses for the networks, names and addresses of nonprofit consumer groups and educational organizations that are concerned about television, groups that provide resources or materials for parents and teachers, and publications about TV's effect on children. We'll talk more about that in chapter 15, "Parents as Talent Scouts."

References

Carlsen, G. Robert, and Anne Sherrill. 1988. *Voices of Readers: How We Come to Love Books*. Champaign-Urbana, IL: National Council of Teachers of English.

Considine, David M., and Gail E. Haley. 1992. *Visual Messages: Integrating Imagery into Instruction*. Englewood, CO: Libraries Unlimited.

Reading Is Fundamental, Inc. 1991. "TV and Reading." Washington, DC: RIF.

Trelease, Jim. 1989. *The New Read-Aloud Handbook*. 2d ed. New York: Penguin Books.

11

There's More Than One Way to Play the Game

When we think of reading, we usually think of books. Can it really be reading without books? Can it be golf if the game doesn't strictly follow the rules of golf—for example, Texas Scramble, Two-Ball Foursome, Best Ball? Of course! Playing the game a little differently adds spice. So let's explore reading without books.

Comics

I've often wondered how many kids get hooked on reading through comic books. They certainly were a start for me. Comic books are, in a sense, illustrated plays that provide excellent opportunities to learn vocabulary and complex concepts through strong visual images. Yet, comics are more than just pictures. The average 22-page comic has about 5,000 words, the length of a short story.

Who reads comics? In *Leading to Reading*, Barbara Lee and Masha Rudman (1982, 85) say that the heaviest consumers of comics are children between the ages of nine and thirteen, and "children in grades four to six devour comics at the rate of ten to twelve per week."

Certainly comics vary in content, complexity, and reading level. As I grew, my interest in comics "matured" along with me. The first comics I remember were ones with humorous friendly creatures such as Casper the Friendly Ghost, usually written at about the second-grade level. I later moved into my superhero/heroine and feminist phase, where my favorite was Wonder Woman (a beautiful, female, superhuman, crime-fighting character). Then I went on to the rather sophisticated *Classic Comics*, which included stories based on classics such as *Treasure Island*, *Heidi*, *Moby Dick*, *The Adventures of Tom Sawyer*, and various Greek myths and legends. In the eighth grade, I remember writing an assigned biography from *Classic Comics'* version of Joan of Arc. Although I hate to admit it, in college I enjoyed the racy, irreverent bad taste of *Mad*, a satirical magazine that parodies popular movies and TV programs, challenges authority, and takes a skeptical view of advertising, government, and most other institutions.

Why do kids like comics?

- Comics offer adventure, escape, and humor.
- Comics are usually clear—good triumphs over evil.
- Comics use the living, dynamic language of everyday speech and current slang.
- Even difficult vocabulary is accessible through pictorial explanations.
- Characters generally have strong emotions.
- Children can identify with the characters and situations—such as the underdog Charlie Brown, the naughty Dennis the Menace, or the imaginary, creative world of Calvin and Hobbes.

Comic books have a place in the literacy classroom. After reviewing many research studies, Stephen Krashen (1993, 60) concludes the following:

- The texts of comics are linguistically appropriate, and pictures can help make the texts comprehensible.
- Research shows that comics have no negative effect on language development and school achievement.
- Comic books readers do at least as much book reading as non-comic book readers. There is, moreover, suggestive evidence that comics may serve as a conduit to book reading.

In addition, comic books can be used to teach story elements, sequencing, characterization, summarization, original comic creation, and writing. They can be a lead into the "real story," as with *Classic Comics*, and they are particularly effective in building background. They can also be used, as I use and enjoy them as an adult, just for fun.

Games

Games that require reading and language arts skills can be used either as a direct teaching tool or as a "curricular-connected" leisure time activity for children. In my classroom, I had the perennial favorites—Scrabble, Probe, Boggle, Word-Yahtzee, and Password; I also kept old copies of *Game* magazine.

My favorite games are those the children create for each other based on books they have read. The kids would stay after school to play Literacy Trivia, which was based on their own reading. The students at Winship School in Grand Forks, North Dakota, created several games from their reading of *Gone Away Lake* (Enright 1957). Mystery stories, books with maps, and books where the characters are trying to get from one place to another make particularly good board games.

Newspapers

Newspapers have been called the living curriculum. Newspapers not only provide material that is accessible, timely, and related to daily life, but they also help students develop a positive and relevant lifetime reading habit.

Newspaper in Education Programs. Much of the impetus for using newspapers in the classrooms came from the Newspapers in Education (NIE) programs sponsored by the Newspaper Association of America (NAA) Foundation. Under the programs, newspapers provide copies to schools, usually at a reduced rate, to use in their classrooms. They also sponsor teacher- and parent-education programs and offer curriculum materials to help schools use the newspaper as a meaningful resource for student learning. The more than 700 NIE programs differ according to the needs of the local educational community. Newspapers are used as learning tools not only in reading but also in language arts, social studies, math, science, and home economics.

In their brochure *Why NIE?* the NAA Foundation (1984, 10)* offers 13 reasons to use newspapers in the classroom:

1. It's an adult medium. No big seventh grader who can't read likes to be seen carrying around "Six Ducks in a Pond," but he's proud to be seen reading the newspaper.

2. It deals in reality, in what is happening here and now. Motivation for reading and discussion are built-in.

3. It bridges the gap between the classroom and the "real" world outside.

4. It contains history as it happens; issues and events reported completely and objectively.

5. It contains something for every student ... editorials, comics, math problems, science, sports, etc.

6. It contains practical vocabulary, the words students will use over and over throughout their lives.

7. It can be marked, cut, pasted, colored—activities important to young children who learn by doing and by seeing.

8. It contains ... the best models for clear, concise, simple writing.

9. It is the perfect model for teaching students to write for a purpose for a particular audience.

10. It is the most up-to-date social studies text there is.

11. It tells what's going on locally, in the youngster's own hometown—the only chronicle of local events.

12. It is the only "text" the majority of children will continue to read throughout their lives.

13. It is an influential and integral part of our free society. Its freedom is guaranteed under the Constitution.

---

*The list of reasons to use newspapers in the classroom is reprinted with permission from the Newspaper Association of America Foundation.

Newspaper in Education Week. Newspaper in Education (NIE) Week is a project jointly sponsored by the International Reading Association (IRA), the National Council for Social Studies (NCSS), and the Newspaper Association of America (NAA) Foundation; it is usually held each year during the first week of March. It provides teachers an opportunity to try newspapers for one week as an introduction to NIE.

Each year the theme and curriculum materials differ. For example, the theme for 1993 is Challenges and Choices. The activities in the curriculum guide are designed to help students examine challenges they face as individuals, as members of their communities, and as citizens of the world. Teachers can select activities from six different areas:

- The Challenge of the Information Explosion
- Personal Challenges
- The Challenge of Citizenship
- Global Challenges
- The Challenge of the Future
- Challenges in the Arts

Lessons integrate reading, writing, speaking, and listening skills in multidisciplinary activities. Six content strands are woven through the challenge units: self-esteem, multicultural education, civic competence, literacy/language, geography, and economics.

For more information about NIE programs, contact

NAA Foundation, The Newspaper Center
11600 Sunrise Valley Drive
Reston, VA 22091

You may also contact your local NAA-affiliated newspaper. If you are interested in organizing a Newspaper in Education Week, you may wish to contact your local newspaper or your local or state IRA or NCSS chapter.

Other Newspaper Activities. Whether you have a formal NIE program or use the newspaper as supplemental material, it is a resource that should not be ignored. Even special features such as horoscopes, advice columns, classified and other ads, weather maps, movie and entertainment reviews, and human interest stories provide rich sources for classroom activities. For several years I have kept a "truth is stranger than fiction" file of fascinating news stories that can be used for reading, writing, and storytelling.

Magazines

Each year more and more magazines are published for preschoolers and school-age children. Kids like them for the same reason that many adults like them:

- They are lightweight, portable, and inexpensive. A full-year's subscription to a teen or children's magazine (10-12 issues) usually costs less than one hardcover book.
- They're lively and entertaining. The writing style is light and a single issue contains an array of articles, stories, activities, and pictures.
- Magazine features are short, so readers have the satisfaction of finishing an article in one sitting. They can pick it up and put it down as time permits without losing the continuity of the story.
- If you are a parent ordering a magazine for home use, you know how much your children love to receive mail addressed to them personally.

Magazines such as *Time*, *Newsweek*, and *National Geographic* can also be helpful in the middle school and high school classroom as source material for research, writing, reading, social studies, and other subjects. In the lower grades, old magazines can be cut apart for rebuses, classification exercises, letter searches, and other activities.

Other Nonbook Sources for Reading

Pins, buttons, signs, and bumper stickers. Have students either collect or write down favorite sayings. I record mine in my journal. For example:

- A sign on an old wagon wheel next to a gas station in Rugby, North Dakota, reads: "Doggie rest stop."
- A sign on a house painted black, green, purple, red, and Day-Glo orange reads: "Maybe I don't like the color of your house either."
- A bumper sticker warns: "Don't wash this car. It is part of a research study in the chemical effect of air pollutants."
- A pin reads: "Life is uncertain so eat dessert first."

Kids can discuss the meaning of the sayings and create their own buttons, T-shirts, or bumper stickers.

Sheet music. I couldn't seem to interest my eighth-grade students in poetry until I brought in song lyrics and sheet music for them to explore. Students can take familiar tunes and compose their own words to fit the rhythm.

Greeting cards. Contemporary greeting cards are fun, funny, and sometimes thought provoking. After putting together a class collection and reviewing them, have students design their own cards.

Souvenir programs. Students and teachers can bring in programs after athletic events, plays, concerts, and special programs. Programs usually contain interesting tidbits about the participants and sometimes historical information and plot summaries.

Driver's manual. This manual was a hit with the eighth-grade students. They make up sample tests for each other with accompanying answer keys. They learned how difficult it is to write an unambiguous question.

Miscellaneous pamphlets. The Government Printing Office is an excellent source of hundreds of inexpensive and free books and pamphlets on a variety of subjects—baby sitting, pet care, winter survival, exotic plants, camping and backpacking, just to name a few.

Maps. Even state road maps are filled with reading material. The North Dakota road map is typical. It lists state park facilities; describes 32 special tourist attractions; gives a mileage chart; lists incorporated cities, county seats, and their population; outlines traffic rules; lists radio stations; tells where to write for more information on historical sites, hunting and fishing, national park and national historic sites, state parks, the International Peace Garden, and road conditions; lists highway patrol offices and phone numbers; and provides a legend to explain the map markings.

Posters. I used hundreds of thought-provoking posters in my classroom. They often came free with book orders or in teacher magazines. We'd use the message of the poster as a stimulus for discussion, writing, and creating new posters.

How-to manuals. Free manuals from craft stores, home extension agencies, magazines, and other sources teach kids how to do any number of things, from growing a bonsai tree to making candles. Students may find it a real challenge to create their own "how-to" manual and test it to see if other students can follow their directions.

Placemats. Have students collect placemats from restaurants. They often contain interesting information about the history and location of the restaurant, places of interest in the area, etc.

Menus. Menus can be used in reading, nutrition, math, and even social studies if students find menus from ethnic restaurants.

Recipes. Have the ingredients handy and turn your kids loose with a simple recipe. They may wish to write down a favorite family recipe as dictated by their parents or grandparents so that someone else can follow it.

Reading is not confined to books, just as running is not confined to track. Materials such as newspapers, magazines, comics, and games invite the reader to interact with print in new and thought-provoking ways.

References

Krashen, Stephen. 1993. *The Power of Reading: Insights from the Research*. Englewood, CO: Libraries Unlimited.

Lee, Barbara, and Masha Kabakow Rudman. 1982. *Leading to Reading*. New York: Berkley.

NAA Foundation. 1984. *Why NIE?* Washington, DC: Newspaper Association of America.

Literature Resources

Enright, Elizabeth. 1957. *Gone Away Lake*. New York: Harcourt Brace Jovanovich.

12

Promoting the Sport

Events and Programs That Promote Reading

Some people say that without the events, there would be no sports; others disagree, saying that most participants enjoy sports for their intrinsic value. Few, however, would disagree that the Bowl games, the Olympics, the World Series, the Stanley Cup, and all the many other special events add interest, excitement, and anticipation and give some athletes a sense of purpose and a goal for their training. Reading is the same. Although reading and responding would certainly occur without special events and programs, those extras can provide interest, excitement, and challenge. In this chapter we'll explore events and programs that promote reading.

Events

Friday Night Prime Time

Dr. Beth Randklev, principal of Belmont School in Grand Forks, North Dakota, and her staff have a Friday Night Prime Time in the spring of each year. She credits D. C. Heath Company with the original idea. Here is the plan.

On a selected Friday night, all interested children in grades 3-6 come back to school at 5:00 P.M. armed with sleeping bags, stuffed animals, and, of course, books. Children are assigned to groups of six to eight students with a parent volunteer. The evening is divided into half-hour blocks of time. Students read for a half hour then participate in an activity for a half hour, read for a half hour, and so on. The activities include exercise; games; entertainment such as a storyteller, a puppeteer, or a performance by a high school drama or musical group; story reading; snacks; and a supper of pizza and ice cream. The parent volunteers keep track of the number of pages read in their groups, and the principal tallies the totals and announces the total at intervals. Around 10:30 A.M., the children pack up books and sleeping bags and head home. Dr. Randklev said Friday Night Prime Time is a real highlight of the year; in fact, even when kids have gone on to junior high, they volunteer to come back to "help." Lake Agassiz Elementary School in Grand Forks also has a Prime Time; however, the event is for lower-grade students and runs from about 5:00 P.M. to 7:30 P.M.

Lock Up

Another variation of the Friday Night Prime Time is the Lock Up slumber party. Jackie DiGennaro, a fourth-grade teacher in Sitka, Alaska, spends the night in the school with her class as a reward for successful class reading projects. During the evening they watch a video of a book and compare the video with the book version, go on a schoolwide treasure hunt, play reading and other board games, share snacks, and read.

In Larimore, North Dakota, fourth-grade teacher Pam Suchor held a similar event, although her class's sleepover was inspired by a book the students had just finished reading, *Help, I'm a Prisoner in the Library*, written by Eth Clifford (1979). The story is about two girls who go to use a library restroom and get locked in just before a snowstorm blows up. After several weird adventures, they're rescued when they shoot off fireworks. The sleepover-reading event was complete with a big sign in the window that read: "Help, I'm a Prisoner in the Library."

Interactive Book Fair

Madonna Schaner, while a librarian at Christ the King Church in Mandan, North Dakota, put together a fun-filled interactive book fair. Elementary children visited more than 30 booths manned by 80 junior high students and participated in book activities planned by Schaner and the students. Each book booth was developed around a theme and included books, an interactive activity, a special present or prize, and occasionally hosts dressed in appropriate costumes. Themes included were popcorn, sports, Beverly Cleary books, fairy tales, fables, balloons, chocolate, animals, *How to Eat Fried Worms* (Rockwell, 1973), apples, horses, award-winning books, grandparents, maps, magic, newspapers and magazines, dinosaurs, space, food, tall tales, ducks, the environment, big books, and the prairie. Students were also invited to participate in a bookwalk (a variation on the cakewalk), puppet shows, story writing, bookbinding, slogan and sign making, and bookmarker making.

Media Fest

Belmont School in Grand Forks, North Dakota, has a one-day media fest, a celebration of the year's reading and writing activities. Every corner of the school is covered with children's writing and special projects. On the special day, younger children are paired with older students, who together visit the exhibits and share with each other their own work and that of their classmates. Last year's fest included:

- Slide shows illustrated and written by students and accompanied by appropriate music
- Story corners where students could sit down and listen to children read the books they had written
- Transparency shows, also illustrated and written by students
- A big bulletin board entitled "Discover the Fun," which invited viewers to read all the haiku written by a class and to write their own to add to the bulletin board
- Student videos either about a book or about a topic researched by the children

- Poetry illustrated by student watercolor painting
- Sharing with a book buddy self-authored books (autobiographies or patterned writing)
- Student writing on every available surface

As Dr. Randklev, the principal, said, "It is a real celebration of literacy." The writing is left up for a week to be enjoyed not only by the children but by the community as well.

Poetry Week

Judy Hager, a librarian in Grand Forks, described a fun-filled poetry week that featured a different theme each day. For example, one day spaghetti was the theme. To begin the day, the cook read "Spaghetti" from Shel Silverstein's *Where the Sidewalk Ends* (1974). She wore a corsage made from decorated noodles and, of course, spaghetti was served at lunch.

During the week, a selected student runner dashed into the classroom several times during the day and yelled "Poetry Break." Either the class members had to stop what they were doing and read poetry, or the teacher shared a poem with the group. All the staff—cooks, custodians, principals, everyone—had a poetry book with them, so if the Poetry Break happened near them, they could participate. Students carried poems in their pockets during the week, and an assigned Mystery Person would stop people throughout the day and ask, "Do you have a poem in your pocket?" If the student had a poem and read it to the Mystery Person, the student received a little prize.

International Theme Day

As one part of the districtwide Spotlight on Authors Program, the principal, Ginny Bollman, the staff, and the parent-teacher organization of Wilder School in Grand Forks, North Dakota, planned an International Day. Each class chose a country to study. Many classes invited people in the community who were native to that country to visit the classroom. After several months of research, each class prepared for visits by tourists. All the children packed their suitcases complete with baggage handling tags, received their passports, and were ready to travel to the foreign countries. Before they entered the host country, students had their passports stamped. The host country shared music, stories, art, plays, poetry, maps, and costumes and displayed cultural artifacts. In each country the tourists sampled native food and were provided "brochures" about the country, which they placed in their suitcases for later reading.

Beach Party

Students at Wilder School were invited to a beach party. In the coldest part of the North Dakota winter, the staff and the parent organization decorated the gym like a beach, complete with sandcastles, fishing piers, waves, beach umbrellas, palm trees, and lounge chairs. Students dressed in beach attire and brought their towels, sunglasses, and books. Each class spent 30 minutes at the "beach" reading.

An Alternative to Halloween Celebrations

Because the jury is out on whether schools should celebrate Halloween, Wilder School came up with a fun alternative. The children had been studying the importance of characterization as a part of story development, so instead of Halloween costumes, the school had a Book Character Day. Children came dressed as their favorite character and the classrooms planned special events around that theme. Principal Ginny Bollman said, "The costumes were so much more inventive and interesting than those we used to see for Halloween. It was a great day."

Moonlight Reading

Wilder School faculty and students planned a special night with parents. Each classroom had a special reading "happening" for visitors, including readers theatre, children reading from their writing, viewing of a class video with commercials for favorite books, and puppet plays.

Crazy Clothes Days

Students at Wilder promote reading through crazy clothes days. For example, on Get Mixed Up in a Good Book Day, kids wear mixed-up clothing; on Sweat It Out with a Good Book Day, students wear sweats; on Sock It to Me with a Good Book Day, kids wear crazy socks; and on Reading Is Cool Day, kids wear sunglasses, shorts, and other "cool" wear.

Book Swaps

Book swaps are great ways to keep books circulating. Certainly there are many ways to do a swap. Here is one.

Students bring in books they'd like to swap and receive a coupon for each book. Sometimes guidelines are drawn up for the books, such as no religious books in a public school. Often there's a shortage of upper-level books, because kids usually bring in the books they've outgrown and look for higher-level reading. Thus, the sponsors will need to think of creative ways to stagger the selection process so every child gets some appropriate choices.

Book Fairs

Many companies offer schools the opportunity to have school-sponsored book fairs. They usually include either a percentage of sales or free books, or both. Sometimes the percentage increases with the amount of gross sales. For example,

Scholastic Books Troll Book Fair generally gives the sponsor 20 percent of the gross sale receipts; however, if the sales are more than $2,000, the percentage increases to 35 percent. Peggy Koppelman, a school librarian in Grand Forks, North Dakota, reports, "With the number of free books we receive, I'd say we're earning about 50% of sales. With book budgets going down the free books are a wonderful way to supplement our offerings."

A local bookstore provided an "in-house" book fair, where the school community was invited to visit the bookstore between 6:00 and 8:00 on Saturday night, when the store is usually closed. The local parent-teacher organization received 20 percent of the revenue from the sales.

Spotlight on Young Authors

The objectives of the year-long (1992-93), districtwide Spotlight on Young Authors event in Grand Forks, North Dakota, were to help students become aware of authors' and illustrators' works, to inspire students to do further reading of authors' and illustrators' works, to engage students in authentic reading and writing experiences, to encourage collaborations between classrooms and libraries and between schools and communities, and to provide literacy role models for children. A steering committee in each school in the district, made up of teachers, parents, and administrators, selected the author to be featured and developed the year-long plan. Becky Thompson, chair of the planning committee for Century School said, "The reason we picked Ann McGovern as our author is that her work spans all grade levels. We've worked hard to tie the books and the activities into our curriculum."

Each school was given $400 for "celebration" activities. Becky Thompson, during an interview early in the year, said, "Our committee raised matching money to give us more flexibility. The parents were wonderful not only for fund raising but for their ideas, energy and leadership. I don't know what we would have done without them."

The kickoff activity for the year-long event was a Bon Voyage party. Students entered the gymnasium decorated with a dock complete with an ocean liner; a train with a train track coursing its way through the school; an airplane with a pilot; and teachers wearing multicolored sweatshirts with the school's theme, "Traveling with Your Imagination." A storyteller shared stories pertaining to the theme and then a "conductor" waited to lead the students back to their classrooms. The students who started their "travels" by reading the author's books on sharks and underwater adventures were conducted by parents in beach attire. Outside their door was a fishnet with a large shark tangled in it.

Upon entering their classroom, all the students in the school received a passport, which included a list of the author's books by category. After each "visit" with a book, students had their passports stamped. Passports also contained students' school pictures, the date of departure (the day of the first event), and the date of return (the day of the author's visit). The students received peanuts to munch on during their voyage and participated in activities related to the class's theme.

The kickoff was just the beginning. Activities continued throughout the year to keep interest alive. One of Ann McGovern's books is *Stone Soup* (1968), so the school developed an incentive program called Reading Is Souper, which works as follows. Each week in the media center, a large black pot is placed to await its ingredients. At each home reading session (the length of a reading session is determined by the parents), parents sign a reading coupon shaped like a vegetable. The children deposit their coupons in the soup pot, and on Friday two names are drawn from the pot for special prizes such as T-shirts or books. Each week the soup pot is emptied and new vegetable coupons are added. Teachers may ask students to focus during a particular week on a literature genre such as biography or historical fiction, or on newspapers or magazines.

Other activities at Century included a book fair, bookmaking project, book sharing, discussion groups, writing, class displays, and a musical based on *Stone Soup* performed by first-graders. Every Friday the teachers would wear their "Traveling with Your Imagination" sweatshirts, and whenever a class focused on an Ann McGovern book during the day, the students would wear a special theme button for all to see.

During the year students selected one of their works from their writers' workshop folder to polish, publish, and bind for the library. The culminating event was, of course, the author's visit. In addition to other activities, the students who had the most stamps in their passports (and therefore were the most familiar with the author's work) were eligible for a special drawing for Lunch with the Author.

The community was very supportive of the event. The local newspaper featured one author every few weeks to give the project communitywide visibility. Parents participated in a fall kickoff event where slides about their school author's life and works were shared. Because a book-signing party was a featured event, one school's parent-teacher organization gave every child one of the author's books as a holiday gift to ensure that every child had a book to be signed.

Ordinarily a project of this magnitude would be beyond the budget of many school districts. The Grand Forks School District has collaborated with the community to develop an Educational Foundation to fund special projects of this nature.

Pastries for Parents or Goodies for Grandparents

On a particular day (which could be called Muffins for Moms Day or Donuts for Dads Day), a parent or grandparent is invited to the school at 7:45 A.M. for a continental breakfast. The children give their guests a tour of the school and invite them to read with the students for the first half hour of the day. This is a good time to have volunteers and school staff, such as cooks and custodians, available so that no child is left out.

Dinner Club

Mary Ellen Peters, librarian in Bisbee-Egeland, North Dakota, has a Garfield Dinner Club with her students. Students are invited to get a book on Monday and, on the following Monday, to bring their lunch to the library to discuss their reading. Peters said, "This means that they have to give up their noon recess but if it happens to be January and 30 degrees below zero, it may not be a difficult decision."

Books are purchased through the school and then offered to the students for purchase at half the book club price. Thus, many of the books cost about $1. Peters said, "Book ownership is important and this helps the kids build a home library of quality books."

Students are given questions to think about as they read. Questions like the following form the framework for the literary discussions:

1. Did this story turn out the way you thought it would? Why or why not?
2. Would you like to have the main character for a friend? Why or why not?
3. How would the story change if it took place in our community?
4. If you were the author, how would you have changed the ending or the beginning of the story?
5. What made this book interesting?
6. Have you ever experienced some of the events or feelings the main character did? Tell about them.
7. What do you think would happen in a sequel to this book?

Mementos of the dinner club are given at the end of the discussion, including Garfield stickers, Garfield bookmarks, and a Garfield comic book for one lucky participant. Peters even makes Garfield cookies with a special cookie cutter. Although Peters started the club with the third grade, soon all the grades asked to participate. That's a lot of cookies!

Programs

Back Pack Reading

Back Pack Reading, a unique kindergarten and first-grade home-school partnership reading program, was conceived by the Grand Forks School District in Grand Forks, North Dakota, and funded by the Knight-Ridder Foundation. The basic idea is to get books into the hands of kids and have parents partner with the school in reading with and to their kindergartners and first-graders.

The planning team decided it was important to have the books easily and quickly accessible to students, so the books were placed in the classrooms rather than in the libraries. At first the librarians thought that the program would cut down on the library circulation, but quite the opposite happened. Library circulation increased from 901,944 before the program to 2,148,000 during the first year of the program. In 1992, the circulation for the elementary libraries was 2,973,523. The number of students in elementary school has not increased significantly but the reading habit clearly has.

The team also felt it was important to involve teachers in book selection. Each teacher was given $225 to select classroom paperback books for students in the teacher's class. A relationship was developed with a local bookstore so teachers would be able to see the books they were purchasing (rather than ordering them from a catalog), and the teachers simply charge the purchase to the Back Pack Reading program. The district reading consultant, Pat Johnston, feels teacher book selection gives the teacher greater ownership in the program and is one of the keys to the success of the project.

Each day the children select one book to take home in their "Back Pack" (actually a special plastic sack). The parents either read with or to the students. The books come back the next day and the children select another book. A team of parent volunteers repairs the books to keep them in circulation.

Each school has an inservice at the beginning of the school year to explain the program to parents. Pat Johnston feels the inservice is critical to the success of the program. Parents love the program. The following comments are typical of those found on the parent survey.

"My daughter's confidence in her ability to read has grown tremendously as a result of this program. Her success has been incentive enough for her to want to read nightly."

"We feel the Back Pack Reading program is a joy to both our child and ourselves. It is a wonderful way to get a child to show an interest in reading. A high plus program!"

"Even though our intentions were always good and we knew the importance of reading, it sometimes was easy to say 'no, we don't have time tonight.' Now we always *make* time. Thanks."

"The Back Pack program not only is beneficial to my first-grader but also to my three-year-old. He can hardly wait for a new book every night and tries to read with my first-grader."

From all indications the program has been very successful in getting children and parents into the book habit right from the beginning of school. Johnston estimates that the 1,600 kindergartners and first-graders read 135,000 Back Pack Reading books during one year in addition to those they took out of the library.

Spin-Off Programs

The Back Pack Reading program was so popular that several spin-off programs developed. For example, a local pediatrician with funding from a hospital community group has started a "Books for Babies" program. Every newborn goes home with a book and a little brochure describing the importance of reading aloud to children. Also the program was expanded to grade 2 in a program called Rainbow Reading.

ELBA (Elementary Library Book Award) Programs

The ELBA, Grand Forks' local equivalent of the Newbery and Caldecott awards, was created to stimulate interest in good children's literature and to encourage children to read. Each spring after reading the books on the nomination list, the students vote for their favorite book. The winning books are announced during National Library Week in April. Seals commemorating the award are placed on the winning books throughout the Grand Forks School

District. The award is presented to one first-place book and one second-place book in each division. The divisions are primary, intermediate, and upper elementary.

Before school begins, the librarians select 15 books for division I and 10 books each for divisions II and III. Here are the rules for the program:

1. Students have from September through March to read the books.

2. The voting takes place during the month of March.

3. The books may be read to the children by the teacher or by another student.

4. Although students are encouraged to read the complete set of books in their division, they are eligible to vote if they have read or had read to them at least seven books in division I, five books in division II, or five books in division III.

5. Students do not have to follow grade-level division. They may read in any division.

6. To vote for a particular book, the students must have read that book or had that book read to them.

7. Each student may vote for only one book.

8. Winning books will be announced during National Library Week in April.

Peggy Koppelman and Judy Hager, librarians in the Grand Forks School District, describe how they stimulate interest in the event. First, the librarians select a theme for the year. Themes such as "A Palette of Colors" (a focus on illustrators), "Reading Is Out of This World" (space), and "A Spotlight on Young Authors" (a connection between reading and writing) have been selected. When the program first began, the group had a mascot made for each school. The mascot, Elba, looks like a huggable little green-and-white-spotted space alien. Elba is then dressed according to the theme. Peggy Koppelman says, "She's been a wizard, a knight in shining armor, a pirate, a clown, a space explorer—whatever fits with the theme."

The librarians and teachers plan activities related to the theme, have mementos and bookmarks made, and write fact sheets for each author; and the librarians prepare booktalks. During the kickoff week, kids participate in the planned activities, the librarians visit each room to do booktalks on the nominated books, and the reading begins. "Kids love the program," said Koppelman, "the only problem is having enough books available for check-out." Last year 3,884 students voted (which means they met the reading criteria and were interested in voting) out of 5,652 eligible students.

Readers' Choice

Several state library associations have statewide equivalents of the Grand Forks' readers' choice ELBA program. In Texas, for example, the library sponsors the Texas Blue Bonnet Award. Thirty titles are selected as the reading base. From those 30 titles the children select their "children's choice." Last year the sponsors reported that the children of the state read more than one million copies of the 30 books in preparation for the award.

Special events add excitement to reading. If you're a player, you can't help but participate. There is no such thing as a bench warmer in the game of reading.

References

Hager, Judy. 1993. Interview with author. Grand Forks, North Dakota, January 4, 1993.

Literature Resources

Clifford, Eth. 1979. *Help, I'm a Prisoner in the Library*. Boston: Houghton Mifflin.

Koppelman, Peggy. 1993. Interview with author. Grand Forks, North Dakota, January 4, 1993.

McGovern, Ann. 1968. *Stone Soup*. New York: Scholastic.

Rockwell, Thomas. 1973. *How to Eat Fried Worms*. New York: Franklin Watts.

Silverstein, Shel. 1974. *Where the Sidewalk Ends*. New York: Harper & Row.

13

Administrators as Cheerleaders

Players need supporters, people who cheer them on. Coaches also need to know that the managers are "on their team." It's not much different in reading. Certainly kids, teachers, and parents can build toward a wonderfully responsive reading environment, but administrators are key to providing leadership, resources, role models, support, and encouragement to ensure that reading is not a spectator sport. Stephen Krashen (1993, 85) says, "Administrators need to know that a print-rich environment is not a luxury but a necessity."

In their study *Becoming a Nation of Readers*, Richard Anderson et al. (1985) studied schools that produced reading achievement beyond expectations, considering the composition of the students. The most effective schools were characterized by vigorous instructional leadership. Although the leader was usually a principal, in some cases it was another administrator, such as a reading supervisor, or a faculty team. Instructional leaders not only led directly, but they also created school environments that nurtured reading and other learning as well. The highly effective schools had these characteristics (112-114):

- Effective schools had high but realistic expectations about student progress in reading.

- Effective schools demonstrated school pride, collegiality, and a sense of community. They had collaborative planning and professional staff development conducted on a schoolwide basis.

- Effective schools were orderly and well disciplined, which helped to maximize the amount of uninterrupted time available for learning.

How do administrators convey their expectations, build school pride and a sense of community, and promote staff development? How can administrators promote reading? In my conversations with administrators and teachers they provided this advice:

- Be a role model for teachers and kids

- Provide resources and support teachers

- Celebrate student progress

- Support home-school reading programs

- Remember the Management Maxim: "What you pay attention to, you get more of"

- Give ownership and credit to faculty

Be a Role Model for Teachers and Kids

The critical importance of the parent and teacher role model in promoting reading is explored in chapters 2 and 15. The administrator also is an important role model for both students and faculty.

Know the Books the Kids Are Reading and Talk About Them with Kids

Notice I didn't necessarily say READ all the books the kids are reading; I said KNOW the books. This can be accomplished by reading book jackets, reviewing book summaries in the resources listed in appendix A, talking with faculty about the books the kids are particularly enjoying, or simply talking to kids. After one year of talking and listening to your students, you'll have a good enough grasp of the literature to carry on a conversation about the books that are the school favorites. Each year you'll expand your repertoire.

Where should you talk with kids about books? Anywhere—in the hall as the kids are coming to class or lining up for the water fountain, in the cafeteria as they are standing in the lunch line, or on the playground. Or how about having a breakfast or lunch club each week? The administrator could invite a different group of students to join the "literary club" each week for book discussions. Students might submit beforehand ideas they'd like to discuss. The administrator should also take the opportunity to share a book with the "club." Students might receive a certificate saying, "(Student's name) is a Member of the Literary Club."

Share Books with Kids

My husband, Ray, who is the assistant superintendent of schools in Grand Forks, North Dakota, makes a regular practice of visiting classrooms to read aloud to kids. He also brings along a canvas bag of treasures to add mystery to the time together. The treasures include a shark jaw, a puffer fish, a shy puppet, and a "talking" conch shell. When reading to Head Start children, he always ends up with several little boys either in his lap or cuddled up as close as they can get. At Christmastime he usually reads *The Best Christmas Pageant Ever* (Robinson 1972) to at least one class.

Ray also did a booktalk with high school students using the theme of the special relationships between grandfathers and grandchildren. As he reflected on his own special relationship with his grandfather, he wove in books appropriate for a high school audience, including *Cold Sassy Tree* (Burns 1984), *The Education of Little Tree* (Forrest 1986), and *Tracker* (Paulsen 1984). I'm proud and pleased that he takes the time for this important activity. Not only do teachers and kids know the importance and pleasure of reading, but the community and the principals know reading is supported from the top.

Sometimes teachers might be reticent to ask a principal to come into their classroom to read. Why not give each teacher a voucher at the beginning of the school year for 30 minutes of reading time?

Walter Beseler, a high school principal in Cando, North Dakota, walks through the halls with a book in his pocket. He reads while supervising the lunchroom or performing hall or bus duty. It has become standard practice for kids to stop and talk with him about his books: "Looks like you started a new one, Mr. Beseler. What's it about?" or "Hey, Mr. Beseler. What book is in your pocket today?"

Support Events That Promote Reading

In chapter 12, we talked about events that promote reading. Nothing speaks more loudly than the administrator's presence. Although the administrator doesn't need to be totally responsible for either the ideas for or the implementation of the events, she or he needs to show support through involvement, commitment of resources, and participation in special reading events.

Ginny Bollman, principal at Wilder Elementary School in Grand Forks, North Dakota, shows her support of DEAR (Drop Everything And Read) time by assigning custodians, cooks, and special teachers (and no doubt herself) to regular classrooms so all can be reading models during DEAR time. She also begins what she calls "Progressive Stories" in three or four classrooms. Each class adds something to the story and passes it on to another class. The finished product is bound and placed in the library.

Give Books as Special Gifts

The administrator might purchase a number of inexpensive books from book clubs and have them available as special gifts for children. For example, the administrator might visit and give a book to every child who is hospitalized during the year.

Provide Resources and Support for Teachers

Build an Environment of Trust

Teachers have to know that their administrators will support them in both their successful and not-so-successful attempts at innovation and creativity. Research tells us that peak performers live on the edge of their competence, so our very best may have a higher "failure" rate than those who stay with the status quo. For example, moving away from a basal-driven language arts program is risky, and teachers have to know that in a trusting environment they are free to change without a demand for first-time perfection. Krashen (1993, 85) says, "Administrators need to know that when teachers are reading to students, and when teachers are relaxing with a good book during sustained silent reading sessions, teachers are doing their job."

Provide Stimulation and Be an Advocate for Change and Innovation

Sharon Gates, principal at Lake Agassiz School in Grand Forks, North Dakota, along with her faculty and a university faculty member, developed a year-long seminar where teachers read many books and articles, discussed issues, and looked at assessment tools as they moved forward to a literature-based reading program. Gates provided the encouragement, the resources, the vehicle for discussion and interaction, and the visiting university expert. "We now have a common language," says Gates, "and we are moving forward."

Administrators should encourage teachers to visit other classrooms and other schools to gain new ideas, and they should support teachers' attendance at conferences and workshops. Also, it is important when teachers return from such meetings to provide a vehicle for them to share the ideas they gathered.

Be Clear About Your Expectations with Both Teachers and Kids

Nothing undermines trust and creates an unsettled environment faster than not being clear about expectations. As Anderson et al. (1985) identified, high but realistic expectations are one of the characteristics of high-achieving schools. It goes without saying that expectations must be conveyed in clear, unambiguous terms for them to be fulfilled.

Give Ownership and Credit to the Faculty

Dr. Beth Randklev, principal of Belmont School in Grand Forks, said during a 1992 interview, "When you give ownership for special events and creative ideas to teachers and students, you take the ceiling off their work. Principals must encourage them to go for it, celebrate it, and credit it." Every school has talented staff members. Often all administrators need to do is hire good people, give them support, and then get out of their way.

Celebrate Student Progress

When students have achieved a reading objective, administrators should celebrate with the student or the class. A principal in Dawson, Minnesota, has reading/popcorn parties with small groups of students who have reached a reading goal. Each student leaves the session with a little card that says, "(Name of student) Read with the Principal Today."

Some principals challenge students to read so many books or pages by a certain date. I've seen many "prizes" for students who "beat the principal." Gary Mitchell, principal of Century School, Grand Forks, North Dakota, said he'd milk a live cow if the kids met his challenge. Other challenges I have read about include the following:

- The principal allowed kids to cut off pieces of his tie as they got closer to their goal.
- The principal sat on top of the school for one day.
- The principal ate a book (the book happened to be made of chocolate).
- The principal shaved her head.
- The principal dyed her hair green.
- The principal sat in a dunking tank and students got a certain number of throws, depending on how much they had read.

Even something as simple as a short note from the administrator acknowledging a student's good work can be a wonderful incentive. Dr. Randklev celebrates with her students, and one day a celebration note came back to her that read, "To Dr. Randklev: Belmont School Is Reading and Writing."

Support and Promote Home-School Reading

As mentioned in previous chapters, children who read at home are farther ahead in the reading game than those who don't. We need parents on our side if the team is going to win. Every principal's newsletter should have a paragraph about reading—good books, book-sharing ideas for home, ideas like those in chapter 15. Parents should be encouraged to participate in special school reading events or home-school reading programs such as Back Pack Reading discussed in chapter 12.

Several schools keep their school libraries open for a few days a week during the summer months. Others open their school libraries one or two nights a week so community members can make use of the facility and check out books with their children or for themselves.

Parents should always be made to feel welcome in the school and a true part of the learning team. The principal has a major role in setting the tone for the home-school collaboration.

Remember the Management Maxim: "What You Pay Attention To, You Get More Of"

Dr. Randklev said, "Where you as a principal put your values is where the people you work with put their time." If principals talk about reading at every staff meeting, share articles about reading on a regular basis, write about reading in every newsletter, talk with children about books every day, support events that promote reading, and live reading through their own role modeling, the team members—teachers, kids, parents and community—are going to get the message.

Administrators truly are the cheer*leaders* in the reading game. Whether by serving as role models, providing support and stimulation, or establishing appropriate expectations, they can lead their schools to be "Reading Places."

References

Anderson, Richard C., Elfrieda H. Hiebert, Judith A. Scott, and Ian A. G. Wilkinson. 1985. *Becoming a Nation of Readers: The Report of the Commission on Reading*. Champaign-Urbana, IL: Center for the Study of Reading.

Krashen, Stephen. 1993. *The Power of Reading: Insights from the Research*. Englewood, CO: Libraries Unlimited.

Randklev, Beth. 1992. Interview with author. Grand Forks, North Dakota, December 14.

Literature Resources

Burns, Olive Ann. 1984. *Cold Sassy Tree*. New York: Dell.

Forrest, Carter. 1986. *The Education of Little Tree*. Albuquerque, NM: University of New Mexico Press.

Paulsen, Gary. 1984. *Tracker*. New York: Bradbury Press.

Robinson, Barbara. 1972. *The Best Christmas Pageant Ever*. New York: Avon Books.

14

Peanuts, Popcorn, and Other Incentives

Certainly many players have a great love of the game and would play whether they were compensated or not; however, most adults work for some compensation, recognition, or reward. Why not provide incentives for reading? Incentive programs can take many forms. The incentive can be the opportunity to participate in special events like those described in chapter 13. They can derive from setting personal or group goals and then striving to exceed the personal or group "best." Or incentive programs can involve competitions among children, among classrooms, or among schools. The rewards can be intrinsic or extrinsic.

Let's start our discussion with the most controversial of the incentive programs, competition. Children may flock to the baseball fields during the summer because they love to hit and run, but many also enjoy the competition. It's hard to imagine a football game without competition or a track meet without contenders. In some individual sports, players may be competing against themselves, trying to beat a personal "best," but that in itself is a kind of competition.

What about reading? Are incentive programs and competition all good or all bad? Ken Goodman (1986, 40) would vote "all bad." He believes that motivation is always intrinsic. "Kids learn to read and write because they need and want to communicate. Extrinsic rewards have no place in a whole language program." Regie Routman (1988, 30) author of *Transitions: From Literature to Literacy*, agrees, relating that she was guilty of "artificial motivation" for many years. "Smelly stickers" for so many books read were her tool. She was desperate to get turned-off kids into real books. When she began a literature-based reading program, the need for the stickers disappeared. She believes, "As long as the task is relevant to the kids, and they can see a real purpose, there is no need for external motivation." Certainly, incentive programs have stirred the ire of many other educators who are squeamish about offering prizes to children for reading.

Jim Trelease (1989, 146), author of *The New Read-Aloud Handbook*, offers a strong rebuttal. "Why, I ask, is there a separate set of standards for children? If incentive programs are good for adults (salespeople, insurance agents, and ballplayers), why not kids? The player who has a $50,000 incentive clause in his contract for winning the batting crown is going to try harder. And experience shows us that students will read longer for a pizza than they will for nothing." Readers of this book who oppose offering incentives for reading may want to skip this chapter. On the other hand, even those who don't like competitions and incentives may find some great ideas that could be converted to "no competition, no external incentive" activities.

BOOK IT! National Reading Incentive Program

The Pizza Hut BOOK IT! program is probably the best known and has had the greatest impact of any of the corporate-sponsored incentive programs. The program began during the 1985-86 school year and has reached 17 million children. Children earn coupons for free pizza, depending on how many books they've read. Although the program costs Pizza Hut more than $100 million in free pizza each year, the company believes that it motivates children to read more by rewarding them for their reading accomplishments. The program, offered to students in grades 1-6, usually runs from October through February. Here is how it works:

Setting the goals. The teacher sets reading goals for the students for each month of the program. The goals can be for each student, for groups of students, or for the class as a whole. The goals can be number of books read, number of pages read, number of minutes read, and so on. They can vary from month to month. For children who have difficulty reading, the teacher can set monthly goals where the children are read to by others, such as a parent, grandparent, sibling, school volunteer, or older student buddy.

Determining how to verify reading assignments. BOOK IT! offers a free program-enhancement booklet filled with imaginative ideas other teachers have used to verify reading assignments. Teachers may also wish to involve parents by sending home a parent reading verification form.

Meeting the goals. As soon as a child meets the monthly reading goal, the teacher gives that child a Pizza Award Certificate. The child takes the certificate to a Pizza Hut restaurant, where he or she is personally congratulated by the manager and given a free, one-topping Personal Pan Pizza. On the first visit the manager also gives the child a BOOK IT! button and a star for the button. The child receives another Personal Pan Pizza, along with a star, on each subsequent visit. It should be noted that no purchase at the restaurant is required and the pizza can be ordered to go.

Class party. If all the children in the class meet their reading goals in any four of the five program months, the entire class, including the teacher, is given a pizza party.

In a 1992 telephone interview, David Darby, a member of the Carson Group, which manages the BOOK IT! program for Pizza Hut, stated that an important component of the program is the interaction of the children with the Pizza Hut manager. The managers are trained to stop by and not only congratulate the children but talk with them about what they are reading. "The praise from an outside person is really important." He also points out that the program stimulates what he calls the "important communication triangle between parent, teacher, and child." For more information about the BOOK IT! program, write to

The BOOK IT! Program
P.O. Box 2999
Wichita, KS 67201
You may also call 1 800 4 BOOK IT.

Spin-Off Programs

Not every community has a Pizza Hut, so several local restaurants have developed programs based on the Pizza Hut model. One restaurant encourages students to "Build a Burger." The class has a Burger Board in the classroom. After reading so many books the kids get the bottom of the bun, then the meat, then the lettuce, and so on. When their burger is complete, they get a certificate entitling them to one burger at the local restaurant. A local ice cream shop has an "I Go Bananas Over Books" program. Students build a banana split—first the bananas, then one flavor of ice cream, then another, then toppings one by one, ending with whipped cream and a cherry on top.

Reading Olympics

During an Olympic year, design a school reading Olympics patterned after the Olympic games. Begin with the Reading Olympic Torch Run, using as many kids as you can for runners (with kids as runners, a torch facsimile might be advisable). Have the Reading Olympic Torch Run from the public library to the school, or around the school and through the halls, or from the main office to the school, with the superintendent running the first lap, or have the run from one child's house to the next, with the torch ending on the track or in the gym. Have a parade of the athletes led by the American and the state flag. Maybe the local National Guard or scout troop would lead the parade in uniform followed by the mayor, the school superintendent, the principals, and so on. Each class would march behind its own specially designed class reading flag wearing sweats or dressed as book characters. Competition could be done within a class or grade level or by categories. Categories might include mysteries, biographies, adventure stories, a favorite author category, best effort, and so on. Next, the Olympic Committee will need to develop criteria for "winning" the various gold, silver, and bronze medals. An awards ceremony with Olympic music and a winners' dais would complete the Olympic games. World records for the games could be kept, to be replaced by new records in subsequent years.

Footsteps Around the World

In this combined reading and math venture, students compute how many steps it takes to get to various places around the school or the community. The class members earn a step for each book read (or, for example, for each 45 minutes spent reading). When the students arrive at the destination, they find a reward—for example:

- Steps to the playground for extra recess time
- Steps to the cafeteria for gingerbread cookies

- Steps to the local ice cream shop for ice cream
- Steps to the principal's office for a special time with the principal
- Steps to the train station for a train ride to the next town (school bus brings the class home)
- Steps to the local YMCA for a pool party
- Steps to McDonald's for lunch
- Steps to the teacher's house for a hot dog cookout in the backyard
- Steps to the high school for a sporting event and popcorn
- Steps to a community place of interest like the zoo, a park, a ferry boat, and the like

Mystery Reader

Once a week, Jackie DiGennaro, a teacher in Sitka, Alaska, has a Mystery Reader Night. On that evening, between 7:00 and 8:00, she randomly calls three students at home. If she "catches" a student reading, the student receives an "I Was Caught Reading" certificate and a coupon. The coupons are good for various prizes such as:

- A 30-minute trip to the library during class time
- One free book of your choice in the next book order
- Lunch in the room with Mrs. D. Bring a friend and a book to discuss.

Individual Reading Logs

Jackie DiGennaro also encourages her students to read at least 15 minutes a day at home. At the beginning of school she sends home a letter challenging parents to turn off the TV for that time each day and read with their kids. The reading can be done either silently or orally. Kids fill out the reading log during the week and return it each Friday with a parent's signature. Students are required to write two sentences about the book they are reading. Mrs. D. keeps a chart with the children's names on it. If they read each day, they get a sticker for the chart and "gold slip" for a weekly drawing that includes, as she says, "What else?!—books and other fun prizes." Students who read all semester get a trip to McDonald's with the teacher. Those who read all year have a slumber party at school.

Battle of the Books

June Gray in Saginaw, Michigan, describes the "Battle of the Books," a districtwide competition sponsored cooperatively by the school district and the public library. The coordinating team selected 30 books appropriate for fourth-, fifth-, and sixth-graders. Students were given three months to read all the books they could. Students then prepared themselves for factual and comprehension questions about the books. Individual schools had mock battles to select the team that would represent their school in the districtwide "battle." Then the teams met in districtwide competition. Gray says, "The competition is a great motivator for reading. A real key to the success for the program is the support by teachers and parents."

How do you get started planning your own "Battle of the Books"? Joanne Kelly (1990) in her book, *The Battle of Books: K-8*, offers more than 800 questions arranged by book type (popular contemporary novels, classics, award books, and so on). Battles can be graded according to the ability levels of students. She also provides reproducible certificates, bookmarks, and display ideas.

Incentive programs aren't for all teachers or all kids; however, used with sensitivity, they do provide one more way to get children excited about books.

References

Darby, David. 1993. Telephone interview with author. Pittsburgh, Pennsylvania, January 21.

Goodman, Ken S. 1986. *What's Whole in Whole Language?* Portsmouth, NH: Heinemann.

Gray, June. 1992. Telephone interview with author. Saginaw, Michigan, December 9.

Kelly, Joanne. 1990. *The Battle of Books: K-8*. Englewood, CO: Teacher Ideas Press.

Routman, Regie. 1988. *Transitions: From Literature to Literacy*. Portsmouth, NH: Heinemann.

Trelease, Jim. 1989. *The New Read-Aloud Handbook*. 2d ed. New York: Penguin Books.

15

Parents as Talent Scouts

Getting Your Players Ready for the Major Leagues

Schools have students for only five hours per day; if your player is to play in the majors, educators and parents have to work together. Children who have tossed and caught balls when they were little will certainly be more prepared for T-league than those children who have not. The skills for baseball—for example, eye-hand coordination for fielding, running, catching, throwing, and batting—can be started at almost any age. Likewise, the skills necessary for reading need to be nurtured long before children get to school and continued long afterward.

What Should Parents Do?

We know that children who come from homes where someone has read to them, talked to them, listened to them, labeled things for them, and spoken in complete sentences to them have a head start on the reading game once they start school. This chapter contains many ideas on how to get your child ready for the major leagues (see summary in fig. 15.1). The best part is that you'll love it, too!

Fig. 15.1. Things parents can do to help children perform well in school.

What Should Parents Do?

If you as parents want to get your players ready for the major leagues in reading, you should:

Read aloud to your children

Act as a role model

Set aside quiet time for reading

Make sure your children have reading material

Encourage book ownership

Allow children the freedom to choose their own books

Limit television

Find creative ways to extend books into other activities

Tell your players stories and listen to theirs

Be aware of your players' physical and emotional well-being

Enjoy your children

Read Aloud to Your Children

Let us once again repeat one of the most important of the findings reported in *Becoming a Nation of Readers*. "The single most important activity for building the knowledge required for eventual success in reading is reading aloud to children" (Anderson et al. 1985, 23). And when should you start? Reading Is Fundamental (1991) offers this advice in their pamphlet entitled "Reading Aloud to Your Children": "Without doubt, reading aloud is a gift you can freely give your children from the day you bring them home from the hospital until the time they leave the nest. Children's reading experts agree that reading aloud offers the easiest and most effective way to turn children into lifelong readers. And it's as much fun for you as it is for your children."

First of all, where can you do it? The answer is ANYWHERE—waiting at the doctor's or dentist's office or in the grocery line (in fact, in any waiting situation), in the backyard, at the park, in a tent, in the car on long trips or during traffic delays—or in more traditional places such as snuggled in bed, on the sofa, in your favorite chair, on the floor—anywhere.

When should you start? From the moment you get the baby home from the hospital. It has even been suggested, but certainly not confirmed, that you can start before the child is born. The idea is apparently that by talking to the baby in the womb, it will respond after birth to the sound of its mother's voice. And don't stop reading to your children until they leave home. Even after the children are grown and return for the holidays, make reading a part of your family tradition. This Christmas my husband plans to read either *Christmas Gift* by Ferrol Sams (1989) or *The Best Christmas Pageant Ever* by Barbara Robinson (1972) to our grown children, their spouses, and our grandchildren. I have three very special children in my life who live in Alaska. Because I can't be there to read to them, I send them stories I record on cassette tapes.

Choose a special time each day to read to your children. Bedtime or naptime are obvious choices. I have great admiration for my friend Karol Hagberg. Her son D. J. was probably 12 or 13 at the time. In the midst of entertaining approximately 25 dinner guests, Karol rose quietly and said, "I hope you'll excuse me for 15 or 20 minutes; it's D. J.'s reading time." I loved overhearing the cadences of her soft voice against the clinking of the wine glasses. I have often wondered if she ever missed a bedtime reading.

What should you read to children? Young children respond well to Mother Goose rhymes and other traditional rhymes and songs because they love the rhythm of the language, but I'm convinced that anything will do. When our grandson was six months old, I found myself alone with him with no books. The best thing I could find was an old *Time* magazine so I read it aloud "with feeling." He stared at me with rapt attention. I can only assume that he enjoyed the sounds of the language rising and falling (or that he's destined to be a news reporter or a politician).

My father and I had a tradition each Sunday. I'd sit either in his lap or at his feet and he'd read me the comic strips or, as Daddy called them, the "funny papers." Then every Sunday he'd say with his rolling southern accent, "Mary Helen, these are funny papers, honey. If they're 'funny' why aren't you laughing?" Then I'd giggle and say, "Oh, Daddy, YOU'RE funny" and snuggle in closer.

Read billboards, menus, maps, directions, mail order catalogs, cereal boxes, anything, so that your children will know the importance of reading in the world and, of course, read books. My husband, Ray, and his brother were avid cereal box readers. In fact, anything with print on it was "consumed" at breakfast.

If you are puzzled as to what type of book is most appropriate for your children at a particular age, my best advice is to experiment—your children will let you know what they like or don't like—or get some guidance from your librarian. The Reading Is Fundamental organization has an inexpensive pamphlet, "Choosing Good Books for Your Children" (1990), which includes tips on what to look for when choosing books for children of specific ages. The address for Reading Is Fundamental is included on page 216.

Reading aloud is fun—let yourself go, ham it up! Suggestions for how to read aloud to children are included on pages 23-24. In addition to those suggestions, here are several more specifically for parents.

1. Be prepared to read a book over and over again. When children have a favorite, they want to read it again and again. Although you may get bored, the repetition is good for the children. After a time, they may know the story well enough for you to stop and let them "read" a part. Encourage them to chime in on a familiar refrain such as, "I'll huff and I'll puff and I'll blow the house down."

2. Have the children sit close to you where they can see the pictures. Point out things in the pictures to them.

3. If it's a new book, stop and let them make predictions about what's going to happen next.

4. Don't be surprised if the children lose interest in old favorites. Children outgrow toys and they outgrow books, too. Save them for your grandchildren.

5. With young children, be prepared for lots of questions. Take time to answer them. The objective is not to finish a book in record time but to have a special time with your children.

6. Encourage your older children to read to the younger ones. It's great practice for parenting and a special time among siblings.

Act as a Role Model

Children have to see you reading. Stephen Krashen (1993), in his metaresearch study, found that children who did more leisure reading had parents who also did more leisure reading. Your actions really do speak louder than your words. When your kids see you reading a newspaper or magazine or see you snuggled in bed with a book, they'll want to follow your example. Let them hear you laugh or see you cry so they'll know the power of literature. Tell them about an article you read in the paper, or read a cartoon out loud at breakfast. Read the recipe out loud when you're cooking. Point out the word *salt* on the box when you take it off the shelf. Show them the word *salt* in the recipe book. If the children see you go to the dictionary to look up a word that puzzles you, they'll eventually do the same without any prompting. My husband's family were great "researchers." He tells me a dinner never passed without someone referring to the nearby encyclopedia to solve the great debate of the evening.

Tell them about your reading strategies. For example, "When I get to a word I don't know, I usually skip over it or guess at the meaning, but if it's really important to the story, I look it up in the dictionary." Or, "This is a good book, but sometimes the author goes into too much detail describing all the intricate details of building the church. Since it doesn't seem to be important to the story I skip over those parts." Or, "These Russian novels have so many characters. Sometimes they go by their first name, sometimes by their second or last name. I kept getting confused, so finally I made a little chart of characters so I can keep them all straight." Teachers need to do the same thing.

Set Aside Quiet Time for Reading

You'll remember from the research reported in chapter 2 that the amount of time children spent reading outside of school was the best predictor of reading comprehension, vocabulary development, and gains in reading achievement. Again, just as in sports, if you practice a skill, you get better at it.

Parents need to set aside time for independent reading, or silent sustained reading (SSR), as we call it in schools. A parent shared one of her ideas with me. She and her family have "green flag" time. At a certain time during the day, she hangs out a green flag. It signals to the other children in the neighborhood that it is quiet reading time. Then she sets the kitchen timer for one hour. (I'd recommend a shorter time for younger children.) If the telephone rings, she either answers it or puts a recorded message on the answering machine, "It's green flag time at the Smith house. Please leave a message, and we'll return your call within one hour." The Smith children may either sleep or read during green flag time, but those are the only options. She, of course, reads during green flag time. A funny thing happened—all the kids in the neighborhood thought it was "cool" and wanted to have green flag time at their houses, too.

As a family you can set up an SSR time when everyone in the family reads. Set the timer—even 10 minutes will do wonders for your child's reading skill and interest. But you can't set your kids to reading and sneak in and watch the Vikings on Monday Night Football. Remember the big *R*: Role model. This is especially important for male members of the household. Too often little boys have gotten the message that reading is a "girl thing." Small wonder that boys are much more likely to have reading difficulties than girls.

One other thing should be noted here. In some households it's hard to find a quiet, private place to read. Not all children have their own bedrooms. Throw a sheet over a couple of chairs to form a tent; put an old refrigerator box in a corner (let the children decorate it); reserve a less-used hallway as a reading alley. I came from a busy, noisy household and for several years shared a bedroom with an equally busy, noisy sister. Mother had a rule: no children in the living room; however, if you were very quiet, you could slip into the easy chair in the far corner of the living room and no one would notice. I'd read for hours. I'm sure now that our ever-watchful mother knew exactly what was going on and was pleased to ignore the infraction of "The Rule."

Another option is to make reading a privilege. "Your regular bedtime is 8:00, but if you go up to your bed and read your book, you may stay up 15 minutes later." Make a big deal of giving your children their very own bed lamp. Even better, have them go with you and let them pick it out themselves. That small investment will pay dividends many times over.

Make Sure Your Children Have Access to Reading Materials

Right after you get your newborn home from the hospital, even before you get the baby's Social Security card, get a library card in the child's name. Anderson et al. (1985, 78) reported, "The amount of reading children from poor homes did and their gains in reading achievement over the summer were related to the distance they lived from the public library." Make regular visits to the library; make them an adventure. Look at the fish in the tank, go to the listening center, listen to story hour, read the posters. Most important, let your children browse through the books and pick out some of their own. Show them how *you* pick out books. Read the titles to them and say, "I'll bet this book is about a silly frog because ... ," or "I think I'd like this one because ..."

Libraries are important, but it's also important to have books at home. In the pamphlet "Building a Family Library," Reading Is Fundamental (1989) offers excellent suggestions for building a family library. You can put together a large collection of books without spending a lot of money. New books can, of course, be purchased in bookstores. Surprisingly, many publishers are now issuing paperback editions of books within a year of the hardcover release. These often sell for one-third the cost of the hardback. I always prowl the discount table, too. I have purchased many excellent anthologies of folktales, fairy tales, ghost stories, or young adult fiction and several "classics" such as *Wind in the Willows*, *King Arthur's Tales*, *Just So Stories*, and *Aesop's Fables* for a fraction of their original cost.

Book clubs offer books at very low prices. They include advertisements that tell a little bit about each book and an order blank. Your children may have access to these through the school; however, there are book clubs for parents, too. A sample of those are included on page 39.

Here are suggestions for locating used books.

Secondhand bookstores. Most cities have used-book stores; these can be readily found in the telephone yellow pages. The children's section can be a treasure trove of good inexpensive books, and the selection is always changing. Suzanne Barchers (1990, 21) found that some collectors were willing to trade books. "[Trading] is a good way to get rid of unusable books from your collection and trade them for more useful titles. You may have to trade away two to get one, but two rejects are worth one good title. If you develop a rapport with a dealer, you might be able to get advance notice of good acquisitions."

Yard sales, flea markets, and church bazaars. Comb through neighborhood newspapers and newsletters for dates and locations. Some organizations even sponsor yearly used-book sales, sometimes with thousands of titles. You can build quite a collection for as little as 25 to 50 cents a book. Yard sales, flea markets, and church bazaars are also terrific sources for puppets (just cut a hole for a hand, take the stuffing out of stuffed animals, and baste the edges) and materials for art projects, such as yarn, wallpaper samples, cloth, and trimmings.

Library sales. Many libraries have annual sales to make room for new titles. Some of the books have a low circulation or are outdated. Others have been donated to the library for resale at annual library sales. Check with your librarian for dates of sales.

Attics and basements. Do you have any of your own books from childhood? Find and add them to your collection. I was delighted when my mother sent me a box of my old books and among them was one of my favorites about a bunny who turned blue when he wiggled his nose.

Informal trading. Encourage your children and their friends to swap books they've read for books they haven't. Or arrange a weekend book swap among families from your children's school or neighborhood. Arranging book swaps is discussed in chapter 12.

Thrift and resale shops. Stores like those run by the Salvation Army, Goodwill Industries, and service and veterans' organizations are good sources for used books. Because the stores have new supplies coming in every day, check them frequently for the best selection. If you get to know the staff at these shops, they may be willing to call you when a good shipment comes in.

Reading material extends beyond books. Make sure you have on hand things like sample menus from local restaurants, catalogs, maps, newspapers, and magazines. When you are pausing between tasks, browse through them. The kids will get the idea. Krashen (1993, 86) suggests, "Parents need to know that children will get far more benefit from being read to, from seeing parents read for pleasure, and from reading comics, magazines, and books, than they will from working through workbooks on sale at the local drugstore."

Encourage Book Ownership

This, of course, goes hand in hand with providing access to books. Encourage your children to participate in book clubs. Allow them to save their allowance or earn extra money to go book shopping. Give books and magazine subscriptions to the children in your life on traditional toy-giving occasions and encourage others to do the same. I try to model that not only in my professional life but in my personal life as well. I give ABC books for baby presents, cookbooks for wedding presents, "love and marriage" books for wedding shower gifts, poetry books for anniversaries, "coffee table" books for house warmings, and so on. My husband and I want our grandchildren to have a very special collection of books, so each year for their birthdays, we give them the Caldecott and Newbery book winners for that year. By the time they are grown up, they'll not only have a wonderful collection of books, but they'll also have first-edition copies that may grow in value as collector's items. If I've not seen a child in a long time and I'm not sure of the child's current interests, I might buy a gift certificate from a bookstore in his or her community where he or she can have the joy of spending it on a special book.

Provide special individual bookshelves or book places for your children to keep their books. They don't have to be elaborate—plastic or wooden crates, cinderblocks, baskets, or sturdy cardboard boxes will do just fine. Let the children decorate them and make them their own. Encourage your children to keep their library books alongside their own books.

Allow Children the Freedom to Choose Their Own Books

We've talked about the importance of freedom of choice in relation to teachers, but I'd like to emphasize a couple of points for parents by telling two stories.

My agreement with my students on Mt. Desert Island, Maine, was this: I would not act as a censor of their reading. We agreed that it was the students' responsibility to discuss possible reading with their parents—if the book was OK with their parents, it was OK with me. This was our covenant. The parents, the students, and I agreed.

Mrs. Thompson charged in red-faced and angry. "Why are you allowing my daughter to read THIS!" She held the blue-covered book by two fingers (as if she might catch a dread disease from it) and thrust it into my face. Actually it was a rather innocuous book about girls her daughter's age who were pregnant and in a home for unwed mothers. Unless I had read the abridged version, I couldn't imagine what her objections were. I judiciously decided that this was not the time to mention our covenant. I'd rather take the flack for the book than have Teri punished for reading the book on the sly.

"What troubles you about the book, Mrs. Thompson?" I asked.

"This is not a happy book. I only want my daughter to read happy books," she snapped. Yes, happy books, I thought. Teri's life was happy—she was a pretty 13-year-old who lived in a large boisterous family with two intelligent, well-educated parents. Her father's lucrative business provided the children with anything they wanted or needed. Children in our little town were safe at any time of the day or night, so safe as to be a little boring, perhaps.

I thought I'd give it one try for Teri. "Mrs. Thompson, you and your family do indeed lead happy lives. Maybe what Teri wants to do is understand how people unlike her live. Maybe she wants to see how girls who have no loving family to turn to survive and care for each other. She'll never experience that kind of world, but she wants and needs to understand it so she can be compassionate and loving, so that she won't turn her back on people unlike her out of fear or ignorance."

"Happy books," repeated Mrs. Thompson, "happy books." I hurt for Teri. I hurt as we checked the "happy quotient" of her readings, and I've often wondered whether Teri will need to experience some of those "unhappy" things because she wasn't allowed to read about them.

Another story. One day when I was about Teri's age, I asked my father whether I could read one of the books on my parents' bookshelf. I pointed to a faded purplish-blue book. He looked at it and nodded, "Certainly, darlin', you may read any books of ours, and if you have any questions you just come ask me." I took *Andersonville*, a book on an infamous Civil war prison, off the shelf and curled up in the living room. I was horrified—why was my father allowing me to read what was to my 13-year-old eyes a raunchy, raw book? Several times over the next few weeks I put it away, wondering each time why Daddy was letting me read it.

Over time I began to understand the profound respect my father had shown me and how much he trusted our relationship. I would read what I needed and wanted to read, and he trusted that if I found it troubling or confusing, I would come to him and we'd talk it over.

The message of the stories is: Talk it over. Find out what your children need, understand the power of vicarious experiences, suspend judgment, and, most important, be there to talk it over.

Limit Television

It's time for Jim Trelease and me to get out our soapboxes. As Trelease (1989, 121) says, "Television is the direct opposite of reading." When the child is watching baseball, the child isn't out there playing it. We are after participation, not spectatorship.

Trelease (121-127) goes on to mention 17 other negative aspects of television, several of which follow:

- Television is an antisocial experience.
- Television, vying for children's time and attention with a constant diet of unchallenging simplest entertainment, stimulates anti-school and antireading feeling among children.
- Television stifles the imagination and discourages creative play.
- Television is psychologically addictive.
- Television presents a continuous distortion of physical and social realities, thus reinforcing false stereotypes.
- Television has been called by a number of people "the greatest babysitter of all time."

So what are we waiting for? Let's turn the darn thing off! Farmington Turn-Off, a month-long campaign staged by the Farmington (Connecticut) Public Library is a community program to do just that. The program was designed to make people aware of television's addictive nature and to provide families with alternative activities. Libraries, schools, churches, and parks and recreation departments work together to plan activities. Since it began in 1984, it's been copied in communities throughout North America.

If you are considering a TV turn-off project, the best book on the subject is Marie Winn's *Unplugging the Plug-In Drug* (1987). The book contains everything you need to know—experiences gained from other turn-offs, activities, organizational tips, publicity, pitfalls, and charts.

Here are some suggestions for TV watching:

1. Give your children a TV budget. They have a TV "allowance" each week of, say, three hours. Get out a TV guide or the local newspaper listing of programs and help them plan how to spend their allowance. If they want to spend it all on Saturday morning cartoons, that's up to them, even though you'd love for them to see the Discovery Channel program on panda bears. Give your children a blank weekly schedule so that they can fill in their time. By doing this, children become discriminating viewers, not individuals who sit down in front of the TV for something to do.

2. Have a TV blackout night when no one watches TV. Play family games that night or bake cookies together.

3. Put the TV in an out-of-the-way, uncomfortable spot.

4. Always turn off the TV when no one is watching it. You don't really need the background noise.

5. Allow TV watching only when all the household chores and the homework are done. My mother was masterful. I didn't get hooked on the TV habit, and to this day I rarely watch it. Here is what she did. Dinner ended and I rose from the table to start doing the dishes. Mother would say, "If you have homework or reading to do, you may be excused to go to your room—otherwise you may stay down here and help me with the dishes and several other chores." Naturally I always went to my room. TV was never an issue. Note that I had choices, but they did not include watching TV.

6. Have a "no TV on school nights" rule.

If you watch TV with your children, you might try some tie-in activities that encourage more creative thinking:

1. Develop a commercial rating sheet. Monitor commercials over a two-week period. Which commercial was the funniest? Which was the dumbest? Which was the most convincing? Which distorted the truth the most? Which product would you never buy? Have a family vote at the end of the two weeks. Family members have to offer supporting

reasons for their decisions. The kids could make up awards and they could act out the award ceremony.

2. Watch the news together and compare the TV coverage of a story with the local newspaper coverage. Discuss the following: Is a picture ALWAYS worth a thousand words?

3. After a TV program on an issue like alcoholism, talk with your children about how they felt about the program.

4. Watch for programs, such as those suggested in chapter 10, that are based on books. Go to the library after such a program to see whether the book is available.

5. Watch for programs that require or invite children to respond. The only program I liked as a child was "Tom Terrific and Mighty Manfred the Wonder Dog." You placed your little plastic sheet (which you had ordered from Mighty Manfred) over the TV screen and got out your Tom Terrific colors. Now you were READY. Horrors, Tom Terrific was about to be gobbled by a space alien. Quickly you had to grab your colors and draw a ladder so he could escape. Oh dear, a child is about to fall off a cliff. Draw a bridge across the ravine so Mighty can save him from certain death. If you weren't up there drawing, the characters were doomed. I wonder how long the program lasted. Even as a child I could imagine the "Big Trouble" if I had, in my enthusiasm, forgotten to put the protective, washable shield on the TV. Tom Terrific colors all over the evening news—not good.

6. Help your children distinguish between fact and fiction. Ask them if they think a situation seems to make sense. Is that how people usually act? Ask them what they would do if they were in that situation.

7. Challenge children's creativity by asking them to create different endings for a program.

Find Creative Ways to Extend Books into Other Activities

Although many of the activities in this book can be used just as well by parents and grandparents as by teachers, I did come across an excellent book just for parents entitled *Involving Parents Through Children's Literature: Grades 1-2*. The author, Anthony D. Fredericks (1992),* gives story summaries of 40 ever-popular children's stories followed by thoughtful discussion questions and fun activities. See figure 15.2, pages 190-191, for one of my favorites.

*Material from Anthony D. Fredericks, *Involving Parents Through Children's Literature: Grades 1-2* (Englewood, CO: Teacher Ideas Press, 1992), copyright © 1992 by Anthony D. Fredericks, is reprinted with permission.

Fig. 15.2. Example of questions and activities to use in conjunction with children's stories.

GREGORY, THE TERRIBLE EATER

Mitchell Sharmat

(New York: Four Winds, 1980)

STORY SUMMARY

Gregory, a goat, is very picky about what he eats. Although most goats like to eat leather shoes and cans, Gregory prefers to eat fruits and vegetables. Finally, a helpful doctor discovers a "cure."

DISCUSSION QUESTIONS

1. What are some of your favorite foods? What are some of your least favorite foods?
2. Do you eat everything your parents tell you to eat? Why do you think they always make you eat things you do not want to?
3. Do you think Gregory would have eventually grown out of his unusual eating habits? Why?
4. What would have happened if Gregory's parents had not worked the "goat food" into his diet? Are there any foods you are glad your parents made you try?

ACTIVITIES (Please choose any two activities.)

1. Ask your child to cut out several pictures from old magazines. The pictures should be foods your child enjoys and some your child does not enjoy. Paste these pictures on a sheet of construction paper in two sections: Foods I Like and Foods I Don't Like.
2. Ask your child to create some menus of their favorite meals at home. Work with your child to compile these into a booklet.
3. Have your child pretend that a goat is coming to dinner. Give your child a paper plate and a variety of craft materials to use for food. For example, have your child create a tinfoil hamburger, button beans, yarn spaghetti, etc.
4. Challenge your child to create a television commercial to "sell" his or her favorite food. Give your child an opportunity to produce the commercial for other family members.
5. Research the actual diet of a goat as well as the diets of other animals. Use *Animal Encyclopedia for Children* by Roger Few (New York: Macmillan, 1991) as a reference. You and your child can make a comparative chart for the diets of the animals.
6. You may enjoy the story *The 300 Pound Cat* by Rosamond Dauer (New York: Avon, 1981). Have your child compare the eating habits of William (in *The 300 Pound Cat*) to Gregory (in *Gregory, the Terrible Eater*). How are the stories similar? How are they different?

RELATED CHILDREN'S BOOKS

An Apple a Day by Judi Barrett
We'll Have a Friend for Lunch by Jane Flory
Sheldon's Lunch by Bruce Lemerise
Alexander's Midnight Snack by Catherine Stock
Alexandra the Rock-Eater by Dorothy Van Woerkon

■ ■ ■ ■ ■

Make the Reading/Writing Connection for Your Players

Write notes to yourself or make grocery lists and read them to your children. Let them select a favorite thing to put on the grocery list, write it down, and show them where it is on the list. If they go with you to the store, let them hold the list while you check the items off. If you can, match the word *soup* to the label on the soup can. When your children are older, put notes in their lunch box, "I love you" notes on their pillow, and notes welcoming them home with a list of their chores and where to find their snack. Encourage them to write notes to you and make sure you respond. If a child gets angry at you, give the child a piece of paper with a sentence that begins, "I'm really, really, really mad at Dad because ..." and let the child write out the frustration. Whether Dad is asked to respond is up to the child.

Our daughter Jill made a book for our grandson Sammy entitled *Sam's Book*. At the time, all the grandparents and several other close relatives lived quite far away. *Sam's Book* had his "important" people in it. My husband's heart melted when, not having seen Sam for six months, two little two-year-old arms shot right up when my husband got off the plane and Sam cried, "Papa!" It seems to me that *Sam's Book* has endless possibilities. All kinds of photographs could be added—a picture of Bubba with "Sam's Bear" written on the page, for example. As the child got older, more photographs could be added. More complicated labels (even a one-paragraph story describing the picture) could be either written or dictated by the child. The pictures, the stories, and the book could take their places beside other important books on the child's shelf—*Sam's Book: Volume 8*.

Tell Your Players Stories and Listen to Theirs

All that can be said about the power of reading aloud to children can also be said about storytelling. Still, storytelling has several distinct advantages. It's portable: You can do it anyplace, anytime. It requires no equipment. You can do it in the dark. You can stretch the story or abbreviate it, depending on the time you have. It's just you and the story, with nothing to act as a barrier between you and the children, even if the barrier is only a book. If you tell a story, the children will want to tell one, too. Storytelling increases children's vocabulary, helps improve their auditory memory, stretches their imagination, gives them a sense of how stories work, and gives them reasons to read.

You can tell your favorite folktales, fairy tales, or scary stories. Don't worry about whether you get it "right." Cinderella has more than 500 different versions, and who's to say your version isn't every bit as "right" as number 87. If your kids say, "Mom, that's not how it went," grab the opportunity for them to tell you *their* version.

You can tell family stories, stories about Grandma and Grandpa's farm before they had running water, or how Great, Great Grandma hid the family treasures in the pecan grove to keep the Union Army from finding them during the Civil War, or about Crazy Uncle Howard who hopped freight trains all over North America and rode with the hoboes throughout the Great Depression.

You can tell them stories of your life, stories of one of your most embarrassing moments, like when your desk tipped over in seventh grade, burying you in five layers of stiff crinoline, and the teacher and several husky lads had trouble turning you right side up because they were laughing so hard; or why Grandpa calls you Cousin Fatso; or about how other people in the family got their nicknames.

You can tell them stories about *them*, stories of the time your daughter rescued the dog who fell through the ice then fell through the ice herself, or of how she loved to dance with Daddy by standing on his feet. Children love it when you make up stories with them as the main character, too. For other storytelling ideas, see chapter 5.

Be Aware of Your Players' Physical and Emotional Well-Being

I'm amazed. I rarely go into a school to work with children when I don't observe at least three or four children squinting from the back of the room. Don't depend on the school to tell you your child needs glasses, a hearing device, or three big hugs a day. You know them best—players who are in good condition have a better chance when they play the game. After all, you are the talent scout!

Enjoy Your Children

Laugh with them. Be interested in what they read, what they think about, what they do. Give them time and attention, and, finally, offer them the gift of love and approval.

Parents are children's first and most important teachers. Children need parents on their team if they are to win in the reading game.

References

Anderson, Richard C., Elfrieda H. Hiebert, Judith A. Scott, and Ian A. G. Wilkinson. 1985. *Becoming a Nation of Readers: The Report of the Commission on Reading*. Champaign-Urbana, IL: Center for the Study of Reading.

Barchers, Suzanne I. 1990. *Creating and Managing the Literate Classroom*. Englewood, CO: Teacher Ideas Press.

Fredericks, Anthony D. 1992. *Involving Parents Through Children's Literature: Grades 1-2*. Englewood, CO: Teacher Ideas Press.

Krashen, Stephen. 1993. *The Power of Reading: Insights from the Research*. Englewood, CO: Libraries Unlimited.

Reading Is Fundamental, Inc. 1991. "Reading Aloud to Your Children." Washington, DC: RIF.

______. 1990. "Choosing Good Books for Your Children." Washington, DC: RIF.

______. 1989. "Building a Family Library." Washington, DC: RIF.

Trelease, Jim. 1989. *The New Read-Aloud Handbook*. 2d ed. New York: Penguin Books.

Winn, Marie. 1987. *Unplugging the Plug-In Drug*. New York: Penguin Books.

Literature Resources

Robinson, Barbara. 1972. *The Best Christmas Pageant Ever*. New York: Avon Books.

Sams, Ferrol. 1989. *Christmas Gift*. Atlanta, GA: Longstreet Press.

16

The Librarian as the General Manager

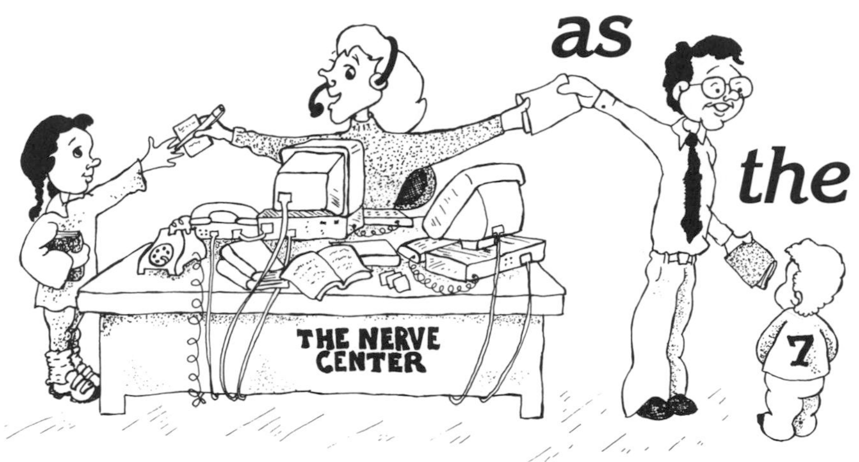

Teams need general managers, whether they are professional baseball teams or reading teams. The job description of a general manager and that of a librarian could have come from the same book: leadership, planning, management, promotion and marketing, personnel, facility management, networking, and cooperation. Certainly, without the general manager the game could go on, but the role of the general manager is critical if resources are going to be made available, if the game is to be promoted, if the play is to be coordinated, and if the sport is to have a good "playing field."

School Librarians/ School Media Specialists

Can you imagine a general manager who thought the job consisted of counting the bats and keeping the helmets dusted? Of course not! What a waste of talent. Yet, thousands of librarians across our country are doing just that—checking the books in and out—that, and only that, is The Job. Actually, some of these librarians would rather the books not go out at all—it messes up the order of things and makes the shelves untidy. And who knows, the books might not come back! Or they might come back with peanut butter and jelly on page 39.

As reading is not a spectator sport, the role of the librarian/media specialist/general manager is not one of a passive spectator. To be worthy of the paycheck, the library media specialist must get involved—the librarian must play the game. Yet, it is more than just playing the game. After all, the term "general manager" may be a misnomer. The general manager may "manage" but that is the lowest level of the responsibilities; actually the general manager must lead, in every sense of the word.

As a way to think about the role and activities of a library media specialist and the media center, David V. Loertscher (1988, 11-14)* presents the following thought-provoking taxonomy in his book *Taxonomies of the School Library Media Program*. As you read through the activities, rate your library. If you are a librarian/media specialist, rate yourself.

■ ■ ■ ■ ■

Level 1—No Involvement: The library media center is bypassed entirely. Students or teachers in this school might have to think hard if asked if their school has a library. It is not a place anyone thinks of visiting.

---

*Excerpt from David V. Loertscher, *Taxonomies of the School Library Media Program* (Englewood, CO: Libraries Unlimited, 1988), copyright © 1988 by Libraries Unlimited, and is reprinted with permission.

Level 2—Self-Help Warehouse: Facilities and materials are available for the self-starter. The library looks inviting, the collection is well organized, but the librarian is grafted onto the checkout desk—or is invisible. The philosophy is "If You Can Find It, Help Yourself."

Level 3—Individual Reference Assistance: The librarian is alive and well and will assist students and teachers when they request information or materials of specific interest. Loertscher describes this as the "magician's role"—from out of the vast reference hat the librarian pulls important and trivial information and materials.

Level 4—Spontaneous Interaction and Gathering: The librarian is awaiting the challenge. On the spur of the moment the librarian charges into action, responding to the instant need for information when a student or a teacher wishes to expand on the subject under discussion. Out comes an article on the pouch life of baby kangaroos, a map showing the battle of Gettysburg, a pamphlet on the care of pot-bellied pigs, two overheads showing the projected population of the world in 2010, and a recording of Robert Frost's poetry read by Robert Frost. Certainly this service is necessary and desirable, but Loertscher (12) warns that it should not serve as an "excuse for lack of planning by teachers or turn into a baby-sitting service."

Level 5—Cursory Planning: The teacher is sitting in the faculty lounge and the librarian walks in, "Say, Helen, seeing you reminds me, next week I'm doing a really dull unit on magnets, do you have any ideas?" The librarian offers sources for help and ideas and activities that should increase interest in the task. The cursory planning level is characterized as informal and brief.

Level 6—Planned Gathering: Here we have the teacher/planner. The teacher talks with the librarian well in advance of the class project, giving the librarian time to gather materials from a variety of sources, including the state and public library. Blanche Woolls (1988, 7) says, "For many school media specialists, the gathering of materials, placement on a book truck, and delivery to the classroom has been the highest level of involvement of the library with the classroom." They are playing the game—but only if they are asked to join in.

Level 7—Evangelistic Outreach: This librarian isn't waiting to be asked whether the library would like to play. The librarian plans teacher inservices to show materials and equipment; provides sample lessons that use books and media from the library; demonstrates supplementary teaching aids; provides library lessons for students on research methods; teaches on-line database searching services to both teachers and students; and helps students find resources that extend their assignments. The library media specialist is looking for converts. If they get to the library media center, maybe they'll see the light.

Level 8—Scheduled Planning in the Support Role: At last, the librarian has made the teaching team. The teachers and students have planned a resource-based teaching unit or project and the librarian is involved in resource development well in advance of the library experience. The library media center is included in the teaching plan, and students are given assignments that make use of materials both in and outside the media center. Students take as much responsibility for their learning as possible. Notice at this level of the taxonomy, the library media specialist is still responding to a planned unit or project. In other words, the librarians are on the playing field but they haven't yet thrown the ball.

Level 9—Instructional Design, Level I: At this level the library media specialist starts to act more like a real general manager, participating in every step of the development, execution, and evaluation of a resource-based teaching unit. Yet, at this level the involvement is still detached and the contribution is considered merely enrichment or supplementary to the core program.

Level 10—Instructional Design, Level II: At this level the entire unit content depends on the resources and activities of the library media center. The library media center staff are no longer just providers of materials, but teachers and evaluators of student progress.

Level 11—Curriculum Development: Now the real general manager steps up front and center. The library media specialist contributes to the planning and structure of what is taught in the school or district. This general manager not only knows how to play the game—knows what players, coaches, and talent scouts need—but is also a convener of resources, the communication link to other teams and leagues, a strategist on learning theory, and the key promoter of the sport.

■ ■ ■ ■ ■

As I read Loertscher's and Woolls's books, I had one of those rare "aha" experiences. My orientation is to the classroom, not to the library, having had five decades of personal experience with library media centers that were mostly on Level 1 or, at best, Level 2 of the taxonomy. (I wonder whether the libraries "lived down" to my expectations.) When I encountered wonderful library media centers like those in the Grand Forks School District or those at the University of North Dakota, I thought they were more rare and precious than emeralds. As I think back to my teaching days, I tremble with excitement at what we might have done if we had had a Level 10 or 11 library media specialist on our team. We would have won the World Series for sure!

It makes so much sense. We live in the so-called Information Age, and libraries, both school and public, are key to our ability to move into the next century. None of us can afford to be passive in this rapidly changing world of information lest we become the technological equivalent of the manual typewriter. Daniel Barron and Timothy J. Bergen, Jr. (1992, 522) call for a restructuring of school libraries to prepare students for personal success in the next century:

> If you want to get your school beyond textbooks and lectures; to participate in whole language instruction; to develop effective programs in critical thinking; to help students survive and thrive in an information-based economy; to increase the chances that your students will become lifelong learners; to integrate television, satellite, and computer technologies into your curriculum; to have access to educational resources and materials beyond the walls of your school;

and to provide yourself and other members of the instructional team with information that will improve efforts to implement site-based management—then you want *information power*. And the place to get it is the restructured school library of the Nineties."

How should that look and how can it be done? In 1988, the American Association of School Librarians and the Association for Educational Communications and Technology produced a book entitled *Information Power: Guidelines for School Library Media Programs*. The guidelines took three years to write and represent not only the best professional thinking in the field but also the best available research. The mission of the school library media program as stated in *Information Power* (1988, 1) is "to ensure that students and staff are effective users of ideas and information." The document continues with the specific objectives (1-2):

1. To provide intellectual access to information
2. To provide physical access to information
3. To provide learning experiences that encourage users to become discriminating consumers and skilled creators of information
4. To provide leadership, instruction, and consulting assistance in the use of instructional and information technology
5. To provide resources and activities that contribute to lifelong learning
6. To provide a facility that functions as the information center of the school, as a focus for integrated, interdisciplinary, intergrade, and school-wide learning activities
7. To provide resources and learning activities that represent a diversity of experiences, opinions, social and cultural experiences, opinions, social and cultural perspectives

What does all this mean in light of this book's premise that reading is not a spectator sport? Several important things come to mind.

Access

Although access to school libraries seems a basic premise, in many schools and communities it becomes a threshold question. In *Becoming a Nation of Readers*, Anderson et al. (1985, 78) report: "Analysis of schools that have been successful in promoting independent reading suggests that one of the keys is ready access to books. However, fully 15 percent of the nation's schools do not have libraries. In most of the remaining schools, the collections are small, averaging just over 13 volumes per student."

Access means that the library is open and staffed so that children can browse and be assisted by qualified professionals. The library media specialist and the teacher schedule time for library visits and plan special events and learning activities.

Access means that the books and materials are attractively displayed, carefully weeded, and in good repair. Research supports that when a collection is weeded, circulation goes up. Beth Fox (1988, 34) estimates that as much as 90 percent of client selection is made through browsing. A weeded collection allows users to find desirable material in a timely way. Jack Humphrey (1992, 538) says, "Books that are no longer relevant to the perceptions and needs of today's young people should be removed from the school collections.... While there may be thousands of books on the shelves, as many as 75 percent of them are probably of little or no use to the students." Woolls (1988, 69-72) offers excellent suggestions for weeding the collection in her book *Managing School Library Media Programs*.

Integration

It should be abundantly clear from all that has been reported that the library media center cannot be an isolated museum for used books. It must be the nerve center for the learning/reading environment if our children are to live and thrive in the Information Age. Woolls (1988, 6) says, "If school library media centers were to have a motto, it might be, 'Integrate with the Curriculum.' Library lessons and library services no longer stand alone but are an integral part of the curriculum." In chapter 8, we discussed integrating reading across the curriculum through thematic units. Certainly, the library media center's role is central to the process. Without the services and resources of the library media center, teachers would be sorely challenged to reach beyond the textbook.

Image and Attitude

As we review Loertscher's taxonomy, is is clear that library media specialists cannot be passive, waiting for someone to ask them to dance. In fact, they may have to organize the dance, promote it, and bring the music, the refreshments, and their partners.

They not only must have the professional competence to be true instructional leaders, but they must also inspire people to trust them, to make them part of the team. Children and adults alike must be made to feel welcome and excited about participating at the library media center. Library media specialists have to be key players if they want to ensure that children are true participants in the reading and learning game.

Programs and Promotion

In addition to participating as a part of the learning team, library media specialists will also want to think of ways to promote reading, the library media center, and their services. Many of the ideas that are scattered throughout this book have originated with librarians. Let's briefly review some of the library media specialists' favorites:

Booktalks. Pages 32-38 describe several different types of booktalks. Librarians and teachers report this as one of the best ways to get books off the shelves and into the hands of kids.

Storytelling. Although we often think of storytelling as something for primary children, storytelling as a pathway to reading is a sure success for students of all ages.

Space and time advertising. Articles can be written for the student newspaper, for the parent newsletter, or for the local newspaper. Because peer recommendations are such an important component, one feature might be "What's (name of student) reading?" with a brief synopsis of the student's favorite book or books. Our local paper has a column called "What's New at the Library?" which features the latest additions to the collection with brief book reviews.

Displays of posters, signs, and show cards. These are excellent ways to advertise the media center. Don't depend on those that have been commercially prepared. Microcomputer software such as Print Shop provides excellent poster and sign graphics.

Contests. Contests and incentive programs were mentioned in chapters 12 and 14, but library media specialists might wish to have special awards for the student research project that best incorporates multimedia into the presentation, for the best project using primary sources, for the best biography project, for the best science research project, and so forth.

Free samples. Who doesn't love free samples? Give away bookmarks, book bags, posters, or products related to a special promotion.

Extended hours. Have evening hours once a week, inviting children to come to the center with their parents. Once a month connect the evening hours with a special event—a readers theatre performance by kids, a storytelling swap, a student-directed puppet play, and other activities.

Loudspeaker advertising. Have a reference question of the day, read a poem, tell a joke (then tell about the book that it came from), do a 30-second booktalk, tell about special media center events of the week—in sum, create the image of a positive, dynamic library media center.

Most important, be proactive! Get involved with teachers and children so they can't imagine learning and reading without you on their team.

Public Librarians

The public librarian is also central to the reading/learning team. Because many school libraries serve students only during school hours, and, as we discovered, 15 percent of schools do not have school libraries, the public library plays an important role in providing access to both print and nonprint material for students and parents. Much of what has been said about making school libraries exciting applies to public libraries as well. In this section let's look at the unique role that public libraries can play in making sure that reading is not a spectator sport. Many national programs that promote reading are discussed in chapter 18. Here are a few ideas for promotion at the local level.

Readiness or Preschool Programs

One of the national goals is for all children to start school ready to learn. The public library may be the only source of books and reading services for preschoolers. Because 50 percent of a child's intellectual development occurs before the age of four, the libraries have a special responsibility to offer activities, services, and materials to help preschoolers develop intellectual and social skills. Successful library preschool programs offer a variety of activities: read-alouds, storytelling time, puppets, crafts, language games, songs, creative dramatics, and creative movement. At an early age children learn the fun, joy, and adventure of reading and books.

Many library preschool programs also involve the parents. Parents are introduced to their important role as the children's first role model and learn the keys to promoting the love of reading.

Certainly, active preschool programs at the library can break the cycle of illiteracy. Libraries that target disadvantaged families take their programs to the families instead of expecting the families to come to them. Pittsburgh's Beginning with Books project gives packets to preschoolers in health clinic waiting rooms, in homeless shelters, in housing developments, and in day care centers. The Mid-Arkansas Regional Library conducts workshops for disadvantaged parents: How to Read to Children, How to Raise a Smarter Child, and Child Development.

Programs for At-Risk Students

Libraries can offer special programs that address teen concerns (how to deal with anger, peer pressure, substance abuse, teen depression). Teen groups might create skits to dramatize teen problems. Appropriate library materials are featured at the programs.

Libraries like the Reuben McMillan Free Library Association in Youngstown, Ohio, conduct special programs on ethnic heritage for at-risk and minority students. The program ideas have included Hispanic crafts, games from around the world, African-American writers, and other topics and activities.

A homework center might be provided to help at-risk students who need additional tutoring. It could be staffed by college and senior citizen volunteers.

Programs That Promote Literacy and Love of Reading

Programs for students can include readers' advisory, cultural explorations, literacy tutoring, reading clubs, summer reading programs, after-school programs, class visits, readers' choice programs, teen programs, contests, family programs, and Reading Is Fundamental book distribution programs. Cooperation can be encouraged among the area school and public libraries and various youth organizations such as Girl Scouts, Boy Scouts, and YMCA.

Programs for Latchkey Children

After-school programs for latchkey children provide recreational and learning opportunities for children who might otherwise be home alone watching television or roaming the streets. The Greenville County (South Carolina) Library operates an active program in cooperation with neighborhood youth centers, the police and fire departments, the humane society, the Red Cross, the county health department, the county extension services, and the city and county recreation departments. The program includes placing cases of books at neighborhood centers, teaching crafts, and presenting lessons on practical topics such as how to prepare nutritious snacks. Other latchkey programs offer games, storytelling, reading activities, and practical skill development, such as pet care and safety. In Chesterland, Ohio, bus transportation is provided for fourth- and fifth-grade students. Students have a designed place to socialize, complete with vending machines for after-school snacks. The library provides youth programming and help with school assignments.

The opportunities for public library, school library media center, and classroom links are limited only by the creativity of the people in charge. It's important to remember that the team is not complete without the general manager. Library media specialists are much more than distributors of books. They are key players in the great game of reading.

References

American Association of School Librarians and Association for Educational Communications and Technology. 1988. *Information Power: Guidelines for School Library Media Programs*. Chicago: American Library Association.

Anderson, Richard C., Elfrieda H. Hiebert, Judith A. Scott, and Ian A. G. Wilkinson. 1985. *Becoming a Nation of Readers: The Report of the Commission on Reading*. Champaign-Urbana, IL: Center for the Study of Reading.

Barron, Daniel, and Timothy J. Bergen, Jr. 1992. "Information Power: The Restructured School Library for the Nineties." *Phi Delta Kappan* 73 (March): 521-525.

Fox, Beth Wheeler. 1988. *The Dynamic Community Library*. Chicago and London: American Library Association.

Humphrey, Jack W. 1992. "The Glitzy Labyrinth of Nonprint Media Is Winning the Battle with Books." *Phi Delta Kappan* 73 (March): 538.

Loertscher, David V. 1988. *Taxonomies of the School Library Media Programs*. Englewood, CO: Libraries Unlimited.

Woolls, Blanche. 1988. *Managing School Library Media Programs*. Englewood, CO: Libraries Unlimited.

17

Communities Supporting the Home Team

Athletic teams thrive on the community's support. The home-team advantage is well known. Readers, too, can thrive on the community's interest in and support of their activities.

Inviting the Community Members In

Celebrity Readers' Day

Invite local celebrities such as political figures, popular entertainers, sports figures, TV and radio personalities, and school administrators to visit the school to talk about why reading is important to them and then share several of their favorite books. When I was invited to participate in such a program, the committee provided the guest readers with a list of books that would be appropriate for the various grade levels. The celebrity readers received their assigned grade level well in advance, so if they wished, they could find some new favorite books. The appropriateness of the reading material helped ensure that the experience would be a positive one for both the children and the guests.

It's important to think of some way to thank the guests. All that is really needed is a "thank you package" from the children with their notes, pictures, or written reactions. Those special notes and pictures from children are among my favorite possessions.

Mystery Reader, or "Guess Who Came to Read Today"

This activity is similar to the one described above, although in this case an opaque screen is set up in the room and a "mystery reader" reads from behind the screen. The children try to guess the identity of the mystery reader. Readers have included a much-loved police officer who has traffic duty near the school, a favorite bus driver, a room mother or father, and a regular volunteer.

The Great American Read Aloud/ Night of a Thousand Stars

This nationwide event, sponsored by the American Library Association, also features celebrity readers. During National Library Week and School Library Media Month, more than 1,000 libraries nationwide participate in what the American Library Association calls "the nation's biggest pro-literacy event." The events planned at local, regional, and national levels focus national attention on

- the pleasures of reading aloud
- the importance of parents and children reading together
- librarians as leaders in promoting literacy
- how books and libraries change lives

Throughout the nation, guest readers share their love of reading by reading aloud from favorite books and sharing how books and libraries have made a difference in their lives. Former First Lady Barbara Bush, Charlton Heston, Kathie Lee Gifford, Ellen Burstyn, Wolfman Jack, Washington Redskin Art Monk, governors, and mayors are among the well-known people who have participated.

Volunteers of Many Talents

Community volunteers can add so much to the school, and they can gain so much from their special relationship with children. Children always need an adult to read to them or listen to them read. Volunteers can help in the reading centers and in the publishing center (reading, editing, typing, binding), can play reading games with the children, and can work with small groups on projects—the list is never ending. It's very important to remember the three *R*'s of working with volunteers: Recruit, Recognize, and Retain. Volunteers will be interested in continuing their work with the schools if they feel valued. Certainly much of the value is intrinsic, but don't neglect the external recognition.

Great Book Discussion Leaders

Community members may be interested in receiving the training to be Junior Great Book discussion leaders. The discussions are great noontime or after-school activities. For information about the program, write to

Junior Great Books Program
35 E. Wacker Drive, Suite 2300
Chicago, IL 60601-2298
You may also call them at 1-800-222-4870.

The Community Welcoming Readers

Bags and Books

Hugo's, a local grocery store in Grand Forks, North Dakota, invited the children to decorate grocery bags with scenes from or advertisements for their favorite books. Judy Hager, the librarian in the participating school, reported the project was a great success; "however, it wouldn't have happened without a good volunteer who was willing to transport 800 sacks to and from the grocery store." Ms. Hager added, "A number of community people wrote to children who had decorated their bag to thank them for their good work and encourage them to continue reading. It meant so much to the children to be recognized by someone they didn't even know."

Window Displays

During a special week such as National Education Week or National Library Week, stores invite children to decorate a store window with a display promoting reading. Some stores assign their window display expert to work with the kids to create something unique and eye appealing. High school distributive education students may also be able to provide the expertise. Many parents and children are seen strolling by the windows to view classroom creations, and a few stop to shop. The Tattered Cover, a Denver bookstore, has real people reading in its window display.

The Mall

Each year the mall in Grand Forks, North Dakota, cooperates with the Lake Agassiz Reading Council to sponsor a reading event. The one I remember best was Rocking Chair Reading. In honor of North Dakota's 100th anniversary, 100 rocking chairs with 100 readers took their places in the mall. Throughout the day volunteers read to small groups of children. Sometimes the children stayed for the whole hour; others stayed for a story or two, then left. Throughout the day, on the hour, 100 new readers came. Colorful storybook characters welcomed the children to the area and helped them find a reader.

Incentive Programs

In chapter 12, I mentioned a few incentive programs provided by local businesses. Look creatively at local businesses and help them look creatively at themselves. A company as mundane as the bus company might provide a "celebrity bus trip" for readers who reach their reading goals. Winners wear a button reading, "I'm a celebrity reader." The trip ends at the local ice cream store or in the office of a store owner or public relations person. There everyone enjoys a cone and the students share a favorite book with the hosts.

School and Business Partnerships

School and business partnerships can be not only a wonderful asset to the school but also a very special opportunity for a business and its employees. In a 1993 personal interview, Mike Johnson, principal at West School in Grand Forks, North Dakota, describes the school's budding relationship with Minnkota Power Company: "We started in September with a challenge. Our big push this year is on reading and writing and we just don't have enough hands to edit and publish." Minnkota Power's publication staff of writers and graphic artists have invited West

School's first-graders to write an anthology and visit the plant for a tour. The tour will end in the publishing department, where students will watch their book being printed and bound. Students in other grades will do the same.

Before the visit the students will learn about the company and the power industry so they can be informed observers. "We hope," stated Mr. Johnson, "that during the tour students will not only learn about the industry first hand but will observe 'real people' using reading and writing every day in the workplace."

It's important to remember that children have things they can offer in a partnership relationship beyond the public relations opportunities. Johnson stresses, "In a partnership, we feel it's very important that we give something back to the company, therefore we've offered to do entertainment programs for the staff at the plant, provide artwork for the offices, and decorate for special company events; we have also invited employees to use our gymnasium for the evening." Johnson hopes one of the graphic artists will develop a logo for the partnership that can be a symbol for both the children and the Minnkota employees of the important work that children and adults can do together.

Companies in other parts of the country have other types of school partnerships. One company built a simple, large display rack and stocked it with about 200 books at various grade levels. Employees were encouraged to take one hour off a month to visit a classroom to read with a child on company time. Another company offered one hour a month to employees who would visit a school to help children edit their writing. I can imagine that the intrinsic rewards to the employees are enormous. Other business partnerships on the national level will be discussed in chapter 18.

Athletic team players love to be cheered on. They need to know the community is behind them. The community can provide the same kind of support for readers, whether it is by volunteering in the school, by inviting readers into their business places, by recognizing and celebrating readers, or by establishing creative school and business partnerships.

References

Johnson, Michael. 1993. Interview with author. Grand Forks, North Dakota, January 11.

18

A Few Equivalents

of the NFL, NBA

National Organizations Supporting and Promoting Reading

Certainly, with or without the national organizations that support and promote athletics, sports would still be played on local fields and in backyards. Balls would still be bounced against backstops attached to garages, and balls would still be hit through Ms. Fredrich's side window, which has the misfortune of facing the schoolyard. Yet, there is something about the big leagues. Does the big league give the sport and the players prestige and visibility? Do the big leaguers provide role models for young athletes, something to reach for? Do the national organizations help create interest in the sport, excitement, and the ultimate forum for the play?

Reading has some big leagues, too: national organizations that support and promote the sport. Some, like the Reading Is Fundamental organization, promote reading as their sole mission; others, like Pizza Hut, support reading through various corporate activities. Many of the organizations not only promote the sport but also get the balls and bats of reading—books and newspapers—into the hands of kids. Without the equipment it's pretty hard to play the game.

Reading Is Fundamental and Its Corporate Supporters

The Reading Is Fundamental annual report for 1991 (1992, 3) tells of RIF's beginning. In 1966, Margaret McNamara worked as a volunteer in Washington's inner-city public schools tutoring children who were struggling to become readers. "She found that most of them had never owned their own books. When she invited one child to choose a book to keep as his own, his enthusiastic response convinced her to act." She and a group of concerned parents went to work, inspired by a simple idea: to make books available to children, books they could choose and keep.

From that single neighborhood project, Reading Is Fundamental has evolved into a nationwide network of more than 4,300 community-based projects. Though local programs work independently and vary among schools, they basically follow the same pattern. RIF volunteers—parents, teachers, librarians—sponsor fundraisers and solicit donations from local business, citizen's groups, even college fraternities. (Matching federal funding is available for some existing programs, but due to budget cutbacks, new programs must raise all their own funds.) Then a committee buys books, at a discount, from publishers. Most groups plan activities to spark interest in books. Three times a year distributions are held; children browse and select a book to keep. RIF's vital statistics for 1991 are shown in figure 18.1.

Fig. 18.1. Reading Is Fundamental program statistics for 1991 (*RIF Newsletter*, Washington, DC, 1992).

RIF Vital Statistics for 1991

	Totals
Children Served	2,828,649
Volunteers Involved	141,890
Projects	4,308
Sites	14,075
Books Distributed	9,046,624

In addition to its regular community-based programs, RIF has created several programs to serve populations with special needs.

Project Open Book. Homeless children are at risk educationally and psychologically. They have little continuity in their disrupted lives and few personal belongings. Project Open Book believes that books can be "friends in strange places" and that owning books can be a real comfort. This RIF project establishes reading corners in homeless shelters, special corners where children can do homework, choose a book to keep, or sit quietly to read a favorite story. In 1991, Project Open Book reached 20,000 children at 65 shelters located in 22 states. At the Open Book sites RIF also distributes a *Family Facts* booklet, which reinforces the parents' role as their children's most important teacher. Open Book receives donations of books from publishers and book distributors and support from Xerox Foundation and several individuals.

Running Start. This program was created with a $2.1 million grant from the Chrysler Corporation Fund. Running Start was designed to give first-graders a tangible goal: to read or have read to them 21 books during a 10-week Reading Challenge. Students receive a free book and a certificate of accomplishment for meeting the Running Start Reading Challenge and have opportunities to win other prizes as well. Families are invited to participate in free reading rallies, festive events featuring tips to encourage reading success. Teachers receive a handbook of creative classroom ideas and send-home activities as well as posters, stickers, bookmarks, and other colorful incentives to make the Reading Challenge fun for students. The program is offered in 10 cities where Chrysler has plants. In 1991, Running Start reached 34,000 first-graders in 361 schools.

Shared Beginnings. In the annual report, RIF (1992, 10) reports, "Every 64 seconds in America an infant is born to a teenage mother. It is unlikely that these young mothers have finished high school. Though they want a better life for themselves and their children, their children are at grave risk of growing up poor and without the literacy skills needed to succeed in school or in life." With a grant from the New York Life Foundation, RIF designed a program to enable teen parents to help create a legacy of reading and learning for their young families. Teen parents learn that literacy skills begin developing when their children are infants. They come to believe that books and reading are important to a baby's well-being. The program empowers these young parents to assume with confidence their role as their children's first and most important teacher. They read, talk, and sing to their babies. Field tests confirm that the program had a tremendous influence on the child-parent bond.

Family of Readers. This pilot project underwritten by Kraft General Foods Foundation, centers on the training of adult learners to run an RIF reading motivation program for their own children. To guide parents through the steps of running a reading motivation program, RIF has developed a Family of Readers Club Handbook. The project is being piloted at 11 sites, where staff provide adult education and parent training.

Reading Is Fundamental Partnerships for Literacy

RIF often works in partnership with corporations and civic organizations who want to make a difference in the lives of children. Here are a few of the partnerships that could serve as models for other national, state, or local organizations.

UGI Corporation. The UGI Corporation, a Pennsylvania utility, not only provides money to support RIF programs but also encourages employees to volunteer to work on RIF projects in their local communities. UGI advertised RIF's Parent Guide brochures in the employee magazine to help parents learn how to motivate their own children to read.

ARCO Foundation. The ARCO Foundation supports grassroots literacy initiatives in communities where ARCO employees live and work. In 1991, ARCO funds helped RIF deliver books and motivational activities throughout Alaska. Many Alaskan villages are remote and isolated and cannot provide young readers with adequate access to books. ARCO supplements book budgets to enable communities to offer children the means to read for pleasure. Since 1990, ARCO has provided funds for projects in Houston and Dallas, Texas, that serve low-income, at-risk, often minority populations, including Native American, Hispanic, and Filipino children.

Santa Fe Pacific Foundation. In 1991, the Foundation supported RIF projects serving more than 59,000 children who live in communities along the Santa Fe Railroad lines in the Midwest and Far West. Santa Fe monies have meant that projects serving mostly disadvantaged youth are able to provide books and activities to prepare these children for literate adulthood.

Kiwanis projects. Kiwanis International, through its Priority One initiative, has provided resources across the country to help children between birth and age five. During the first year, there were 153 new Kiwanis-sponsored RIF programs serving nearly 33,000 preschoolers. Kiwanis International also provided the funds to print 50,000 copies of the *Family Facts* booklet, which is given to every family served by the Kiwanis Priority One program. The booklet provides a place for parents to keep track of essential information relating to their children's health and educational needs and includes tips to help parents encourage their children's reading and learning.

Hallmark Corporate Foundation. This foundation sponsors RIF's National Poster Contest inviting hundreds of thousands of children to celebrate the joys of reading through art. A national panel of judges selects a winning poster, a number of runners-up, and honorable mentions from every state. These posters are exhibited at different locations around the country. And the winning artist comes to Washington, D.C., to be honored during RIF Week, to celebrate and represent the many thousands of RIF kids who entered the contest.

Student Loan Marketing Association (Sallie Mae). This organization provided the challenge grant that launched RIF's Arkansas initiative aimed at reaching fourth-grade public school students to help them avert "the fourth-grade slump." By the second year of the project, nearly 80 percent of Arkansas's fourth-graders were participating in projects at their local schools.

Metropolitan Life Foundation. RIF and the Metropolitan Life Foundation sponsor an annual event, In Celebration of Reading. Children from every RIF project are invited to participate in the program. During a specified two-week period, RIF children read for pleasure and qualify to be entered in their local Celebration drawing. Local winners' names are sent to the national RIF office for a final drawing to select the National RIF Reader. The National RIF Reader goes to Washington, D.C., to be honored during RIF Week and to represent the other RIF kids who participated.

MCA/Universal Studios, Amblin Entertainment, and Nabisco Biscuit Company. These companies sponsored a nationwide campaign to encourage young people to choose a buddy and read. It all began with a mouse named Fievel Mouskewitz, star of Steven Spielberg's *An American Tail*. Spielberg's Amblin Entertainment allowed Fievel to become the official "mousecot" of the new literacy program. The Reading Buddies program encourages students to choose a reading buddy, as long as one of the buddies is between 2 and 12 years old and they have fun reading together. After the program was announced in Los Angeles, Nabisco followed up with a national promotion of free Reading Buddies kits featuring Fievel and including a Reading Buddies newsletter, bookmarks, bookplated membership cards, and a host of other incentives to encourage students to become reading buddies. Hundreds of thousands of reading buddies sent away for Reading Buddies kits. The partnership sponsored other related activities, including:

- An all-day event that included a world premiere screening of Fievel's movie, *An American Tail—Fievel Goes West*, followed by a party with a western theme, where students were invited to create and publish their own books about the Old West.

- A four-page advertorial in *Parenting Magazine* entitled "How to Raise a Reader," which included information on the Reading Buddies program.

- A 10-minute program about Reading Buddies viewed by 37 million viewers watching Spielberg's *E.T.*

These are just a few of the many organizations and corporations who sponsor promotional campaigns and special events to help fund RIF activities. If you are like me, you like to support businesses who support kids. You can obtain a list of those activities and programs by writing to RIF at

Reading Is Fundamental, Inc.
Smithsonian Institution
600 Maryland Avenue, Suite 500
Washington, DC 20024
Or you may call them at (202) 287-3220.

RIF also offers a number of attractive, inexpensive, and practical books, booklets, and parent guide brochures. Many of their materials have been referred to in other parts of this book. For a complete list of their materials, you may write to RIF at the above address.

Center for the Book

The Center for the Book in the Library of Congress was established in 1977 to strengthen and celebrate the role of books in the human endeavor. The coalition brings authors, publishers, booksellers, librarians, readers, and interested corporations and foundations together. Through its projects and publications, it stimulates public interest in books and in reading. The Center is a successful public-private partnership; the Library of Congress supports the four full-time positions, but its programs and publications are funded through contributions from individuals, corporations, professional associations, civic organizations, libraries, schools, labor units, and foundations. In the *Encyclopedia of Library and Information Science* (U.S. Library of Congress 1992, 2), John Cole states, "In promoting the concept of a 'community of the book' that works cooperatively on behalf of book culture, the Center for the Book has become a public voice and a national advocate of books, reading, and libraries."

The Center's program includes reading promotion projects with four national television networks, symposia, lectures, exhibits, publications, multimedia projects, and special events that honor anniversaries or individual achievement in the world of books. The Center for the Book has a partner for each of its activities. Examples of partnership programs include National Young Reader's Day, Read More About It, and Literary Heritage of the States project.

National Young Reader's Day. Each November, in cooperation with the Center for the Book, Pizza Hut sponsors the annual celebration of National Young Reader's Day. Pizza Hut also produced a beautiful four-fold brochure promoting the 1992 theme, "Explore New Worlds—READ!" The brochure presented practical ideas for individuals and families, schools and libraries, national and state organizations and their affiliates, and business and labor organizations to remind Americans of the joys and importance of reading as a way of learning about the world.

Read More About It. The Library of Congress/CBS Television's Read More About It may be the best-known promotion. Thirty-second reading messages from the Library of Congress send viewers to their local libraries and bookstores to "read more about" the subject of the program. An estimated 20 million viewers, the largest audience ever reached by a "Read More About It" message, saw the announcement that suggested books about baseball during the fourth game of the World Series on October 20, 1990.

Literary Heritage of the States. The Library of Congress received a $503,329 grant from the Lila Wallace-Reader's Digest Fund for The Literary Heritage of the States, a three-year education and traveling exhibition. The project will develop literary maps depicting places and people that are part of America's literary heritage. Beginning in the spring of 1993, two traveling exhibitions featuring reproductions of these colorful maps will travel from coast to coast. The grant will also support an illustrated exhibit catalog, research in the Library of Congress's collections about the literary heritage of each state, and the development of new forms and educational uses of literary maps.

Each year the Center for the Book initiates national reading promotion themes that can be used by organizations throughout America to promote books; for example, the theme for 1991 was "The Year of the Lifetime Reader"; 1992, "Explore New Worlds—READ!"; and 1993, "Books Change Lives." More than 100 educational and civic organizations are partners; each uses the theme and develops projects at the national or local level.

In addition to national organizations and corporate sponsors, participation in national reading promotion campaigns comes from the 27 state Centers for the Book. Each state center is a voluntary statewide coalition that has been formed to work with the national Center for the Book to promote books, reading, and the state's intellectual and literary heritage. State centers plan and fund their own projects, drawing from the state's "community of the book," including authors, publishers, educators, librarians, and lovers of books and reading.

Since its establishment, the Center for the Book has sponsored more than 65 publications, ranging from small pamphlets to major scholarly works. The subjects vary, demonstrating the Center's interest in all aspects of the world of books.

For more information about the Center for the Book, write to

John Y. Cole
Director
Center for the Book
Library of Congress
Washington, DC 20540

A Sample of Other Organizations That Support Reading

Cargill

Cargill, a Minneapolis-based merchandiser and processor of agricultural commodities, has joined with the 53,000-member American Library Association to develop an international literacy outreach project. The heart of the project is Cargill volunteers developing their own projects in partnership with local librarians and literacy groups to encourage reading and literacy skills among family members in local communities. Partners For Family Literacy resource kits have been distributed to over 800 Cargill offices worldwide and to public libraries in those countries and communities where Cargill has a presence. The kit provides information on how to develop activities that bring parents and children together to cultivate reading and literacy skills. Included are

- Ideas for family literacy projects
- Tips on how to organize a volunteer project
- Recruiting tips
- Media tips
- Tips for parents

Since the partnership was launched in January 1992, the company has had many noteworthy successes. Cargill's North Star Steel facility in Houston presented a $5,000 gift to the local library for a parents' reading room, where parents learn to read to their children. In addition, the Cargill Grain office and the Rantoul (Illinois) Public Library are working together with local groups to get every member of the community to stop doing whatever he or she is doing at a specific time and read together. Local radio and press media have pledged their support.

As of October 1992, Cargill had registered more than 135 projects in 25 states. Typical local community partners include the 4-H, Girl Scouts, local literacy councils, elementary schools, homeless shelters, Head Start, and Literacy Volunteers of America.

Osram Sylvania

In the fall of 1992, Sylvania launched a program called America's Official Reading Time.™ Robert Brands, the company's marketing manager, said, "As we viewed the statistics on the country's illiteracy rate we became very concerned and knew we wanted to do something." From that concern, the company developed a three-tier program to promote a family reading time from 7:00 to 8:00 every night. Brands said, "We wanted it to be a specific 'tangible' time so people could focus and it could become an 'official' reading time."

During the first phase, the program focused on public awareness concerning the illiteracy issues in the United States. In the second phase, the program encouraged parents to promote reading. Along with RIF, the company developed a 16-page booklet entitled *How to Get Kids Excited About Reading*, which included a guide to materials and creative ideas for parents. By early 1993, over a half million copies had been distributed through retail distributors and schools. The last phase of the project is, as described by Brands, a grass-roots effort by local retailers. For example, when a consumer buys a Sylvania lighting product, the consumer can send in a coupon for the free parent booklet. Banners appear in retail stores, "Reading Is a Bright Thing to Do." Other promotional activities are being planned at the local level.

Chrysler

Chrysler Corporation has joined together with Meredith Publishing, the American Federation of Teachers, and the Association for Supervision and Curriculum Development in a program called the Chrysler Learning Connection. In addition to the Running Start program, which we have already discussed, the coalition is sponsoring a number of other activities and publications.

Learning at Every Turn and *Recipes for Reading Success*. *Learning at Every Turn*, a 30-minute video, and *Recipes for Reading Success*, a 24-page company booklet, shows how families can build reading fun into every family activity. The video and booklet are free to interested families as long as supplies last. Order blanks can be obtained at local Chrysler product dealerships.

Three Advertorials. Three advertorials will be published in 12 family-oriented magazines, which have a combined circulation of 21,970,000. The theme for January of 1993 was "Making Reading a Family Affair." The 12-page advertorial includes topics such as "Reading Together for a Change," "Don't Wait for the School to Involve You, Involve the School," "Is Your Child Ready to Learn," "Tips for TV Use," "Home Is Where Reading Happens," "Five Questions to Ask Your Child's Teacher," and "Parent's Bookshelf." In March 1993, the theme for the advertorial was "Reading About What Matters" and in May 1993, the theme was "Reading, Writing and Creativity."

Sweepstakes. Parents may enter their children's school (K-8) to win a $1,000 School Library Award. Fifty schools will be chosen at random for the award.

Newspaper Association of America Foundation

Through its educational services department, the NAA Foundation sponsors three interrelated programs in literacy and education: Newspaper in Education, Family Focus, and Press to Read. Each addresses a key objective of the Foundation: "developing informed and intelligent newspaper readers."

Newspaper in Education. Since 1965, the Foundation has maintained a leadership role as a clearinghouse of information on Newspaper in Education (NIE) programs across North America. The NIE program is a cooperative effort of newspapers working with local schools to use the newspaper as a tool for instruction. Under the program, newspapers provide copies, usually at a reduced rate, to schools for use in their classrooms. They also sponsor teacher-education programs and offer curriculum materials to help schools use the newspaper as a meaningful resource for student learning. More information about this program can be found in chapter 11.

Family Focus. This intergenerational literacy program was designed to help parents use the newspaper with their children to promote reading and communications skills. Family Focus is a collaborative effort of the NAA Foundation, the International Reading Association, the National Association of Elementary School Principals, the National PTA, the National Association of Secondary School Principals, the National Middle School Association, and the American Association of School Administrators. The Family Focus project encourages representatives from each of the sponsoring organizations to get together to carry out the parent program in the local elementary or middle school. The Family Focus kits provide materials for 90-minute presentations for parents. It has a leader's guide, including sample programs and publishing aids, and a reproducible brochure for parents.

Press to Read. The Press to Read program encourages and assists newspapers in the development of adult literacy programs. Although this is not a child-oriented program, it deserves mention. When we help an adult become literate, we may be providing one more positive role model for children.

In addition to the activities mentioned above, the NAA Foundation in conjunction with local newspapers, the Center for the Book, and 27 sponsors produced an eight-page special supplement entitled *To Read*, which was delivered to millions of homes on Sunday, September 6, 1992. The supplement, which included a read-aloud story, also contained articles on national goals, reading at home, reading success programs, and other topics. Another special supplement is planned for 1993.

For information about these and other programs sponsored by the NAA Foundation, write to

The Newspaper Center
1160 Sunrise Valley Drive
Reston, VA 22091
You may also call (703) 648-1251.

It is beyond the scope of this book to mention the hundreds of corporations, civic organizations, professional associations, and labor unions that support reading, books, and children. The list is long, prestigious, and a bit awe-inspiring. Parents, teachers, administrators, and kids are not alone. These organizations do more than cheer. They get books into the hands of kids, they support programs for parents, they keep reading on the national agenda, and they promote events that inspire and reward readers.

References

Brands, Robert. 1993. Telephone interview with author. January 21.

Reading Is Fundamental, Inc. 1992. *Reading Is Fundamental Annual Report, 1991*. Washington, DC: RIF.

U.S. Library of Congress, Center for the Book. 1992. *Encyclopedia of Library and Information Science*. Vol. 49. Washington, DC: Library of Congress.

19

Every Player a Winner

The children step out into center field blinded by the blaze of lights. At first they are terrified, unsure whether they have "the right stuff."

Then they see, standing in the shadows, some of the players who have gone before them, players who have played and won. One gives the children the thumbs-up sign.

Their parents are in the front row, partially hidden by the Coca-Cola sign. They've done the right things for their children, encouraging and nurturing their budding talent. But will it be enough for the big game?

Their coach sits quietly, reflecting on the time spent with the children. The children nod their heads almost imperceptibly to the coach as they take their positions on the field. The coach's confident smile makes each player stand a little taller.

Though they stand for the first moment as individuals, they are honed to be a team. They know how to make the best of each player's talent. The playing field is just right tonight. Special care was taken for the big game.

The children know the game inside and out. They've worked as sports writers, announcers, and publicists, so they understand all aspects of the game. They've reviewed play-by-plays; they've worked out religiously in the weight room—they're ready!

What a promotion the national league has given the event! The stands are overflowing. The cheerleaders race onto the field. The enthusiastic roar of the hometown fans shatters the children's introspection.

The umpire shouts, "Play ball!" And the game begins.

■ ■ ■ ■ ■

In this game, in the great sport of reading, there are no losers. If we get books into the hands of kids, encourage them, give them reasons to read, and create opportunities for them to respond, they will indeed be participants and players in the reading game. The only way to lose is not to play the game. For after all, Reading Is Not a Spectator Sport.

Appendix A
Booklists

Annual Lists

The following organizations publish annual lists of recommended books. Some are comprehensive lists of favorites, marked *(C)*; others include only books published in the previous year. Bulk rates are also available. (SASE indicates that a self-addressed, stamped 4¼-by-9½-inch envelope should be included with order.)

The American Library Association (ALA), 50 East Huron Street, Chicago, IL 60611. Enclose SASE with 2 oz. postage for each copy ordered.

Best Books for Young Adults. $.50 with SASE.

Notable Children's Books (annual). Titles with short descriptions. $.50 with SASE.

Recommended Books for Reluctant Readers. $1 with SASE.

The Child Study Children's Book Committee (CSCBC), Bank Street College, 610 West 112th Street, New York, NY 10025.

Children's Books of the Year, 1990 edition. Describes more than 500 titles. $4.

Paperback Books for Children: A Selected List Through Age 13. *(C)* Titles with short descriptions. $4.

Children's Book Council, CBC Order Center, 350 Scotland Road, Orange, NJ 07050.

Notable Children's Trade Books in the Field of Social Studies. Appears in April/May issue of *Social Education*. Send SASE.

Outstanding Science Trade Books for Children. Appears in March issue of *Science and Children*. Send SASE.

Cooperative Children's Books, P.O. Box 5288, Madison, WI 53705-0288.

CCBC Choices (annual spring). Annotated booklist. Send SASE.

The Horn Book, Inc. 14 Beacon Street, Boston, MA 02108.

Children's Classics: A Book List for Parents. *(C)* Lists favorite titles for babies and toddlers through young adults. $3, plus $.50 postage and handling.

The International Reading Association-Children's Book Council Joint Committee (IRA-CBC), 800 Barksdale Road, P.O. Box 8139, Newark, DE 19714-8139.

Children's Choices (annual). Titles with short descriptions. $1. From the Superintendent of Documents, U.S. Government Printing Office, Washington, DC 20402.

Teacher's Choices (annual). Lists books recommended by teachers. Enclose a 9-by-12-inch SASE with 2 oz. postage for each copy ordered.

Books and Indexes

Adventuring with Books: A Booklist for Pre-K-Grade 6. Mary Jett-Simpson, ed. Champaign-Urbana, IL: NCTE, 1989.

Contains notations on nearly 1,800 recommended children's books published between 1984 and 1988.

Alternative Press Publishers of Children's Books: A Directory. 4th ed. K. T. Horning, ed. Madison, WI: Friends of the CCBC, 1991.

Lists names and addresses of small presses in the United States and Canada that publish one or more books for children and indicates the types of books published by each.

Beyond Picture Books: A Guide to First Readers. B. Barstow and J. Riggle, eds. New York: R. R. Bowker, 1989.

Annotates 1,610 recommended books published between 1951 and 1989 written for beginning readers or first- or second-grade children.

The Bookfinder: When Kids Need Books. Sharen Spredemann Dreyer, ed. Champaign-Urbana, IL: NCTE, 1989.

Matches books to the needs and problems of children and young people.

"Books for Junior High Years," *Focus* (Spring 1989): 115. James E. Davis and Hazel K. Davis, eds.

This special issue of *Focus* is devoted to literature especially suited to the junior high and middle school years and ways to approach that literature with students.

Books for You: A Booklist for Senior High Students. Richard E. Abrahamson and Betty Carter, eds. Champaign-Urbana, IL: NCTE, 1988.

Nearly 1,200 new books of high literary quality and high interest to teenage readers.

Books for You: A Booklist for Senior High Students. Shirley Wurth, ed. Champaign-Urbana, IL: NCTE, 1992.

Contains nearly 800 plot summaries of current books for young adults.

Children's Books in Print. New York: R. R. Bowker. Published annually.

Provides index of juvenile titles that are listed in publishers' catalogs as "in print," but it doesn't always include smaller publishing companies.

The Children's Catalog. 16th ed. J. Yaakov, ed. New York: H. W. Wilson, 1991.

Part 1 lists books and magazines recommended for preschool children through sixth grade. The descriptive entries often include quotes from book reviews. Part 2 includes author, title, subject, and analytical listings. A new edition is published every five years with supplements provided by subscribers annually.

Dreyer, S. S. *The Bookfinder: A Guide to Children's Literature About the Needs and Problems of Youth Aged 2-15*. Circle Pines, MN: American Guidance Service, 1977, 1981, 1985, 1989.

The book is arranged so users can locate books on a particular subject relating to children's needs and problems.

The Elementary School Library Collection: A Guide to Books and Other Media. 18th ed. L. Lee, ed. Williamsport, PA: Brodart, 1992.

In addition to books and periodicals, this volume also recommends all kinds of nonprint media and resources for teachers and parents. It includes reading and interest levels. Revised edition is published biennially.

Gillespie, J. T., and C. J. Naden. *Best Books for Children: Preschool Through Grade 6*. 4th ed. New York: R. R. Bowker, 1990.

Contains one-sentence annotations for more than 11,000 books recommended by at least one reviewer that were still in print in 1989.

High Interest, Easy Reading: A Booklist for Junior and Senior High School Students. William J. McBride, ed. Champaign-Urbana, IL: NCTE, 1990.

Contains 400 concise annotations of books that have been highly recommended for reluctant adolescent readers.

Lima, C. W., and J. A. Lima. *A to Zoo: Subject Access to Children's Picture Books*. 3d ed. New York: R. R. Bowker, 1989.

Indicates the subject matter of 12,000 picture books with access through author, illustration, title, and 700 subjects.

Lipson, Eden. *The New York Times Parent's Guide to the Best Books for Children*. New York: Times Books, 1988.

Literature by and About the American Indians: An Annotated Bibliography. Anna Lee Stenslud, ed. Champaign-Urbana, IL: NCTE, 1979.

Identifies 775 sources that can familiarize the reader with American Indian literature. Introductory essays discuss such themes as the suppression of American Indian culture, literary stereotypes of Indians, and the problem of selecting literature that conveys an accurate picture of Native American life.

Magazines for Children. D. R. Stoll, ed. Newark, DE: IRA, 1990.

Gives addresses for and information about 120 children's periodicals.

Pilla, M. L. *The Best: High/Low Books for Reluctant Readers*. Englewood, CO: Libraries Unlimited, 1990.

Contains brief annotations of 374 quality books that are of interest to reluctant readers. The work is indexed by title, subject, grade level, and reading level.

Richardson, S. K. *Magazines for Children: A Guide for Parents, Teachers, and Librarians*. 2d ed. Chicago: ALA, 1991.

Includes detailed descriptive annotations of 112 magazines for children up to age 14.

The RIF Guide to Encouraging Young Readers. Ruth Graves, ed. Garden City, NY: Doubleday, 1987.

Ryder, R. J., B. B. Graves, and M. F. Graves. *Easy Reading: Book Series and Periodicals for Less Able Readers*. 2d ed. Newark, DE: IRA, 1989.

Evaluates 44 book series and 15 periodicals.

Subject Guide to Children's Books in Print. Published annually. New York: R. R. Bowker.

Provides a subject approach to children's books in print.

Sutherland, Z., B. Hearne, and R. Sutton. *The Best in Children's Books: The University of Chicago Guide to Children's Literature 1985-1990*. Chicago: University of Chicago Press, 1991.

Compiled from reviews of books originally designated as "recommended" in the Bulletin of the Center for Children's Books, each volume annotates the best books published during the inclusive years. See also earlier volumes edited by Zena Sutherland (1973, 1980, 1986) covering, respectively, books published from 1966 to 1972, 1973 to 1978, 1979 to 1984.

Your Reading: A Booklist for Junior High and Middle School Students. A. P. Nilsen, ed. Champaign-Urbana, IL: NCTE, 1991.

Includes annotation of titles published between 1988 and 1990.

Special Topics

Adamson, L. G. *A Reference Guide to Historical Fiction for Children and Young Adults*. New York: Greenwood Press, 1987.

Provides plot summaries of historical fiction written by 80 award-winning authors since 1940.

The Black Experience in Children's Books. New York: New York Public Library, 1989.

Annotates folklore, fiction, and nonfiction that portrays Black life; written for children from preschool to age 12.

Kobrin, G. *Eyeopeners! How to Choose and Use Children's Books About Real People, Places, and Things*. New York: Penguin Books, 1988.

Lists 500 informational books, annotated and organized for access through an index.

Kruse, G. M., and K. T. Horning. *Multicultural Literature for Children and Young Adults: A Selected Listing of Books 1980-1990 by and About People of Color*. 3d ed. Madison, WI: Wisconsin Department of Public Instruction, 1991.

Annotates recently published multicultural books recommended for their high quality by the Children's Cooperative Book Center.

Miller-Lachman, L. *Our Family, Our Friends, Our World: An Annotated Guide to Significant Multicultural Books for Children and Teenagers*. New Providence, NJ: R. R. Bowker, 1991.

Provides critical evaluations of approximately 1,000 fiction and nonfiction books published between 1970 and 1990, with a multicultural and/or international focus.

Appendix B
Bound Books*

Step 1

Determine how many pages will be in the book. Remember to include title, copyright, dedication, and "All About the Author" pages. Also count the number of illustrations you will need and how many pages they will take.

Step 2

Get the determined number of pieces of paper and fold each in half. Stack the pages so the folded edges are on the outside and the open edges are in the center of the book. (This makes the pages sturdier.)

Step 3

Write or type your complete book and put your illustrations onto the pages. Leave a one inch border on the outside edge, the top, and the bottom. Leave a one and a half inch border on the inside. (This allows room for the binding.) Staple the completed, stacked pages together.

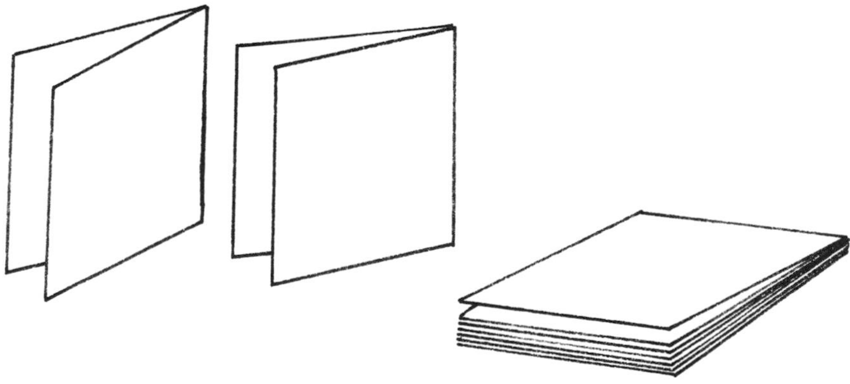

Step 4

Cut two pieces of poster board or cardboard a half inch larger than the folded pages.

*"Bound Books" appears in Deborah Robertson and Patricia Barry, *Super Kids Publishing Company* (Englewood, CO: Teacher Ideas Press, 1990), copyright © 1990 by Libraries Unlimited, and is reprinted with permission.

Step 5

Cut out a piece of wallpaper, contact paper, wrapping paper, or cloth to be your cover. It should be two inches wider all the way around than the combined area of both pieces of poster board or cardboard.

Place the outer covering right side down on the table. Glue the poster board or cardboard side by side on top, with a finger space between the two pieces.

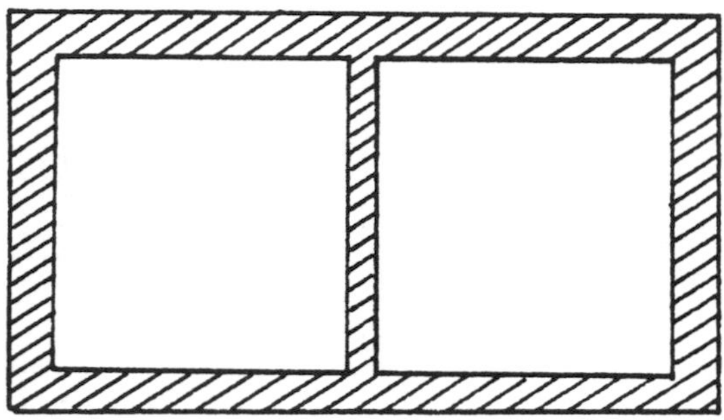

Step 6

Fold the corners of the covering in, then fold the lengthwise edges in, and finally fold the side edges of the covering over the cardboard.

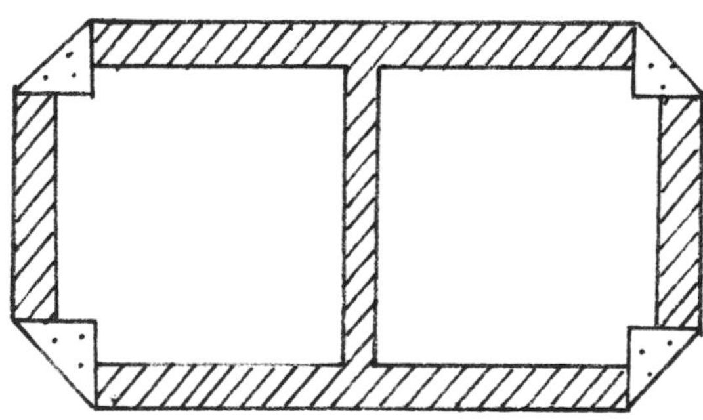

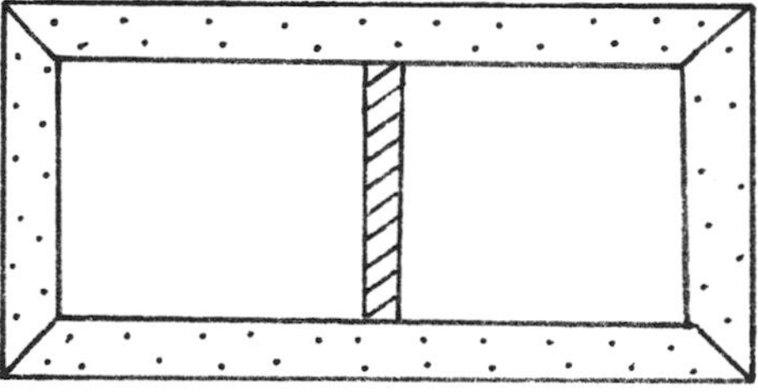

Step 7

Cut a piece of wallpaper, contact paper, wrapping paper, or cloth one-half inch smaller than the poster board or cardboard pieces. Attach to the uncovered side.

You now have a book cover.

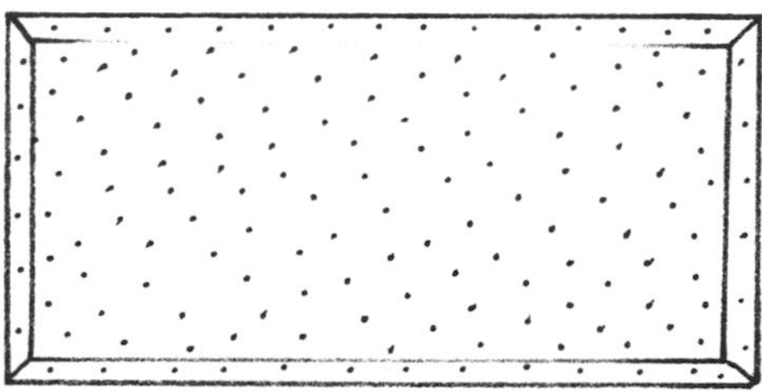

Step 8

Place the completed, stapled pages inside the book cover, directly in the spine.

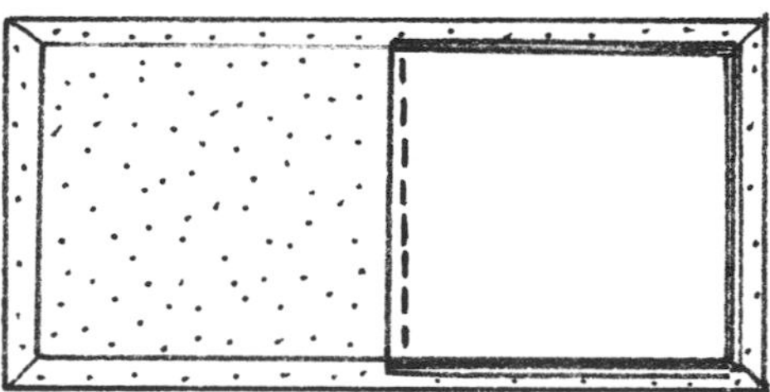

Step 9

Cut two strips of covering materials one inch wide × the length of the book (or use colored plastic tape). Secure the stacked pages to the book cover in the front and the back.

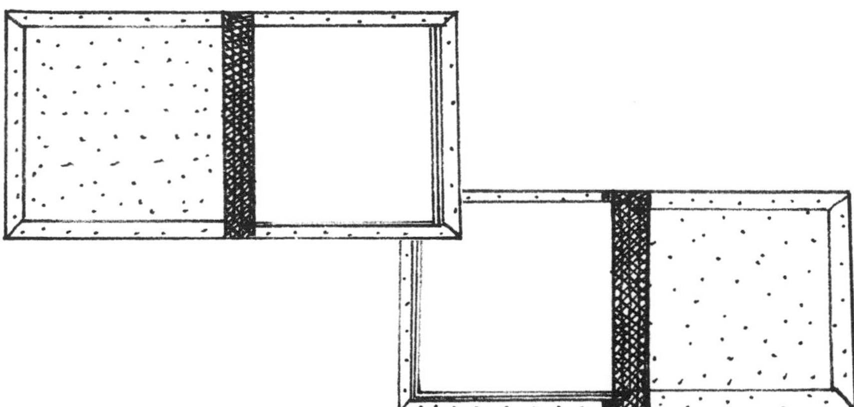

Appendix C
Television Resources

Letters requesting information about programming or advertising can be sent to the networks, government agencies, and the broadcasting industry's trade organization. Also, many of these groups have excellent pamphlets that provide information on the general use of television in teaching.

ABC
1330 Avenue of the Americas
New York, NY 10019
Pamphlet: "Watching Television with Your Children"

CBS
51 West 52nd Street
New York, NY 10019
Pamphlet: "Take a Lesson from TV"

Federal Communications Commission
1919 M Street, NW
Washington, DC 20554

Federal Trade Commission
Bureau of Consumer Protection
Pennsylvania Avenue and Sixth Street, NW
Washington, DC 20036

NBC
RCA Building
New York, NY 10020

PBS
485 L'Enfant Plaza West
Washington, DC 20024

Television Information Office
745 Fifth Avenue
New York, NY 10151
Pamphlet: "How to Help Your Children Get More Out of Television"

Information about memberships, activities, publications, and educational material can be obtained from the following nonprofit consumer groups and educational organizations. Each of these national groups has its own philosophy and priorities for action. You may, therefore, feel more comfortable with one organization than another; or a local group may meet your interests.

Action for Children's Television
20 University Road
Cambridge, MA 02138

International Reading Association
800 Barksdale Road
P.O. Box 8139
Newark, DE 19711

National Black Media Coalition
38 New York Avenue, NE
Washington, DC 20002

National TeleMedia Council
120 East Wilson Street
Madison, WI 53703

National Coalition on Television Violence
P.O. Box 2157
Champaign, IL 61820

National Council for Families and Television
20 Nassau Street
Suite 200
Princeton, NJ 08542

The National PTA
700 North Rush Street
Chicago, IL 60611

People for the American Way
1424 16th Street, NW
Suite 601
Washington, DC 20036

Telecommunications Research and Action Center
P.O. Box 12038
Washington, DC 20005

Four regional centers have developed Critical Television Viewing Skills material for parents, students, and teachers. The centers produce resources for use by different age groups.

(Elementary School)
Southwest Educational Development Laboratory
211 East Seventh Street
Austin, TX 78701

(Middle Grades)
WNET/Thirteen
356 West 58th Street
New York, NY 10019

(High School)
Far West Laboratory for Educational Research and Development
1855 Folsom Street
San Francisco, CA 94103

(Postsecondary)
Boston University School of Public Communications
128 Bay State Road
Boston, MA 02215

Another organization offering materials or courses for parents on how to use television effectively is

Media Action Research Center
475 Riverside Drive
Suite 1370
New York, NY 10027

The following groups provide resources for teachers who want to use television in the school.

Agency for Instructional Television
Box A
Bloomington, IN 47402

On Television Limited
388 Broadway
New York, NY 10013

Prime Time School Television
2427 North Orchard
Chicago, IL 60614

Teacher's Guides to Television
699 Madison Avenue
New York, NY 10021

The following publications, some more critical than others of television and its effect on children, offer suggestions for parents.

Cole, John Y., ed. *Television, the Book and the Classroom*. Washington, DC: Library of Congress, 1978.

Considine, David M., and Gail E. Haley. *Visual Messages: Integrating Imagery into Instruction*. Englewood, CO: Teacher Ideas Press, 1992.

Higgins, Norman, and Howard Sullivan, eds. *Educational Technology Research and Development*. Vol. 38. Washington, DC: Association for Educational Communications and Technology, 1990.

Kaye, Evelyn. *The ACT Guide to Children's Television*. Boston: Beacon Press, 1979.

Logan, Ben, and Kate Moody, eds. *Television Awareness Training: The Viewer's Guide for Family and Community*. New York: Media Action Research Center, 1979.

Moody, Kate. *Growing Up on Television*. New York: Times Books, 1980.

Polk, Lee, and Eda LeShan. *The Incredible Television Machine*. New York: Macmillan, 1977.

Singer, Dorothy, Jerome Singer, and Diana Zuckerman. *Teaching Television: How to Use TV to Your Child's Advantage*. New York: Dial Press, 1981.

Winn, Marie. *Unplugging the Plug-In Drug*. New York: Penguin Books, 1987.

______. *The Plug-In Drug*. New York: Bantam Books, 1984.

Bibliography

Aborn, Carlene. "The Newberys: Getting Them to Read (It Isn't Easy)." In *Motivating Children and Young Adults to Read*, vol. 1, edited by James L. Thomas and Ruth M. Loring. Phoenix, AZ: Oryx Press, 1979.

American Association of School Librarians and Association for Educational Communications and Technology. *Information Power: Guidelines for School Library Media Programs*. Chicago: American Library Association, 1988.

Anderson, Richard, Linda Fielding, and Paul Wilson. "Growth in Reading and How Children Spend Their Time Outside of School." *Reading Research Quarterly* (Summer 1988): 285-303.

Anderson, Richard C., Elfrieda H. Hiebert, Judith A. Scott, and Ian A. G. Wilkinson. *Becoming a Nation of Readers: The Report of the Commission on Reading*. Champaign-Urbana, IL: Center for the Study of Reading, 1985.

Anderson, Walter. *Read with Me: The Power of Reading and How It Transforms Lives*. Boston: Houghton Mifflin, 1990.

Anthony, Rose Marie. *Fun with Choral Speaking*. Englewood, CO: Libraries Unlimited, 1990.

Artley, A. S. "Good Teachers of Reading—Who Are They?" *The Reading Teacher* 29 (1975): 26-31.

Atkinson, Margaret, ed. *The Children's Bookroom*. Staffordshire, England: Trentham, 1989.

Atwell, Nancie. *In the Middle: Writing, Reading, and Learning with Adolescents*. Portsmouth, NH: Heinemann, 1987.

Bachner, Saul. "Sports Literature and the Teaching of Reading: Grab Them and Move Them." *Clearing House* 57 (March 1984): 313-314.

Barchers, Suzanne I. *Creating and Managing the Literate Classroom*. Englewood, CO: Teacher Ideas Press, 1990.

Barchers, Suzanne I., and Patricia C. Marden. *Cooking Up U.S. History: Recipes and Research to Share with Children*. Englewood, CO: Teacher Ideas Press, 1991.

Barron, Daniel, and Timothy J. Bergen, Jr. "Information Power: The Restructured School Library for the Nineties." *Phi Delta Kappan* 73 (March 1992): 521-525.

Barton, Bob, and David Booth. *Stories in the Classroom: Storytelling, Reading Aloud and Roleplaying with Children*. Portsmouth, NH: Heinemann, 1990.

Bauer, Caroline Feller. *This Way to Books*. New York: H. W. Wilson, 1983.

Beers, G. K. "Choosing Not to Read: An Ethnographic Study of Seventh-Grade Aliterate Students." Ph.D. diss., University of Houston, 1990.

Berglund, Roberta L., Richard J. Telfer, and Joan E. Heimlich. "Developing a Love of Reading: What Helps, What Hurts." *Northern Illinois University Literacy Research Report No. 7* (July 1991).

Bloom, Wendy, Tony Martin, and Mick Waters. *Managing to Read*. London: Mary Glasgow Publications, 1988.

Bodart, Joni Richards. *The New Booktalker*. Vol. 2. Englewood, CO: Libraries Unlimited, 1993.

______. *The New Booktalker*. Vol. 1. Englewood, CO: Libraries Unlimited, 1992.

______. *Booktalking*. New York: H. W. Wilson, 1986. Video.

______. *Booktalk! 2*. 2d ed. New York: H. W. Wilson, 1985.

Borba, Michele, and Dan Ungaro. *Bookends: Activities, Centers, Contracts, and Ideas Galore to Enhance Children's Literature*. Watervliet, NY: Crest Litho, 1982.

Branston, Peter, and Mark Provis. *Children and Parents Enjoying Reading*. London: Hodder & Stoughton, 1986.

Bromley, Karen D'Angelo. *Webbing with Literature*. Needham Heights, MA: Allyn & Bacon, 1991.

Brown, Hazel, and Brian Cambourne. *Read and Retell*. Portsmouth, NH: Heinemann, 1987.

Bruckerhoff, C. "What Do Students Say About Reading Instruction?" *Clearing House* 51 (1977): 104-107.

Burns, Paul C., and Betty D. Roe. *Reading Activities for Today's Elementary Schools*. Chicago: Rand McNally, 1979.

Butler, Dorothy. *Cushla and Her Books*. Boston: Horn Book, 1975. (First American edition 1980).

Butler, Francelia. *Sharing Literature with Children: A Thematic Anthology*. New York: David M. Kay, 1977.

Butzow, Carol M., and John W. Butzow. *Science Through Children's Literature: An Integrated Approach*. Englewood, CO: Teacher Ideas Press, 1989.

Cairney, Trevor H. *Other Worlds: The Endless Possibilities of Literature*. Portsmouth, NH: Heinemann, 1990.

Callahan, Tom. "Dreaming the Big Dreams: One-Handed Jim Abbott Shines at Spring Training." *Time* 133 (March 20, 1989): 78.

Callaway, Byron. "What Turns Children 'On' or 'Off' in Reading." *Reading Improvement* 18 (Fall 1981): 214-217.

Carlsen, G. Robert, and Anne Sherrill. *Voices of Readers: How We Come to Love Books*. Champaign-Urbana, IL: National Council of Teachers of English, 1988.

Carlton, Lessie, and Robert H. Moore. *Reading, Self-Directive Dramatization and Self-Concept*. Columbus, OH: Charles E. Merrill, 1968.

Carroll, Joyce Armstrong. *Picture Books: Integrated Teaching of Reading, Writing, Listening, Speaking, Viewing, and Thinking*. Englewood, CO: Teacher Ideas Press, 1991.

Carson, Ben, with Cecil Murphey. *Gifted Hands*. Grand Rapids, MI: Zondervan, 1990.

Carter, Betty, and Richard F. Abrahamson. "Nonfiction in a Read-Aloud Program." *Journal of Reading* 34 (May 1991): 638-642.

Champlin, Connie, and Nancy Renfro. *Storytelling with Puppets*. Chicago: American Library Association, 1985.

Ciani, Alfred J. *Motivating Reluctant Readers*. Newark, DE: International Reading Association, 1981.

Clary, Linda Mixon. "Getting Adolescents to Read." *Journal of Reading* 34 (February 1991): 340-345.

Cochrane, Orin, Donna Cochrane, Sharon Scalena, and Ethel Buchanan. *Reading, Writing and Caring*. Winnipeg, Canada: Whole Language Consultants, 1984.

Conley, Patricia R., and Berdell J. Akin. *Comprehension Checkups Grades 1-5: Strategies for Success*. Englewood, CO: Teacher Ideas Press, 1991.

Considine, David M., and Gail E. Haley. *Visual Messages: Integrating Imagery into Instruction*. Englewood, CO: Teacher Ideas Press, 1992.

Covey, Stephen R. *The 7 Habits of Highly Effective People*. New York: Simon & Schuster, 1989.

Criscuolo, Nicholas P. "Motivating the Unmotivated to Read." *Clearing House* 61 (May 1988): 403-405.

Cullum, Carolyn N. *The Storytime Sourcebook*. New York and London: Neal-Schuman, 1990.

Davidson, Josephine. *Teaching and Dramatizing Greek Myths*. Englewood, CO: Teacher Ideas Press, 1989.

Davies, Ruth Ann. *The School Library Media Program: Instructional Force for Excellence*. 3d ed. New York and London: R. R. Bowker, 1979.

Deford, Frank. "A Track Full of Miracles." *Newsweek* 120 (August 10, 1992): 29.

Durant, Will. *Transition: A Sentimental Story of One Mind and One Era*. New York: Simon & Schuster, 1927.

Durkin, D. *Teaching Them to Read*. 4th ed. Boston: Allyn & Bacon, 1983.

Ecroyd, Catherine Ann. "Motivating Students Through Reading Aloud." *English Journal* 80 (October 1991): 76-78.

Egan, Philip J. "Frequent Short Writing: Motivating the Passive Reader." *College Teaching* 37 (Winter 1989): 15-16.

Estes, Thomas, and Julie Johnson. "Twelve Easy Ways to Make Readers Hate Reading (and One Difficult Way to Make Them Love It)." In *Motivating Children and Young Adults to Read*, vol. 2, edited by James L. Thomas and Ruth M. Loring. Phoenix, AZ: Oryx Press, 1983.

Fader, Daniel N., and Elton B. McNeil. *Hooked on Books: Program and Proof*. New York: G. P. Putnam's Sons, 1968.

Fader, Daniel N., James Duggin, Tom Finn, and Elton B. McNeil. *The New Hooked on Books*. New York: Berkley, 1976.

Flack, Jerry D. *Mystery and Detection*. Englewood, CO: Teacher Ideas Press, 1990.

Fox, Beth Wheeler. *The Dynamic Community Library*. Chicago and London: American Library Association, 1988.

Fredericks, Anthony D. *The Integrated Curriculum*. Englewood, CO: Teacher Ideas Press, 1992.

———. *Involving Parents Through Children's Literature: Grades 1-2*. Englewood, CO: Teacher Ideas Press, 1992.

———. *Social Studies Through Children's Literature: An Integrated Approach*. Englewood, CO: Teacher Ideas Press, 1991.

Galda, Lee. "Playing About a Story: Its Impact on Comprehension." *The Reading Teacher* 36, no. 1 (1982): 52-55

"Ghostwriter." New York: Children's Television Workshop, 1992.

Gilbar, Steven. *The Open Door: When Writers First Learned to Read*. Boston: Godine (in association with the Center for the Book in the Library of Congress), 1989.

Gilliland, H. *A Practical Guide to Remedial Reading*. Columbus, OH: Charles E. Merrill, 1978.

Gold, Judith, Linda Greengrass, and Eleanor R. Kulleseid. "Whole Language and Teacher/Librarian Partnerships." *Phi Delta Kappan* 73 (March 1992): 536-537.

Goodland, John I. *A Place Called School: Prospects for the Future*. New York: McGraw-Hill, 1984.

Goodman, Ken S. *What's Whole in Whole Language?* Portsmouth, NH: Heinemann, 1986.

———. "Unity in Reading." In *Theoretical Models and Processes of Reading*, 3d ed., edited by H. Singer and R. Ruddell. Newark, DE: International Reading Association, 1973.

Granowsky, Alvin. "Can I Guarantee My Child's Love of Learning?" *PTA Today* 14 (February 1989): 25.

Graves, Ruth, ed. *The RIF Guide to Encouraging Young Readers*. Garden City, NY: Doubleday, 1987.

Grimes, Marijo. "Finding Hooks to Catch Reluctant Readers." *English Journal* 80 (January 1991): 45-47.

Heathington, B. S., and J. E. Alexander. "Do Classroom Teachers Emphasize Attitudes Toward Reading?" *The Reading Teacher* 37 (1984): 484-488.

Hennings, Dorothy Grant. *Beyond the Read Aloud: Learning to Read Through Listening to and Reflecting on Literature*. Bloomington, IN: The Phi Delta Kappa Educational Foundation, 1992.

Hirumi, Atsusi, and Dennis R. Bowers. "Enhancing Motivation and Acquisition of Coordinate Concepts by Using Concept Trees." *Journal of Educational Research* 84 (May-June 1991): 273-279.

Holbrook, Hilary Taylor. "Motivating Reluctant Readers: A Gentle Push." In *Motivating Children and Young Adults to Read*, vol. 1, edited by James L. Thomas and Ruth M. Loring. Phoenix, AZ: Oryx Press, 1979.

Humphrey, Jack W. "The Glitzy Labyrinth of Nonprint Media Is Winning the Battle with Books." *Phi Delta Kappan* 73 (March 1992): 538.

Jefferson, Casa Thomas. "21 Teacher Tested Ways to Encourage Voluntary Reading." *Journal of Reading* 33 (December 1989): 222-223. (Modified from the *CTJ Journal* 16 (December 1987): 29-30.

Jensen, Julie M., ed. *Stories to Grow On: Developing Effective Learning Environments*. Portsmouth, NH: Heinemann, 1989.

Jett-Simpson, M. "Students' Attitudes Toward Reading Motivational Activities." Paper presented at the 70th annual conference of the National Association of Teachers of English, Cincinnati, November 1980.

Johnson, D. W., and R. T. Johnson. *Cooperation and Competition: Theory and Research*. Edina, MN: Interaction, 1989.

______. *Learning Together and Alone: Cooperation, Competition and Individualization*. 2d ed. Englewood Cliffs, NJ: Prentice-Hall, 1987.

Johnson, D. W., R. T. Johnson, and E. Holubec. *Circles of Learning: Cooperation in the Classroom*. Rev. ed. Edina, MN: Interaction, 1986.

Johnson, Terry D., and Daphne R. Louis. *Literacy Through Literature*. Portsmouth, NH: Heinemann, 1987.

Karlin, R. *Teaching Elementary Reading*. New York: Harcourt Brace Jovanovich, 1971

Katzer, Sonia, and Christine A. Crnkovich. *From Scribblers to Scribes: Young Writers Use the Computer*. Englewood, CO: Teacher Ideas Press, 1991.

Kelly, Joanne. *The Battle of Books: K-8*. Englewood, CO: Teacher Ideas Press, 1990.

Kinghorn, Harriet R., and Mary Helen Pelton. *Every Child a Storyteller*. Englewood, CO: Teacher Ideas Press, 1991.

Krashen, Stephen. *The Power of Reading: Insights from the Research*. Englewood, CO: Libraries Unlimited, 1993.

Kuhlthau, Carol Collier. *School Librarian's Grade-by-Grade Activities Program*. New York: Library of Congress, 1981.

Larrick, Nancy. *A Parent's Guide to Children's Reading*. 5th ed. New York: Bantam Books, 1982.

Latrobe, Kathy Howard, and Mildred Knight Laughlin. *Readers Theatre for Young Adults*. Englewood, CO: Teacher Ideas Press, 1989.

Laughlin, Mildred Knight, and Kathy Howard Latrobe. *Readers Theatre for Children*. Englewood, CO: Teacher Ideas Press, 1990.

LeBlanc, Elaine Papandrea, and Anthony D. Fredericks. *The Reading Motivation Idea Book*. Glenview, IL: Scott, Foresman, 1986.

Lee, Barbara, and Masha Kabakow Rudman. *Leading to Reading*. New York: Berkley, 1982.

Lesesne, Teri S. "Developing Lifetime Readers: Suggestions from Fifty Years of Research." *English Journal* 80 (October 1991): 61-64.

Levesque, Jeri. "ELVES: A Read-Aloud Strategy to Develop Listening Comprehension (In the Classroom)." *The Reading Teacher* 43 (October 1989): 93-94.

Levine, Caroline A. *41 Creative Book Report Ideas*. Hagerstown, MD: Freline, 1986.

Lindskoog, John, and Kay Lindskoog. *How to Grow a Young Reader*. Elgin, IL: David C. Cook, 1978.

Lipson, Eden Ross. *The New York Times Parents Guide to the Best Books for Children*. New York: Times Books, 1988.

Livaudes, M. F. "A Survey of Secondary (Grades 7-12) Students' Attitudes Toward Reading Motivational Activities." Ph.D. diss., University of Houston, 1985.

Loertscher, David V. *Taxonomies of the School Library Media Program*. Englewood, CO: Libraries Unlimited, 1988.

Loughlin, Catherine E., and Mavis D. Martin. *Supporting Literacy: Developing Effective Learning Environments*. New York: Teachers College Press, 1987.

Lynch, Douglas J. "Reading Comprehension Under Listening, Silent, and Round Robin Reading Conditions as a Function of Text Difficulty." *Reading Improvement* 25 (Summer 1988): 98-104.

Lynch-Brown, Carol, and Carl M. Tomlinson. *Essentials of Children's Literature*. Needham Heights, MA: Allyn & Bacon, 1993.

Mancall, Jacqueline C., Erica K. Lodish, and Judith Springer. "Searching Across the Curriculum." *Phi Delta Kappan* 73 (March 1992): 526-528.

Manley, Will. *Snowballs in the Bookdrop*. Hamden, CT: Library Professional Publications, 1982.

Manning, Gary, Maryann Manning, and Roberta Long. *Reading and Writing in the Middle Grades: A Whole Language View*. Washington, DC: National Education Association Professional Library, 1990.

Martin, Pat, Joanne Kelly, and Kay Grabow. *Rebuses for Readers*. Englewood, CO: Teacher Ideas Press, 1992.

Martinez, Miriam, and Marcia F. Nash. "Seatwork Alternatives Through Literature (Bookalogues)." *Language Arts* 68 (February 1991): 140-147.

Matthews, Charles E. "Lap Reading for Teenagers." *Journal of Reading* 30 (February 1987): 410-413.

McCaslin, Nellie. *Creative Drama in the Classroom*. 4th ed. New York: Longman, 1984.

McElmeel, Sharron L. *An Author a Month (for Pennies)*. Englewood, CO: Libraries Unlimited, 1988.

McGlathery, Glenn, and Norma J. Livo. *Who's Endangered on Noah's Ark: Literary and Scientific Activities for Teachers and Parents*. Englewood, CO: Teacher Ideas Press, 1992.

Montgomery, Paula Kay. "Integrating Library, Media, Research, and Information Skills." *Phi Delta Kappan* 73 (March 1992): 529-532.

Morris, Betty J., John T. Gillespie, and Diana L. Spirt. *Administering the School Library Media Center*. 3d ed. New York: R. R. Bowker, 1992.

Morrow, Lesley Mandel. *Literary Development in the Early Years*. Boston: Allyn & Bacon, 1993.

NAA Foundation. *Why NIE?* Washington, DC: Newspaper Association of America, 1984.

Neamen, Mimi, and Mary Strong. *Literature Circles: Cooperative Learning for Grades 3-8*. Englewood, CO: Teacher Ideas Press, 1992.

Newman, Judith M. *Whole Language: Theory in Use*. Portsmouth, NH: Heinemann, 1985.

Pelton, Mary Helen, and Jacqueline DiGennaro. *Images of a People: Tlingit Myths and Legends*. Englewood, CO: Libraries Unlimited, 1992.

The Public Library Mission Statement and Its Imperatives for Service. Chicago: American Library Association, 1979.

Raines, Shirley C., and Robert J. Canady. *Story Stretchers*. Mt. Rainier, MD: Gryphon House, 1989.

Reading Is Fundamental, Inc. "Family Storytelling." Washington, DC: RIF, 1992.

______. *Reading Is Fundamental Annual Report, 1991*. Washington, DC: RIF, 1992.

______. *A Guide to RIF's Family Literacy Programs*. Washington, DC: RIF, 1991.

______. "Reading Aloud to Your Children." Washington, DC: RIF, 1991.

______. "Teenagers and Reading." Washington, DC: RIF, 1991.

______. "TV and Reading." Washington, DC: RIF, 1991.

______. "Choosing Good Books for Young Children." Washington, DC: RIF, 1990.

______. "UPbeat and OFFbeat Activities to Encourage Reading." Washington, DC: RIF, 1990.

______. "Building a Family Library." Washington, DC: RIF, 1989.

______. "Encouraging Young Writers." Washington, DC: RIF, 1989.

______. "Summertime Reading: How to Encourage Your Children to Keep Books Open After School Doors Close." Washington, DC: RIF, 1989.

______. "Magazines and Family Reading." Washington, DC: RIF, 1988.

______. "Children Who Can Read, But Don't." Washington, DC: RIF, 1987.

______. "Encouraging Soon-to-Be Readers: How to Excite Preschoolers About Books." Washington, DC: RIF, 1987.

Rhoades, Lynn, and George Rhoades. *Teaching with Newspapers: The Living Curriculum*. Bloomington, IN: Phi Delta Kappa Educational Foundation, 1980.

Robertson, Deborah, and Patricia Barry. *Super Kids Publishing Company*. Englewood, CO: Teacher Ideas Press, 1990.

Robertson, J. "Use Oral Reading Wisely." *Instructor* 83 (June 1974): 29.

Rothe, Anna, and Constance Ellis. *Current Biography: Who's News and Why*. New York: H. W. Wilson, 1947.

Routman, Regie. *Transitions: From Literature to Literacy*. Portsmouth, NH: Heinemann, 1988.

Rudman, Masha, and Anna Markus Pearce. *For Love of Reading*. New York: Mount Vernon, 1986.

Rupley, W. H., and J. W. Logan. "Elementary Teachers' Beliefs About Reading and Knowledge of Reading Content: Relationships to Decisions About Reading Outcomes." *Reading Psychology* 6 (1985): 145-156.

Sabine, Gordon, and Patricia Sabine. *Books That Made the Difference: What People Told Us*. Hamden, CT: Library Professional Publications, 1983.

Short, Kathy Gnagey, and Kathryn Mitchell Pierce, eds. *Talking About Books: Creating Literate Communities*. Portsmouth, NH: Heinemann, 1990.

Smith, Frank. *Reading Without Nonsense*. New York: Teachers College Press, 1984.

______. *Writing and the Writer*. Portsmouth, NH: Heinemann, 1982.

______. "12 Easy Ways to Make Reading Hard." In *Psycholinguistics and Reading*. New York: Holt, Rinehart & Winston, 1974.

______. *Understanding Reading*. New York: Holt, Rinehart & Winston, 1971.

Smith, F. R., and K. M. Feathers. "Teacher and Student Perceptions of Content Area Reading." *Journal of Reading* 26 (1983): 348-354.

Smith, Gary. "The Man Who Couldn't Read." *Esquire* (August 1990): 85-95.

Spencer, Patricia Sylvester. "Recovering Innocence: Growing Up Reading." *English Journal* 80 (October 1991): 65-69.

Steinberg, Heinz. "Reading and TV Viewing—Complementary Activities." *Journal of Reading* 26 (March 1983): 510-514.

Steiner, Barbara, and Kathleen C. Phillips. *Journal Keeping with Young People*. Englewood, CO: Teacher Ideas Press, 1991.

Stripling, Barbara K. *Libraries for the National Education Goals*. Syracuse, NY: Clearinghouse on Information Resources, April 1992.

Sullivan, Anne McCrary. "The Natural Reading Life: A High-School Anomaly." *English Journal* 80 (October 1991): 40-46.

Thimmesch, Nick, ed. *Aliteracy: People Who Can Read But Won't*. Washington, DC: American Enterprise Institute for Public Policy Research, 1984.

Thomas, James L., and A. Elaine Goldsmith. "A Necessary Partnership: The Early Childhood Educator and the School Librarian." *Phi Delta Kappan* 73 (March 1992): 533-536.

Thomas, James L., and Ruth M. Loring, eds. *Motivating Children and Young Adults to Read*. Vol. 2. Phoenix, AZ: Oryx Press, 1983.

______. *Motivating Children and Young Adults to Read*. Vol. 1. Phoenix, AZ: Oryx Press, 1979.

Thorn, John, and Pete Palmer, with David Reuther. *Total Baseball*. New York: Warner Books, 1989.

Totten, Samuel, et al. *Cooperative Learning: A Guide to Research*. New York: Garland, 1991.

Trelease, Jim. *The New Read-Aloud Handbook*. 2d ed. New York: Penguin Books, 1989.

Turner, Philip M. *Helping Teachers Teach: A School Library Media Specialist's Role*. Littleton, CO: Libraries Unlimited, 1985.

Urbanik, Mary Kay. *Curriculum Planning and Teaching: Using the Library Media Center*. Metuchen, NJ, and London: Scarecrow Press, 1989.

U.S. Library of Congress, Center for the Book. *Encyclopedia of Library and Information Science*. Vol. 49. Washington, DC: Library of Congress, 1992.

Van Orden, Phyllis J. *The Collection Program in Schools*. Englewood, CO: Libraries Unlimited, 1988.

Vogel, Mark, and Don Zancanella. "The Story World of Adolescents in and out of the Classroom." *English Journal* 80 (October 1991): 54-60.

Warner, John F., and Margaret B. Warner. *Apparitions: 21 Stories of Ghosts, Spirits, and Mysterious Manifestations*. Providence, RI: Jamestown, 1987.

Watson, Dorothy J. *Ideas and Insights: Language Arts in the Elementary School*. Champaign-Urbana, IL: National Council of Teachers of English, 1987.

Williams, Joe, ed. "The Community Relations Report." Bartlesville, OK: Joe Williams Communications, 1992.

Winn, Marie. *Unplugging the Plug-In Drug*. New York: Penguin Books, 1987.

Woolls, Blanche. *Managing School Library Media Programs*. Englewood, CO: Libraries Unlimited, 1988.

Wright, Richard. *Black Boy*. New York: Harper & Row, 1966.

Zill, Nicholas, and Marianne Wingles. *Who Reads Literature? The Future of the United States as a Nation of Readers*. Cabin John, MD: Seven Locks Press, 1990.

Books About Magic

Baker, James W. *April Fool's Day Magic*. Minneapolis, MN: Lerner, 1989.

Bird, Malcolm, and Alan Dart. *The Magic Handbook*. San Francisco: Chronicle Books, 1992.

______. *New Year's Magic*. Minneapolis, MN: Lerner, 1989.

______. *President's Day Magic*. Minneapolis, MN: Lerner, 1989.

______. *Thanksgiving Magic*. Minneapolis, MN: Lerner, 1989.

Cassidy, John, and Michael Stroud. *The Klutz Book of Magic*. Palo Alto, CA: Klutz Press, 1990.

Cobb, Vicki. *Magic ... Naturally: Science Entertainments and Amusements*. Philadelphia: Lippincott, 1976.

Friedhoffer, Bob. *Magic Tricks, Science Facts*. New York: Franklin Watts, 1990.

Creation Myths

Caduto, Michael J., and Joseph Bruchac. *Keepers of the Earth: Native American Stories and Environmental Activities for Children*. Golden, CO: Fulcrum, 1988.

Cohlene, Terri. *Quillworker: A Cheyenne Legend*. Mahwah, NJ: Watermill Press, 1990.

Connolly, James E., collector. *Why the Possum's Tail Is Bare and Other North American Indian Nature Tales*. Owings Mills, MD: Stemmer House, 1985.

D'Aulaire, Ingri, and Edgar D'Aulaire. *Book of Greek Myths*. New York: Doubleday, 1962.

Erdoes, Richard, and Alfonso Ortiz, eds. *American Indian Myths and Legends*. New York: Pantheon Books, 1984.

Fisher, Aileen Lucia. *I Stood Upon a Mountain*. New York: Thomas Y. Crowell, 1979.

Giddings, Ruth Warner, collector. *Yaqui Myths and Legends*. Tucson, AZ: University of Arizona Press, 1983.

Goble, Paul. *Buffalo Woman*. Scarsdale, NY: Bradbury Press, 1984.

Hamilton, Virginia. *In the Beginning: Creation Stories from Around the World*. New York: Harcourt Brace Jovanovich, 1988.

Hughes, Ted. *Tales of the Early World*. New York: Farrar, Straus & Giroux, 1991.

Knutson, Barbara. *Why the Crab Has No Head*. Minneapolis, MN: Carolrhoda Books, 1987.

Wood, Douglas. *Old Turtle*. Duluth, MN: Pfeifer-Hamilton, 1992.

Picture Writing References

Mallery, Farrick. *Picture-Writing of the American Indians*. New York: Dover, 1972.

Tomkins, William. *Universal Indian Sign Language of the Plains Indians of North America*. San Diego, CA: Neyenesch Printers, 1970.

______. *Indian Sign Language*. New York: Dover, 1969.

Literature Resources

Aardema, Verna. *Who's in Rabbit's House?* New York: Dial Press, 1977.

Ahlberg, Janet, and Allan Ahlberg. *The Jolly Postman or Other People's Letters*. Boston: Little, Brown, 1986.

Armstrong, Sperry. *Call It Courage*. New York: Macmillan, 1940.

Armstrong, William. *Sounder*. New York: Harper & Row, 1969.

Buchanan, Ethel. *Three Little Pigs*. Steinbach, Canada: Derksen, 1990.

Burns, Olive Ann. *Cold Sassy Tree*. New York: Dell, 1984.

Carle, Eric. *The Very Quiet Cricket*. New York: Philomel, 1990.

Charlip, Remy. *Fortunately*. New York: Four Winds Press, 1964.

Clarkson, Atelia, and Gilbert B. Cross. *World Folktales: A Treasury of Over Sixty of the World's Best-Loved Folktales*. New York: Scribner, 1980.

Cleary, Beverly. *Henry Higgins*. New York: Dell, 1979.

______. *Ramona the Pest*. New York: William Morrow, 1968.

Clifford, Eth. *Help, I'm a Prisoner in the Library*. Boston: Houghton Mifflin, 1979.

Cochrane, Orin. *Cinderella Chant*. Steinbach, Canada: Derksen, 1988.

dePaola, Tomie. *The Legend of the Bluebonnet*. New York: G. P. Putnam's Sons, 1983.

Duncan, Lois. *Killing Mr. Griffin*. New York: Dell, 1978.

Enright, Elizabeth. *Gone Away Lake*. New York: Harcourt Brace Jovanovich, 1957.

Fatio, Louise. *The Happy Lion*. New York: Scholastic, 1954.

Fitzhugh, Louise. *Harriet, the Spy*. New York: Harper & Row, 1964.

Fleischman, Paul. *Joyful Noise: Poems for Two Voices*. New York: Harper & Row, 1988.

Forbes, Esther. *Johnny Tremain*. New York: Coward, McCann & Geoghegan, 1967.

Forrest, Carter. *The Education of Little Tree*. Albuquerque, NM: University of New Mexico Press, 1986.

George, Jean Craighead. *My Side of the Mountain*. New York: E. P. Dutton, 1975.

______. *Julie of the Wolves*. New York: Harper & Row, 1972.

Grahame, Kenneth. *The Wind in the Willows*. New York: Heritage, 1944.

Hastings, Selina. *Sir Gawain and the Loathly Lady*. New York: Lothrop, Lee & Shepard, 1985.

Hemingway, Ernest. *The Old Man and the Sea*. New York: Scribner, 1952.

Hilton, Lisa, and Sandra L. Kirkpatrick. *If Dinosaurs Were Alive Today*. Los Angeles: Price Stern Sloan, 1988.

Hutchins, Pat. *The Very Worst Monster*. New York: Mulberry Books, 1985.

Kerr, M. E. *Dinky Hocker Shoots Smack*. New York: Harper & Row, 1972.

Kipling, Rudyard. *Just So Stories*. New York: Weathervane Books, 1978.

Leedy, Loreen. *The Furry News: How to Make a Newspaper*. New York: Holiday House, 1990.

L'Engle, Madeleine. *A Wrinkle in Time*. New York: Dell, 1962.

Lionni, Leo. *Swimmy*. New York: Pantheon Books, 1963.

Lowry, Lois. *Number the Stars*. Boston: Houghton Mifflin, 1989.

Martin, Bill. *Brown Bear, Brown Bear, What Do You See?* New York: Holt, Rinehart & Winston, 1970.

Mayer, Mercer. *There's a Nightmare in My Closet*. New York: Dial Press, 1968.

McCloskey, Robert. *Make Way for Ducklings*. New York: Viking, 1941.

McGovern, Ann. *Stone Soup*. New York: Scholastic, 1968.

Milne, A. A. *Winnie-the-Pooh*. New York: E. P. Dutton, 1926.

Moss, Jeff. *The Other Side of the Door*. New York: Bantam Books, 1991.

______. *The Butterfly Jar*. New York: Bantam Books, 1989.

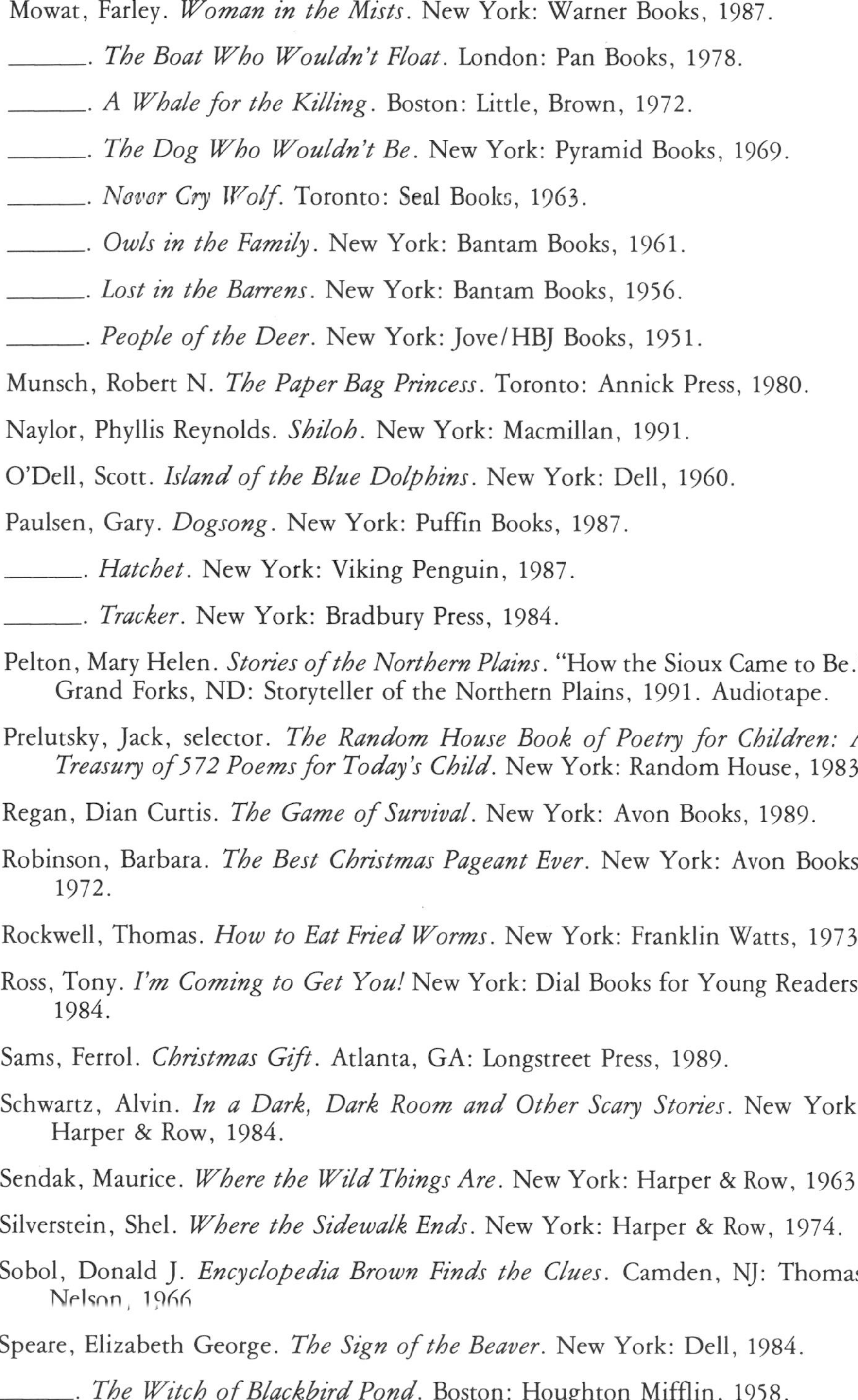

Mowat, Farley. *Woman in the Mists*. New York: Warner Books, 1987.

______. *The Boat Who Wouldn't Float*. London: Pan Books, 1978.

______. *A Whale for the Killing*. Boston: Little, Brown, 1972.

______. *The Dog Who Wouldn't Be*. New York: Pyramid Books, 1969.

______. *Never Cry Wolf*. Toronto: Seal Books, 1963.

______. *Owls in the Family*. New York: Bantam Books, 1961.

______. *Lost in the Barrens*. New York: Bantam Books, 1956.

______. *People of the Deer*. New York: Jove/HBJ Books, 1951.

Munsch, Robert N. *The Paper Bag Princess*. Toronto: Annick Press, 1980.

Naylor, Phyllis Reynolds. *Shiloh*. New York: Macmillan, 1991.

O'Dell, Scott. *Island of the Blue Dolphins*. New York: Dell, 1960.

Paulsen, Gary. *Dogsong*. New York: Puffin Books, 1987.

______. *Hatchet*. New York: Viking Penguin, 1987.

______. *Tracker*. New York: Bradbury Press, 1984.

Pelton, Mary Helen. *Stories of the Northern Plains*. "How the Sioux Came to Be." Grand Forks, ND: Storyteller of the Northern Plains, 1991. Audiotape.

Prelutsky, Jack, selector. *The Random House Book of Poetry for Children: A Treasury of 572 Poems for Today's Child*. New York: Random House, 1983.

Regan, Dian Curtis. *The Game of Survival*. New York: Avon Books, 1989.

Robinson, Barbara. *The Best Christmas Pageant Ever*. New York: Avon Books, 1972.

Rockwell, Thomas. *How to Eat Fried Worms*. New York: Franklin Watts, 1973.

Ross, Tony. *I'm Coming to Get You!* New York: Dial Books for Young Readers, 1984.

Sams, Ferrol. *Christmas Gift*. Atlanta, GA: Longstreet Press, 1989.

Schwartz, Alvin. *In a Dark, Dark Room and Other Scary Stories*. New York: Harper & Row, 1984.

Sendak, Maurice. *Where the Wild Things Are*. New York: Harper & Row, 1963.

Silverstein, Shel. *Where the Sidewalk Ends*. New York: Harper & Row, 1974.

Sobol, Donald J. *Encyclopedia Brown Finds the Clues*. Camden, NJ: Thomas Nelson, 1966

Speare, Elizabeth George. *The Sign of the Beaver*. New York: Dell, 1984.

______. *The Witch of Blackbird Pond*. Boston: Houghton Mifflin, 1958.

Sperry, Armstrong. *Call It Courage*. New York: Macmillan, 1940.

Spinelli, Jerry. *Maniac Magee*. New York: HarperTrophy, 1990.

Steig, William. *Sylvester and the Magic Pebble*. New York: Scholastic, 1969.

Tazewell, Charles. *The Littlest Angel*. Nashville, TN: Ideals, 1946.

Tolkien, J. R. R. *The Hobbit*. New York: Ballantine Books, 1966.

Ungerer, Tomi. *Crictor*. New York: Harper & Row, 1958.

Van Allsburg, Chris. *The Widow's Broom*. Boston: Houghton Mifflin, 1992.

Viorst, Judith. *My Mama Says There Aren't Any Zombies, Ghosts, Vampires, Creatures, Demons, Monsters, Fiends, Goblins, or Things*. New York: Atheneum, 1973.

______. *Alexander and the Terrible, Horrible, No Good, Very Bad Day*. New York: Atheneum, 1972.

Weisner, David. *Tuesday*. New York: Clarion Books, 1991.

Wright, Richard. *Native Son*. New York: Harper, 1940.

Yorinks, Arthur. *Hey Al*. New York: Farrar, Straus & Giroux, 1986.

Zindel, Paul. *The Pigman*. New York: Harper & Row, 1968.

Index

About the Author

Mary Helen Pelton holds a doctorate from the University of Denver. She has been a classroom teacher in Colorado, Minnesota, and Maine; a district superintendent of schools in Maine; and is the assistant dean of the Division of Continuing Education at the University of North Dakota. She teaches graduate courses in storytelling and use of oral language, as well as a course titled "Turning Kids on to Reading." She has been a professional storyteller since 1983, performing locally, regionally, and nationally.

She has coauthored three other books, including two published by Libraries Unlimited: *Every Child a Storyteller* and *Images of a People: Tlingit Myths and Legends*. In writing this book, she draws from her own experience as a classroom teacher and from the experiences of the hundreds of teachers and colleagues who have been a part of her life.